Explaining Beliefs

Explaining Beliefs
Lynne Rudder Baker and Her Critics

Anthonie Meijers

CSLI PUBLICATIONS

Center for the Study of
Language and Information
Stanford, California

Library of Congress Cataloging-in-Publication Data

Explaining beliefs : Lynne Rudder Baker and her critics /
edited by Anthonie Meijers.
p.   cm. — (CSLI lecture notes ; no. 133)
Includes bibliographical references and index.

ISBN 1-57586-351-0 (cloth : alk. paper)
ISBN 1-57586-350-2 (paper : alk. paper)

1. Baker, Lynne Rudder, 1944–   2. Belief and doubt. 3. Philosophy of mind.
I. Meijers, Anthonie. II. Series.
B945.B184 E97   2001
128'.2—dc21   2001043597
CIP

CSLI was founded early in 1983 by researchers from Stanford University, SRI International, and
Xerox PARC to further research and development of integrated theories of language, information,
and computation. CSLI headquarters and CSLI Publications are located on the campus of
Stanford University.

CSLI Publications reports new developments in the study of language, information, and
computation. In addition to lecture notes, our publications include monographs, working papers,
revised dissertations, and conference proceedings. Our aim is to make new results, ideas, and
approaches available as quickly as possible. Please visit our web site at
http://cslipublications.stanford.edu/
for comments on this and other titles, as well as for changes and corrections by the author and
publisher.

Contents

Preface and Acknowledgements

The philosophy of mind has been dominated in recent decades by the idea that ultimately mental states are identical to or constituted by brain states. Lynne Rudder Baker has been a persistent critic of this view. Ever since her book *Saving Belief; A Critique of Physicalism* (1987) she has attacked leading philosophers defending the view. In her book *Explaining Attitudes. A Practical Approach to the Mind* (1995), Baker developed her own alternative called Practical Realism. In her view, propositional attitudes such as beliefs, desires and intentions are not identical to brain states, but are global states of whole persons. What a person believes is determined by what that person would do, say and think in various circumstances. In her latest book *Persons and Bodies; A Constitution View* (2000), Baker elaborated these views by providing a metaphysical account of personhood. Taken together, these books constitute a set of interconnected metaphysical and epistemological views about the nature of mental phenomena and human practices. Practical Realism, one might say, developed into a full-fledged alternative to the received view in the philosophy of mind.

This collection of essays aims at a systematic discussion of Baker's provocative views. Its authors share the conviction that an evaluation of her penetrating criticism of the standard view and of her own alternative is truly needed. The book covers a whole range of issues intimately connected to the analysis of propositional attitudes, including semantic externalism, the autonomy of intentional explanations, the importance of human practices (in a metaphysical and methodological sense), the idea that genuine causal explanations must involve reference to *locally* efficacious causal powers, the relevance of macro-micro reduction and of neuroscience for explaining behavior, the irreducibility of relational properties, and the strengths and weaknesses of the token-identity theory.

vii

The idea of the volume was born at a conference on Lynne Rudder Baker's book *Explaining Attitudes* in the Netherlands in 1997, organized by the joint philosophy of science group of the University of Tilburg and the University of Nijmegen. Subsequent work on this volume was carried out during a period of extensive professional and personal commitments, which delayed its publication. I am very grateful to Jan Bransen and Marc Slors for their encouragement and never-failing help with this project. I also would like to thank Rianne Schaaf, Angèle Pieters and Marc de Vries for their excellent work in the preparation of the final manuscript. Kim Lewis Brown and Christine Sosa did a perfect job at CSLI Publications.

Utrecht, September 2001
Anthonie Meijers

Contributors

LOUISE ANTONY is Professor of Philosophy at Ohio State University. Her areas of specialization are philosophy of language, epistemology, and the philosophy of mind. Recent articles include: 'Feeling Fine about The Mind' (*Philosophy and Phenomenological Research,* 1997), 'Making Room for the Mental' (*Philosophical Studies,* 1999), 'Multiple Realizability, Projectibility, and the Reality of Mental Properties' (*Philosophical Topics,*) and 'Natures and Norms' (*Ethics,* 2000*)*.
Email: antony.3@osu.edu

LYNNE RUDDER BAKER is Professor of Philosophy at the University of Massachusetts at Amherst. She is the author of three books: *Saving Belief: A Critique of Physicalism* (1987), *Explaining Attitudes: A Practical Approach to the Mind* (1995) and *Persons and Bodies: A Constitution View* (2000). She published numerous articles in the main philosophical journals. Her research interest is in metaphysics and the philosophy of mind.
Email: lrbaker@philos.umass.edu

ANSGAR BECKERMANN is Professor of Philosophy at the University of Bielefeld, Germany. His research focuses on the philosophy of mind, the philosophy of action and epistemology. He is the author of *Analytische Einführung in die Philosophie des Geistes,* (2001, 2nd ed.), and the editor of *Emergence or Reduction?* (1992). His articles include 'Is There a Problem about Intentionality?' (*Erkenntnis,* 1996), and 'Property Physicalism, Reduction and Realization' (*Mindscapes,* eds. Carrier and Machamer,1997)
Email: abeckerm@philosophie.uni-bielefeld.de

JAN BRANSEN is Socrates Professor of Philosophy at the University of Leiden, the Editor in Chief and co-founder of *Philosophical Explorations* and

Lecturer in Moral Psychology and Philosophical Anthropology at Utrecht University, the Netherlands. Recent articles on autonomy, self-knowledge and practical reasoning include: 'Alternatives of Oneself: Recasting Some of Our Practical Problems' (*Philosophy and Phenomenological Research*, 2000), and 'On Exploring Normative Constraints in New Situations' (*Inquiry*, 2001). He is the author of a book on post-Kantian skepticism (*The Antinomy of Thought*, 1991), and edited a volume on value realism and a volume on human action.
Email: Jan.Bransen@phil.uu.nl

FRED DRETSKE is the author of several books, including (most recently) *Explaining Behavior* (1988), *Naturalizing the Mind* (1955), and a collection of essays, *Perception, Knowledge, and Belief* (2000). He retired from Stanford in 1998 and is currently a Senior Research Scholar at Duke University. He is presently working on problems of introspection.
Email: fred.dretske@duke.edu

REINALDO ELUGARDO is Professor of Philosophy at the University of Oklahoma. His recent publications include: 'Logical Form and the Vernacular' (co-authored with Robert J. Stainton, *Mind & Language* 2001), 'Samesaying' (in *Discussions with Donald Davidson: Truth, Meaning, and Knowledge,* ed. U. Zeglen, 1999), 'Descriptions, Indexicals, and Speaker Meaning' (*ProtoSociology*, 1997) and 'Burge on Content' (*Philosophy and Phenomenological Research*, 1993). His main research interests are in the philosophy of language, and the philosophy of mind.
Email: relugardo@ou.edu

THEO MEYERING is Associate Professor of Philosophy at Leiden University, the Netherlands. He has published in the areas of the history of philosophy, the history and philosophy of science, as well as in theoretical psychology and cognitive science. He is the author of *Historical Roots of Cognitive Science* (1989), and co-editor (with R. Russell, N. Murphy and M. Arbib) of *Neuroscience and the Person* (1999).
Email: th.c.meyering@let.leidenuniv.nl

ANTHONIE MEIJERS is Professor of Philosophy at the Universities of Eindhoven and Delft in the Netherlands. His research focuses on the theory of artifacts, the philosophy of mind, and the philosophy of language. He is the editor of *Belief, Cognition and the Will* (1999), and *The Empirical Turn in the Philosophy of Technology* (with Peter Kroes, 2000). Recent articles include: 'Mental Causation and Searle's Impossible Conception of Unconscious Intentionality' (*International Journal of Philosophical Studies,*

2000), 'Dialogue, Understanding and Collective Intentionality' (*Grazer Philosophische Studien*, 2001), 'Collective Agents and Cognitive Attitudes', (Protosociology, forthcoming 2001). He is associate editor and co-founder of *Philosophical Explorations*.
Email: a.w.m.meijers@tm.tue.nl

ALBERT NEWEN is Assistant Professor of Philosophy at the University of Bonn, Germany. He is the author of *Kontext, Referenz und Bedeutung. Eine Bedeutungstheorie singulärer Terme* (1996), and the co-editor of *Selbst und Gehirn* (2000) and *Building on Frege* (2001). In addition, he is co-editor and founder of the bilingual journal *Philosophiegeschichte und logische Analyse / Logical Analysis and History of Philosophy*.
Email: newen@uni-bonn.de

1

Introduction

JAN BRANSEN AND ANTHONIE MEIJERS

Bedouins are famous for their storytelling. One of the stories they tell is about Daoud, the owner of the fastest camel in the Sinai desert.[1] He was a very poor man and lived by himself in an old, shabby tent in the middle of the desert. But he did have one precious thing: His camel. Whenever the Bedouins held a camel race, Daoud's won. Always. But then it was a very special camel: It was completely white, and had long thin legs. Nobody remembered the camel's name, nor that of its owner. But that didn't matter: Everybody knew Daoud as the owner of the fastest camel in the desert. Even when Daoud went far, far away to other places in the desert, people recognized him and said: 'Ah, there's the owner of the fastest camel in the desert.' And they respected him for that.

Each morning when Daoud got up, the first thing he would do - even before drinking tea, which Bedouins always do as soon as they get up - was check on his camel. He would go to his camel's sleeping place, look at the beast, touch its head and face, and ask whether it had slept well and had enough food and water. Only then would he go back to his tent and make tea.

One day, Daoud got up as usual, left his tent and went to check his camel - and discovered it was gone. He saw a man's footprints next to where his camel had been sleeping, and realized that someone had stolen

---

[1] As told by our Israeli guide Swika.

Explaining Beliefs: Lynne Rudder Baker and Her Critics.
Anthonie Meijers (ed.).

his camel. He started to follow his camel's footprints, determined to catch the thief and bring his camel back.

Daoud walked on and on and on, for four, five hours, until he came to a place where the footprints of his camel had been obscured by those of many, many other camels. He was at loss, until a Bedouin sheik came riding along. Daoud asked the sheik: 'Have you seen my camel, a white one?' The sheik said yes, about half an hour earlier. Daoud asked where it had gone, and the sheik pointed towards the horizon. So the owner of the fastest camel in the desert went on, walking and walking, until he met a young Bedouin man. He asked him: 'Have you seen my camel?' The young Bedouin nodded: He'd seen it heading off along a wadi about fifteen minutes earlier. So Daoud set off again, this time along the wadi, but still could not find his camel. Later, he met a Bedouin girl and asked whether she'd seen his camel. She said she had, and showed Daoud the direction the camel had gone. So he went on looking for his camel, and asking every person he met on the way whether they'd seen his camel.

Many hours later, he came upon a Bedouin tent and asked the old man sitting inside: 'Have you seen my camel, a white one?' The man replied: 'Yes, it went past here just one cigarette ago,' and pointed in the direction it had gone. Daoud told the man it had been stolen and asked to borrow his camel. Since Bedouins cannot refuse when someone asks for something, the old man agreed to lend his camel to Daoud.

So Daoud mounted the old man's camel and set off to find his own. He rode the camel as fast as he could in the direction he'd been shown, and after a while he saw a huge cloud of dust ahead. He spurred the camel on, thinking: 'Only *my* camel can raise such a cloud of dust!' He rode on and on, and came closer and closer, and finally entered the cloud of dust. He whipped his borrowed camel, and the beast flew over the sand, hoofs barely touching it, until Daoud could see his camel and the thief riding it, and the thief could see him. He rode faster and faster until he was close enough to pull the thief from his camel. He reached out to grab the man - but then suddenly stopped.

Daoud sat there watching his camel and the thief until they disappeared into the distance, then turned and rode back to the Bedouin's tent. When the old man asked what had happened, Daoud shrugged and said: 'I could not catch him, he was too fast. You see, my camel is the fastest camel in the desert. And I am the owner of that camel.'

1 The Fastest Camel in the Philosophy of Mind

The philosophical analysis of mental states has been dominated in recent decades by the idea that one way or another these states are identical with, constituted by, or grounded in brain states. This view underlies many theories currently around in the philosophy of mind: Type-identity theories, token-identity theories, constitution theories, functionalist theories, and eliminative materialist theories. These theories vary in the way they conceptualize the relation between mental states and brain states, but they share the conviction that there must be an intimate connection between the two. Almost everybody in the field regards this view as the most promising one, if we are to make progress in our understanding of such mental phenomena as intentions, beliefs, and desires. It is thus considered to be the fastest camel in the desert.

Lynne Rudder Baker formulates this view, which she calls the Standard View, as follows: 'For all persons S and propositions p, S believes [desires, intends] that p only if there is some neural token, n, such that (i) n has the content that p, or means that p, and (ii) S tokens n.'[2] Although her formulation is not uncontroversial, as several contributions to this volume make evident, it does express the guiding intuition behind mainstream theorizing in the philosophy mind, which is that, ultimately, propositional attitudes are to be understood to a large extent in terms of brain states.

Baker has been a persistent critic of the Standard View. Ever since her book *Saving Belief; A Critique of Physicalism* (1987) she has attacked leading philosophers who defend the view, including David Amstrong, Paul and Patricia Churchland, Daniel Dennett, Donald Davidson, Fred Dretske, Jerry Fodor, Jaegwon Kim, David Lewis, William Lycan, Ruth Millikan, Hillary Putnam, and Stephen Stich. Her arguments have been directed at a cluster of ideas. These include the idea of commonsense psychology as a proto-scientific theory subject to empirical (dis)confirmation; the idea that practical knowledge is second-class knowledge at best; the idea of physical science as the exclusive arbiter of reality; the idea that there are non-intentional and non-semantic sufficient conditions for intentional states; the idea of beliefs as syntactically structured brain states; the idea that genuine causal explanations must involve reference to *locally* efficacious causal powers; the idea that genuine causes have to be physical states or events; and the idea of narrow content as causally explanatory of human action.

Surprisingly enough, though the quality of Baker's arguments is generally acknowledged, they have not resulted in significant changes in the mainstream physicalist orthodoxy. It is as though most philosophers appreciate her arguments for the intellectual challenge they provide, but see no reason to reconsider their own basic intuitions. They tend to keep fine-

---

[2] See Baker in this volume, p. 18.

tuning their theories, without realizing that their camel is in danger of being caught. Perhaps it will not take long before another camel is able to run as fast as, or even faster than, the so-called fastest camel in the desert. Such a camel might be Lynne Baker's theory of mind, called Practical Realism. It offers a provocative and promising perspective in contemporary philosophy of mind, a field which is dominated by a physicalist orthodoxy and which seems to go through a period of relative stagnation.

2   Practical Realism: The New Metaphysics of the Mind

When Lynne Baker published *Explaining Attitudes. A Practical Approach to the Mind* (1995), her aim was not only to criticize the Standard View, but also to develop her own alternative called Practical Realism.(20).[3] It has a number of features that distinguishes it from the Standard View.

Firstly, it is a metaphysics based on practice (31). The notion of a practice is a key notion for understanding Baker's theory of the attitudes. Beliefs, intentions, and desires have their natural habitat, so to speak, in our practices, i.e., in what we do, say, think, and would do, say, and think in various circumstances. This is not a form of behaviorism, since these dispositions are to be described intentionally, but it is a rejection of internalism. It is inspired by what has been called 'the pragmatic turn' in the philosophy of mind, to be associated with the work of Ryle and Wittgenstein.

Practices are also crucial for Practical Realism in a methodological sense. Contrary to the Standard View with its a priori physicalist constraints on causes, Lynne Baker's analysis starts from our successful explanatory practices in everyday life. Whether or not the attitudes should be regarded as *real* causes of human behavior depends on whether or not we need them in our explanatory practices. Baker aims at giving an account that does justice to the role of the attitudes (29). Belief explanations figure prominently in everyday practices, but also in the cognitive practices of the behavioral sciences. Non-psychological intentional explanations, for example, which appeal to beliefs as causes, can be found in abundance in social, legal, political, and economic explanations (29). Baker also defends the idea that our everyday practices do not need a scientific foundation, as adherents of the Standard View tend to think, since they stand on their own. The sciences can criticize and correct commonsense, but cannot supplant it wholesale.

Secondly, Practical Realism offers a metaphysics of the mind *not* based on the idea that propositional attitudes are brain states. Mental states are conceived as global states of whole persons. Whether or not someone be-

---

[3] References between brackets are to Lynne Rudder Baker, *Explaining Attitudes; A Practical Approach to the Mind,* Cambridge: Cambridge University Press 1995.

lieves that p does not consist in whether or not this person's brain (or, for that matter, any other sub-personal part of this person) is in a particular state. Baker supports the Strawsonian claim that persons are primitive entities, though with qualifications.[4] Persons are to be characterized in terms of their global properties, properties that make a difference on the personal level, i.e. on the level at which it makes sense to talk factually and counterfactually about what the person as an intelligible whole will or will not do in the situations in which they might find themselves. Such global properties, of which the propositional attitudes form an important class, cannot intelligently be accounted for in terms of the properties of sub-personal parts.

A third feature is that attitudes, as global states of persons, can be accounted for in terms of relevant counterfactuals being true of these persons, where these counterfactuals are to be specified in intentional terms. Whether or not a certain person believes that p, or desires or intends that p, is determined in Baker's view by what this person does, says, thinks, and would do, say, and think in various circumstances. Thus, whether or not I believe that camels are fast is shown in the kind of things I do, say, and think with respect to camels. The fact that I believe this is therefore not primarily a fact about some of the states my brain might or might not be in.

Practical Realism does not claim 'that facts about beliefs are nothing over and above facts about counterfactuals, but rather that the nature of belief is revealed by counterfactuals about the believer' (21). Counterfactual statements are to be understood as similar to dispositional statements, in that both are ontologically committing. Dispositions to say, think, or act in certain ways are not only *indicative* of the global state of belief. '[S]uch dispositions are metaphysically *connected* to belief. If one failed to have any dispositions to say, think, or act in relevant ways, then one does not have the belief in question. Indeed, relevant dispositions are both necessary and sufficient (in a noncausal sense) for having a belief that p.'[5]

Baker's counterfactual analysis of 'believing that p' does not imply that there is a unique set of counterfactuals true for a particular belief. It may well be that my believing that p is indicated by a set of counterfactuals which are true of me, though none, or almost none, of these counterfactuals are true of someone else having the very same belief. For example, the counterfactuals that are true of Daoud when he believes that the fastest

---

[4] Baker has developed a full metaphysical account of persons in her recent book *Persons as Bodies; A Constitution View*, Cambridge: Cambridge University Press 2000.

[5] See Baker's reply to Meijers in this volume (emphasis added).

camel in the desert has been stolen, will be very different from those that are true of the thief who has the very same belief about this camel.

Fourthly, beliefs are nonentities. Literally speaking, nothing *is* a belief; all there is, is the *believing*. This feature of the theory is nicely captured in Baker's preference for the term 'attitude.' An attitude is always an attitude *of* a person - it can never exist *on its own*. Ordinary language endows the term 'belief' with connotations that tend to obscure this fact, resulting in a (misleading) reification. We tend to think that a belief is just what it is - even if it is no-one's belief.

A fifth feature is nicely captured in Lynne Baker's own description of her position as 'radical relationalism' (156). Mental states, i.e. states with content, are intrinsically relational states involving persons, possible scenarios and suitable activities, or practices, that often cannot but be described using an intentional vocabulary. Practical realism aims to give relational properties their metaphysical due (63). This is evident not only from its adherence to semantic externalism, but also from its conception of the attitudes as relational states that are *causally* efficacious.

A final feature of Practical Realism that needs to be mentioned is the kind of realism favored by Baker. Practical Realism is 'realistic because it affirms the unvarnished truth of the language that partially constitutes successful practice' (22). Something is real, according to Baker, if it is causally explanatory and observer-independent. If the presence or absence of an attitude A makes a difference to the course of events, this is sufficient evidence to maintain that A is real. Since the attitudes are causally explanatory in this way, they are real, according to Baker, independent of whether or not we take them to be realized in brain states.

The emphasis on explanatory practices seems to imply that reality is not mind-independent. But it is important to make a distinction here between mind-dependency and observer-dependency. In Baker's view, part of reality is mind-dependent, but not observer-dependent. Part of reality, notably reality that cannot be described but with the help of an intentional vocabulary, requires minds for being what it is. But this does not at all mean that this part of reality merely exists in the eye of the beholder. Thus it makes perfect sense to imagine a world in which I have a belief in the sense that there is a set of relevant counterfactuals true of me, even though no one, not even me, nor the one imagining this world, is in a position to know that this set of counterfactuals is indeed true of me.

3 Baker's Master Argument

The sketch given above shows that Practical Realism is a set of interconnected metaphysical and epistemological views about the nature of mental phenomena and human practices. Baker's views have been around for some time now, as have her penetrating arguments against the Standard View. Hence, a systematic discussion and evaluation of her position is called for. What is the real strength of her arguments against the received view and what are the weaknesses of the alternative view called Practical Realism?

Given the character of Baker's publications up to and including *Explaining Attitudes* it is only natural to start this collection of critical essays with an exposition of her arguments against the Standard View. In a new article, 'Are Beliefs Brain States?' Baker presents a Master Argument against what she considers to be the two main versions of the Standard View: Eliminativism and non-reductive token-identity theory. Her 'scholastic' approach is very useful for adherents of the Standard View, because its detailed character makes it abundantly clear where the controversies really lie.

Baker argues that non-eliminativist identity theories only make sense as contingent, empirical theories subject to confirmation by neuroscience. Her rejection of the position of those who defend such a type of theory is ultimately based on an empirical conjecture about the future of neuroscience: Neuroscientists will in the long run *not* be able, she presumes, to identify particular neural *tokens* as tokens of the belief that p (for any belief that p). Type-identity theories are very unlikely to be confirmed, for there are very many differences among the brains of adult humans who may have the same beliefs. Sharing a belief is not a matter of having similarly structured brain states (ms 6). For the token-identity version of non-eliminativism, such a confirmation would consist in finding a salient neurophysiological feature that is exhibited each time a person manifests a belief of a certain type, and that would warrant calling particular neural tokens of *different* types each a 'realization' of the *same* belief that p. As Baker says: 'The relevant neural tokens must have something in common other than the fact that they are all said to constitute tokens of a particular type of belief. If the brain states in question were totally heterogeneous, there would be nor reason to suppose that their tokens all constituted of the same belief-type (this volume p. 23). Her empirical conjecture is that such a neurophysiological feature will not be found.

Baker's rejection of eliminativism is twofold. She criticizes an argument in favor of eliminativism, which she considers to be unsound, viz., that if connectionism is true, then eliminativism is true. This conditional presupposes the Standard View, and the failure to recognize this question-begging presupposition is one more instance of the dogmatic belief that the Standard View is the fastest camel in the desert. Baker then argues that if eliminativism were correct, no one would ever have believed, desired, or intended to do anything. This she finds an absurd and self-defeating position. Accepting eliminative materialism would be a form of cognitive suicide (this volume p. 25).

4   Two Grounds for Suspicion

In the second part of 'Are Beliefs Brain States?', Lynne Baker discusses the main opposition against her arguments, and provides additional reasons not to be carried away with the impressive force of her opponents' reservations against Practical Realism. This part anticipates much of the discussion with her critics in this volume. It is very useful, because it provides a division of the opposition along two different lines - lines that we shall elaborate upon in the remainder of this introduction.

According to Baker, her opponents basically have two potential grounds for suspicion: Practical Realism might be thought to involve a rejection of 'the relevance of neuroscience to understanding behavior', and it might be thought 'to make it impossible that beliefs causally explain behavior'. (this volume p. 30-31) In order to provide a general scheme for the discussions to follow, we would like to rephrase these grounds for opposition in terms of two alarming questions that should draw the attention of everyone working in the philosophy of mind and action:

1   Are the salient characteristics of commonsense psychology (i.e. the radical relationalism or semantic externalism it involves, the autonomy of intentional explanations it implies, and the irreducible relevance of higher-order patterns it acknowledges) ultimately incompatible with neurophysiological explanations of human behavior?

2   Do we have any chance to account for the successes of those causal explanations of behavior that involve reference to our propositional attitudes, if we deny that somehow propositional attitudes just *are* brain states?

In the remainder of this introduction we will say more about these two major issues, mainly in an attempt to locate the topics dealt with in the essays collected in this volume. For reasons of clarity we will split up the first question under three related headings.

4.1 Is Common Sense Psychology Incompatible with Neuro-physiological Explanations of Behavior?

Radical Relationalism and Semantic Externalism

Lynne Baker is one of the very many philosophers who nowadays accept and defend semantic externalism. According to this doctrine, what makes a belief the particular belief it *is*, with the content that allows it to be individuated as *this* belief, is not a fact about what goes on in the head of the believer, but a fact about the believer and a certain external state of affairs. This doctrine ('meaning is not in the head') results from Hillary Putnam's well-known and powerful twin-earth arguments and the arguments given by Tyler Burge in favor of social externalism.[6]

Baker uses the plausibility of semantic externalism, or 'relationalism' as she usually calls it, as evidence that there is something seriously problematic with the Standard View. Although she doesn't think that relationalism rules out any possible defense of the Standard View, she does think that relationalism should worry everyone inclined to believe that beliefs just have to be brain states. And she thinks, as we've sketched above, that Practical Realism is a very attractive alternative metaphysics of the mind that fully does justice to the relational character of propositional attitudes.

A number of contributors to this volume argue that Baker's move from semantic externalism to Practical Realism is a matter of jumping to conclusions. They agree with Baker that the plausibility of externalism forces us to rethink and revise some versions of the Standard View, but they see ample possibilities for more sophisticated versions that are compatible with our sciences. Fred Dretske, for one, argues in his contribution 'Where is the Mind?' that Practical Realism has not much to offer to the standard theorist of the relational sort. Such a standard theorist (and Dretske thinks he is just one of many) is happy to accept semantic externalism. But this does not, Dretske claims contrary to Baker, imply that we should give up the idea that mental states are in the head. Indeed, Dretske urges us not to give up this idea, because it is only by holding on to it that we can make sense mental causation.

Dretske accepts, as Baker and others have argued, that defending both semantic externalism and the idea that mental states are brain states, implies the need to answer to the threat of epiphenomenalism. Dretske thinks he can answer this threat, and, in any case, considers such an attempt to defend the standard theory much more promising than giving up, as he thinks Baker does, the causal efficacy of the mental. Dretske accepts that externalism

---

[6] See H. Putnam (1975), 'The Meaning of "Meaning"'; and T. Burge (1979), 'Individualism and the Mental'.

might involve that neurophysiology will not give us the best scientific understanding of intentional behavior. What we need is a story about the right relations between what is inside and what is outside, not a particular story merely about what is inside. And it is quite possible, Dretske asserts, that evolutionary biology or the learning history of the organism, rather than neurophysiology, are the disciplines that will provide the needed story about the relations between inner states and external affairs.

Louise Anthony and Albert Newen agree with Dretske that Baker's externalist objections to the Standard View do not refute the more sophisticated versions of it. Anthony argues in her essay 'Brain States, with Attitude' that the fact that beliefs supervene on a wider social and linguistic context can be made compatible with the view that beliefs are in an interesting and relevant way realized by brain states. She tries to convince us that we should, and can, have confidence in the future of neurophysiology. Given their relational character it is an empirical 'risk that it will turn out that intentional kinds do not map onto nonintentional kinds in the right way.' (ms. 28) But given the reliability of our commonsensical explanatory practices that Baker stresses so much, the risk is not great. We should trust that the appropriate inter-level connections exist.

Newen introduces the notion of context to show in a similar vein that Baker's radical relationalism is not an argument against the Standard View. In his essay 'Contextual Realism: The Context-dependency and the Relational Character of Beliefs' he contrasts Practical Realism with his own position, which he calls Contextual Realism. Newen argues that Lynne Baker is certainly right in that the Standard View mistakenly disregards the role of the context of beliefs. However, once context is *properly* taken into account, her arguments do not show that the basic claim of the Standard View - i.e., that human beliefs are constituted by neural states - is wrong.

At issue here is the distinction between relational and contextual: Baker defends a form of radical relationalism with respect to beliefs, whereas Newen argues for contextualism. In Newen's view, a property p is relational if the fact that some entity has the property p requires the existence of some other system to which S stands in a certain relation. A property is contextual if changing the context can modify this particular property. To give an example, the property of being married is both relational - in that it requires the existence of another person - and it is contextual, in that it is dependent upon a specific social and cultural context (changing the context may modify the social rules for marriage; for example, whether or not it is allowed to divorce). Using this distinction, Newen argues that beliefs are contextually dependent, but not relational. They are dependent upon their physical, social, and linguistic context.

Theo Meyering and Anthonie Meijers also discuss Baker's relationalism, but with different aims in mind. In his essay 'The Causal Powers of Belief' Meyering argues that we should think twice before we accept semantic externalism because it might well involve something we cannot but distrust as obscurantism: action-at-a-distance. In addition Meyering argues that even if we do think we have good reasons to accept externalism, we should keep in mind that we do need even better reasons to conclude from the plausibility of semantic externalism that we have to give up our intuition that causal powers are locally operative. Meyering doesn't think Baker has much to offer in this respect.

Meijers is much more sympathetic to Baker's relationalism and to her Practical Realism more generally. But, as he argues in his essay 'Collective Beliefs and Practical Realism: Giving Relations their Proper Metaphysical Due', Baker has, so far, not much more to offer than a convincing argument *against non*-relationalism. Her Practical Realism lacks a positive account of relations, and in particular of the relata (persons and practices?) that constitute the attitudes *qua being* relations. As a result, Meijers argues, too many questions remain unanswered to already conclude that Baker's Practical Realism is the fastest camel in the desert.

The Autonomy of Intentional Explanations
An important strategy of Lynne Baker is to highlight the autonomy of intentional explanations. She makes use of many examples in which we are unproblematically happy to accept very serious economic, social, legal and political explanations that heavily depend on intentional terms no one knows how to make sense of in a nonintentional, physicalistic vocabulary. Such autonomous intentional explanations are indeed, according to Baker, part and parcel of the practices that make everyday life possible at all, and that are studied by the social sciences. Baker likes to argue that adherents of the Standard View should feel uncomfortable by the abundance of these successful intentional explanatory practices. She likes to think that there is some kind of argument in favor of Practical Realism implied by the ease with which we are happy to accept the adequacy of autonomous intentional explanations. For if there is no need (and, sometimes admittedly, no *possibility*) to ask for the non-intentional, physical, causal patterns underlying, or realizing, an intentional pattern involving, for example the fact of being a convicted felon and having one's gun permit being turned down[7], then it seems, according to Baker, equally unimportant to expect anything from the search for such underlying neurophysiological patterns in the case of expla-

---

[7] See *Explaining Attitudes*, p. 100.

nations involving propositional attitudes. In short, Baker sometimes seems to think that the autonomy of intentional explanations does provide support for the kind of metaphysics she has labeled 'Practical Realism'.

Some of the contributors to this volume challenge this conclusion. Louise Anthony argues that Baker fails to appreciate the significance of differences among various Standard View theories. The more interesting of these versions are non-reductive, and someone defending such a theory, Anthony claims, has all the means to argue that the Standard View is compatible with the view that intentional explanations are in a sense autonomous. Theo Meyering claims something similar. He agrees with Baker that macro-explanations have an important and more or less autonomous role to play in many of our explanatory practices (though they are not *radically* autonomous). Yet, contrary to Baker, he argues that the successes of these practices do not provide grounds for revising our metaphysical insights into causation. After all, the corrective forces between practices and insights always function in both ways. Our 'localist' intuition gives us reason to think that macro-explanations cannot just stand on their own. And it seems to be a fact that, whenever we make progress in understanding causal processes, we do so by distinguishing pseudo-processes from genuine causal processes in which the causal powers operate locally. Because of this, according to Meyering, it is uncalled for - and actually quite dogmatic - to conclude, as Baker proposes, to treat causation as merely an explanatory notion. It would deprive us, Meyering argues, of a possible empirical finding: That belief explanations are trumped by future insights into the internal economy of the brain.

Contrary to Anthony and Meyering, Anthonie Meijers argues that Practical Realism's capacity to make sense of autonomous intentional explanations, makes it, much more than the Standard View, a metaphysical picture that can account for the reality of collective actions and cooperation. Meijers argues that we need collective attitudes, such as the UN Security Council's belief that sending troops is necessary to restore law and order in the Balkans, in order to be able to explain collective actions. Collective actions, i.e. actions performed by a group that is neither a simple aggregate nor a super-agent, make up a substantial part of social reality. If this is so, and if we need to refer to groups in order to be able to explain collective actions, it seems that Meijers has a point in arguing that Baker's Practical Realism will do better than the Standard View as a metaphysics of social reality.

Irreducible Higher-order Patterns
Both semantic externalism and the autonomy of intentional explanations can be seen as arguments *for* the irreducibility of higher-order patterns, and,

by the same token, as arguments *against* reductionist strategies in the philosophy of mind. And indeed, as we have seen, it is a common strategy of adherents of the Standard View such as Anthony and Newen to meet Lynne Baker's criticism by pointing out that there are plausible non-reductive accounts of propositional attitudes.

Not all defenders of the Standard View, however, are inclined to go along with Baker in accepting irreducible higher-order patterns. In his essay 'The Real Reasons for the Standard View' Ansgar Beckermann argues that Lynne Baker ignores the real motivation for the Standard View, i.e., the *prima facie* plausibility that nuclear physics is not a weird science, but that it would *become* a weird science if it were to allow for emergent properties and downward causation. It is the implausibility of downward causation, according to Beckermann, that motivates standard theorists to stick to the idea that 'mental properties are either identical with or reducible to physical properties,' as Beckermann prefers to formulate the Standard View.

Beckermann carefully discusses and refines C.D. Broad's distinction between mechanically explainable and emergent properties. He argues that this distinction allows us to capture in very precise terms what is meant by reduction, realization, and identity between the macro-properties and microstructures of complex systems. Beckermann claims that unless mental properties are reducible to or identical with the micro-structural physical properties, we will have to admit that they are emergent properties. A complex system that has such emergent properties, possesses features that do not follow from the general laws of nature that are applicable to the microstructural components of the system. If such features are in part characterized by the fact that the system *moves in a certain way* (and this seems to be the case with respect to mental properties that are in part characterized by the ways in which they cause bodily movements), this means, according to Beckermann, that we have to admit that nuclear physics is, with respect to such a system, incomplete in a disturbing way. Beckermann sees the attempt to escape from this unacceptable conclusion as the main reason for standard theorists to hold on to their views and reject Baker's Practical Realism as a viable option.

4.2 Is the 'Brain-Explain' Thesis Necessary for the Causal Explanation of Human Action?

The themes discussed so far concern Baker's suggestion that the most significant features of commonsense psychology point in the direction of Practical Realism as a better metaphysics of the mind than the physicalism involved in the Standard View. Her critics mainly argue that her arguments do not really force the adherents of the orthodoxy to give up the Standard

View. Baker's camel might be fast, one might say, but she still can only sit down and watch the fastest camel disappear in the distance.

A second set of themes concentrates on the reasons why to accept this orthodox metaphysical picture in the first place. Lynne Baker's strategy here is to argue that it is mainly an untenable dogmatism that leads most contemporary philosophers of mind to hold on to the claim that beliefs are brain states. Baker's critics, however, consider this largely a matter of self-deceptive rhetoric, that she should feel uncomfortable with once she would fully appreciate the strong grounds for accepting the physicalist metaphysics of the Standard View.

Something of this line has already been foreshadowed in our sketch of Beckermann's argument that we do need a 'brain-explain' thesis to prevent nuclear physics from becoming a weird science. In addition to Beckermann's argument, as was only to be expected, most contributors to this volume come up with further arguments to the effect that Lynne Baker's denial of the 'brain-explain' thesis deprives us of any chance to account for the successes of causal explanations of behavior involving propositional attitudes. Thus, as Dretske puts it: 'It is hard to see how a belief with this content ['the beer is in the fridge'] can determine the trajectory through space of a 200 pound person without the belief residing *inside* the person.'

On this question Dretske departs most clearly from Baker's Practical Realism, and determines what he considers to be the most crucial implication and advantage of the standard theory: that it is able to account for mental causation. As he argues, a story merely about patterns out there in the world and about non-entities that are to be characterized in terms of counterfactuals articulating these patterns is too obscure to have a chance to pass for a theory of mental causation.

Reinaldo Elugardo takes up what we have called Baker's second challenge in two separate ways. His essay 'Brains with an Attitude' consists of two relatively independent parts. In the first part Elugardo makes a methodological point by questioning what might be called Baker's reproach that contemporary philosophers of mind are basically just dogmatic in accepting a physicalist metaphysics of the mind. Elugardo concentrates on Baker's premise that token-identity theories are true only if they will be confirmed by neuroscience. As we have seen, Baker's empirical conjecture is that these theories will *not* be confirmed by the neurosciences. Elugardo distinguishes between two senses of confirmation: Wide and narrow. Wide confirmation means a coherentist form of justification, and narrow confirmation means direct experimental confirmation. Baker's premise, if interpreted in the narrow sense of confirmation, is far too stringent, even for actual scientific practice. In the wide sense, however, a Standard View theory might well be confirmed. Elugardo also argues, in this first part of his contribution, that theories need not be confirmed (in the narrow sense) in order for them to be true, since the truth of a theory is logically independent of its being actually confirmed in the future (ms 11).

In the second part of his essay, Elugardo directly addresses Baker's refutation of the brain-explain thesis, i.e. the thesis that unless beliefs are (either identical to or constituted by) brain states, they cannot causally explain behavior. Baker rejects both this thesis and the replacement thesis she thinks is entailed by it, i.e., that all belief explanations are replaceable by brain state explanations of the same phenomena. Elugardo questions this entailment. He argues that given Baker's own pragmatic conception of explanation, what counts as the *same* phenomena is relative to the context and the inquirer's explanatory goals and interests. This makes it impossible to replace belief explanations by brain state explanations. In addition, the falsity of the replacement thesis does not yet imply the falsity of the brain-explain thesis, which shows again that there is no entailment involved.

Elugardo also extensively addresses the nature of causal explanation. He argues that Baker's counterfactual analysis is not likely to provide a logically sufficient condition for an explanation's being a *causal* explanation. What is lacking in Baker's theory of the attitudes is an account of how there can be genuine causal connections between our attitudes and our actions in the first place, if these attitudes are not identical with or constituted by lower level brain states.

Theo Meyering continues this line of argument against Baker's rejection of the 'brain-explain' thesis, by stressing that Baker's defense of radical relationalism does not give us good enough reasons to give up our very strong and basic metaphysical intuition that causal processes have a local *hic-et-nunc* character. To account for that character we need the idea of beliefs as brain states. In Meyering's view, Baker 'throws in the towel much too early', since there are ways to resolve the dilemma between our metaphysical intuitions on the one hand and our plausible explanatory practices on the other (this volume p. 123).

5 Baker's Reply

These challenges to Baker's views call for an extensive reply and further clarification of her own position. In the final essay of this volume, 'Practical Realism Defended: Reply to Critics,' Lynne Baker provides such a reply and shows that she has answers to the objections of her opponents. She discusses the causal explanatoriness of the attitudes, the brain-explain thesis, the metaphysical constraints on causal explanation, the causal powers of beliefs, the idea of macro-micro reduction, the problems of non-emergent, non-reductive materialism, as well as extensions of Practical Realism.

Baker's in depth discussion offers the reader valuable insights into Practical Realism as a set of interconnected metaphysical and epistemological views about mental phenomena and human action.

As always, her style of argumentation in this reply is straightforward and open-minded, and the arguments themselves are sharp, to the point, and a sincere attempt to come to terms with the real issues. It is philosophy at its best - a great camel, whatever its speed. In the same spirit, a conference devoted to her book *Explaining Attitudes* was held in Leusden (the Netherlands) in 1997. Earlier versions of four essays in this volume (Beckermann, Meijers, Meyering, and Newen) were presented at this conference, as was Baker's opening essay.

References

Baker, L.R. 1987. *Saving Belief; A Critique of Physicalism.* Princeton: Princeton University Press.

Baker, L.R. 1995. *Explaining Attitudes; A Practical Approach to the Mind.* Cambridge: Cambridge University Press.

Baker, L.R. 2000. *Persons and Bodies; A Constitution View.* Cambridge: Cambridge University Press.

Burge, T. (1979), 'Individualism and the Mental', *Midwest Studies in Philosophy* 4, pp. 73-121.

Putnam, H. (1975), 'The Meaning of "Meaning"', in *Mind, Language and Reality. Philosophical Papers*, vol. 2, Cambridge University Press, Cambridge), pp. 215-271.

2

Are Beliefs Brain States?

LYNNE RUDDER BAKER

During the past couple of decades, philosophy of mind - with its siblings, philosophy of psychology and cognitive science - has been one of the most exciting areas of philosophy. Yet, in that time, I have come to think that there is a deep flaw in the basic conception of its object of study - a deep flaw in its conception of the so-called propositional attitudes, like belief, desire, and intention. Taking belief as the fundamental propositional attitude, scientifically minded philosophers hold that beliefs, if there are any, are brain states. I call this conception of belief 'the Standard View'.

As readers of my book, *Explaining Attitudes*, know, I have rejected the Standard View and proposed an alternative, according to which a belief may explain a bit of behavior even if there is no particular state of the brain that corresponds to having that belief. What I want to do today is to present a direct argument against the Standard View that conceives of beliefs as brain states. I shall lay out a set of simple arguments, each of which is obviously valid, in tedious detail in order to make the structure absolutely clear. This labored presentation should make it easy for those who reject my conclusion to locate the exact points of disagreement. What I hope to accomplish with these arguments - if I cannot win you over altogether - is to make explicit a line of thought that has motivated me, at least, to seek an alternative conception of belief to the Standard View. As I defend the premises, some of my methodological convictions will become apparent. Getting clear about exactly where the controversies lie, and how important they are, seems to me a worthwhile undertaking.

Explaining Beliefs: Lynne Rudder Baker and Her Critics.
Anthonie Meijers (ed.).
Copyright © 2001, CSLI Publications.

1. The Standard View

There are two forms of the Standard View - eliminative materialism, which entails that, strictly speaking, no one has ever believed anything; and noneliminative materialism, which tries to give an account of beliefs as brain states. As I am using the term, the Standard View covers an array of well-known theories (some of which may be combined in various ways): Type-identity theories, according to which types of belief are identical to types of brain states; token-identity theories, according to which particular instances (or tokens) of belief are identical to tokens of brain states; 'constitution' theories, according to which beliefs are constituted by brain states, as pebbles are constituted by aggregates of molecules; functionalist theories, according to which beliefs are causal roles occupied by brain states; and eliminative-materialist theories, according to which beliefs, if there *were* any, would be brain states.

The Standard View does not require that beliefs be construed individualistically, or narrowly. What makes a particular brain state a belief that p (say, a belief that water is good to drink) may be determined partly by the believer's relations to her environment, as so-called externalists have it, or may be determined wholly by the intrinsic properties of the believer, as so-called internalists have it. Finally, the Standard View both underlies theories that postulate a language of thought and underlies theories that do not. So, the Standard View provides the background conception of belief for an extremely wide spectrum of theories.

The minimal commitment of all these theories is this:

(SV)   For all persons S and propositions p, S believes that p only if there is some neural token, n, such that (i) n has the content that p, or means that p, and (ii) S tokens n.

According to (SV), the Standard View is committed to holding that for every belief, there is a particular brain state that 'realizes' that belief.[1] The Standard View holds not simply that neural mechanisms underlie or subserve mental processes, but more specifically that in order to have a belief, desire or intention that p, one has a particular brain state that is identical to, or constitutes, or realizes that belief, desire or intention.

Noneliminativist Standard Viewers, who hold that many instances of 'S believes that p' are true, perform a *modus ponens* inference on (SV). Eliminativist Standard Viewers, who hold that nobody has ever believed any-

---

[1] Realization is a theoretical relation that different philosophers construe in different ways. See Ansgar Beckermann, 'Introduction: Reductive and Nonreductive Physicalism' in *Emergence or Reduction? Essays on the Prospects of Nonreductive Physicalism*, Ansgar Beckermann, Hans Flohr, Jaegwon Kim, eds.: 18.

thing or had an attitude with propositional content, perform a *modus tollens* on (SV), and conclude that no instances of 'S believes that p' are true. But both would agree that if there *were* beliefs, they would be brain states.

2. An Argument Against the Standard View

My argument against the Standard View is simple; the defense of its premises, however, is more complex. Here is the master argument:

1. If any form of the Standard View is true, then either some noneliminativist theory according to which beliefs are brain states is true, or eliminative materialism is true.
2. No noneliminativist theory according to which beliefs are brain states is true.
3. Eliminative materialism is not true.
∴4. No form of the Standard View is true.

Before defending the premises, let me say informally how my reasoning goes. My argument for 2 - that no noneliminativist theory according to which beliefs are brain states is true - is ultimately based on an empirical conjecture about the future of neuroscience: If a noneliminativist Standard-View theory is correct, then it is an empirical theory that should be confirmed by neuroscience. But neuroscientists, I predict, will not find the relevant brain states that would confirm any noneliminativist Standard-View theory. My argument for 3 - that eliminative materialism is not true - is on a different plane: If nobody ever believed anything, then many commonplace phenomena (such as philosophy conferences) could not occur. But clearly they do occur. So, eliminative materialism is false.

Now I want to lay out these arguments in some detail. I am going to set out a simple argument, first, for premise 2, then defend the controversial premise of the argument for premise 2, then defend a controversial premise of that argument, and so on. I hope that this approach of nesting simple arguments will make the logical structure of my rejection of the Standard View as clear as possible.

Argument for 2:
Let T be any noneliminative theory according to which particular beliefs are particular brain states:

2.1   If any noneliminativist theory according to which beliefs are brain states is true, then T is true.

2.2   T is not true.

∴.2.   No noneliminativist theory according to which beliefs are brain states is true.

Since T can be any noneliminativist Standard-View theory whatever, there is some theory for which 2.1 is true. The argument that no noneliminativist Standard-View theory is true rests on 2.2. So, here is a simple argument for 2.2:

Argument for 2.2:

2.21   If T is true, then T is either necessarily true or contingently true.

2.22   T is not necessarily true.

2.23   T is not contingently true.

∴.2.2   T is not true.

The first premise of the argument for 2.2 - 2.21 - is self-evident. The second premise - 2.22 - itself requires an argument.

Argument for 2.22

2.221   If T is necessarily true, then it is necessary that human brains are organized in the way that T claims.

2.222   It is not necessary that human brains are organized in the way that T claims.

∴.2.22 T is not necessarily true.

Since T is a noneliminative theory of beliefs as brain states, T includes an account of how the human brain is organized. So, if it is necessary that T is true, and according to T, the brain is organized in a certain way, then it is necessary that the brain is organized in that way. So, 2.221 is true. But however the brain is organized, it is not necessary that it is organized in that way. Under different environmental pressures, presumably the human brain would have evolved in a different way (and still have been a human brain). So, even if the human brain is in fact organized in the way that T claims, it is not necessary that the brain is so organized. Hence, 2.222 is true.

Since 2.22 follows from 2.221 and 2.222, I take it that 2.22 is established: T is not necessarily true. This establishes the second premise in the argument for 2.2, the conclusion that T is not true. So, any particular theory that is a noneliminative form of the Standard View should be understood as contingent. That is, T is an empirical theory - as I think most Standard

Viewers would agree. Indeed, at least part of the motivation for the SV is to bring belief - and every aspect of mental life - within the purview of empirical science. And many versions of the Standard View explicitly aim to be scientific theories. Now turn to the third premise in the argument for 2.2 - 2.23 - according to which T is not contingently true either. This is where my empirical conjecture will come in. Here is the argument:

Argument for 2.23:
    2.231   If T is contingently true, then T will be confirmed by neuroscience.
    2.232   T will not be confirmed by neuroscience.
    ∴2.23   T is not contingently true.

Again, the first premise - 2.231 - seems uncontroversial. If noneliminative versions of the Standard View are contingent (indeed, they purport to be empirical scientific theories), then they stand subject to confirmation or disconfirmation by the relevant science, which in this case is neuroscience. It is logically possible that T be a true empirical theory that is never confirmed by neuroscience; but in that case, I do not think that anyone should believe T. We expect, rightly, that empirical theories be confirmed. So, as 2.231 implies, if T is a true empirical theory about the brain, then T will be confirmed by neuroscience. 2.232, however, is more problematic. So, here is an argument that T will not be confirmed by neuroscience:

Argument for 2.232
    2.2321   if T is a type-identity theory, then T will not be confirmed by neuroscience.
    2.2322   if T is not a type-identity theory (e.g., if T is a token-identity theory), then T will not be confirmed by neuroscience.
    ∴2.232   T will not be confirmed by neuroscience.

Since any noneliminativist theory of beliefs as brain states will either be a type-identity theory or will not be a type-identity theory, the conclusion 2.232 follows from the premises. But both premises in the argument for 2.232 need defense. Start with 2.2321: If T is a type-identity theory, then T will not be confirmed by neuroscience.

According to type-identity theories, for every belief-type, there is a type of brain state N such that necessarily, S believes that p if and only if S's brain is in a state of type N. Even relativized to species, type-identity seems way too strong. For type-identity would require that there be a single brain state such that everyone who believes, e.g., that millions died in World War II, be in that state. But that seems wrong. Suppose that as an infant, Smith, had significant brain damage; but since it occurred when he was so young, his brain compensated for the impairment, so that different neural structures took over functions that otherwise would have been lost. So, although the adult Smith shows few signs in ordinary life of his early injury, his brain is organized in a significantly different way from, say, mine. Surely, if Smith and I read the same newspaper, we could both believe that U.S.-Japanese trade relations have deteriorated - even though there is no possibility of our being in the same brain state. Sharing a belief is not a matter of having similarly structured brains. Indeed, there are many differences among the brains of adult humans, who may share beliefs. Some left-handed people have less functional lateralization than right-handed people. So, even if we restrict type-identity theories to the species *Homo sapiens*, it is not the case that there is a single type of brain state for every type belief, such that every adult human being who has that type of belief is in that type of brain state.

Finally, if a type-identity theory were correct, then the difference between a belief that failure to de-ice your sidewalk almost always constitutes negligence and a belief that failure to de-ice your sidewalk only sometimes constitutes negligence - a difference which may be crucial in a courtroom - would have to be discernible from a neurophysiological point of view. Nothing that I have ever read about neurophysiology remotely suggests that it has detection of such differences on its agenda. For all these reasons, I do not think that any type-identity theory will be confirmed by neuroscience. So, if T is a true theory, it will not be a type-identity theory, and hence a type-identity theory will not be confirmed by neuroscience. So, I think that 2.2321 is true. Turn to 2.2322: If T is not a type-identity theory (e.g., if T is a token-identity theory), then T will not be confirmed by neuroscience. Here is an argument for 2.2322:

Argument for 2.2322:
    2.23221   If T is not a type-identity theory, then T will be confirmed by neuroscience only if: neuroscientists in the long run are able to identify particular neural tokens as tokens of the belief that p (for any belief that p).
    2.23222   It is false that: neuroscientists in the long run are able to identify particular neural tokens as tokens of the belief that p (for any belief that p). (Empirical Conjecture)
    ∴.2.2322   If T is not a type-identity theory (e.g., if T is a token-identity theory), then T will not be confirmed by neuroscience.

2.23221 seems obviously true. Confirmation of a noneliminative version of the Standard View that is weaker than type-identity would consist of neuroscientists' identifying particular neural tokens (of *different* neural types) as tokens of a particular type of belief. The behavioral evidence would tell the neuroscientists what type of belief is in question, and the neuroscientists would look for the neural tokens that could be said to be identical to, or to constitute, tokens of that belief-type. I do not see how anything less than actual discovery of relevant brain states to regard as beliefs would confirm T. But - and the next premise 2.23222 is my empirical conjecture - neuroscientists in the long run will *not* be able to identify particular neural tokens as tokens of the belief that p (for any belief that p).

In order for particular neural tokens to be identified as constituting tokens of a belief that p, the relevant neural tokens must have in common some property recognized by neurophysiologists - even if there is not a single type of brain state shared by everyone who has a single type of belief. In order for neuroscientists to *confirm* a noneliminative version of the Standard View, the neural tokens that are supposed to constitute tokens of a particular belief-type cannot be a complete motley. They must be nonheterogeneous: The relevant neural tokens must have something in common other than the fact that they are all said to constitute tokens of a particular type of belief. If the brain states in question were totally heterogeneous, there would be no reason to suppose that their tokens all constituted tokens of the same belief-type. The claim of token-identity (or token-constitution) would be purely *ad hoc*. My empirical conjecture is that there will not be any salient neurophysiological feature (1) that is exhibited on each occasion on which a person manifests a belief of a certain type, and (2) that would warrant calling particular neural tokens of different types each a 'realization' of that belief.

Perhaps an example will make this clearer. Suppose that, a person, call him 'Fox' got himself elected to the school board; and by all ordinary standards of evidence, Fox appeared to believe that the proposed school budget would raise taxes too much. In the board meeting, he kept complaining about rising taxes, which he had pledged to fight in his campaign; he wrote letters to the editor advocating elimination of the Latin program as too costly for the taxpayer; he joined an organization dedicated to cutting taxes; he confided to his confidential diary that he wanted a school budget that did not require any higher taxes; after the vote, he said on a TV interview that he had voted against the budget because it would raise taxes. Given this behavioral evidence, it is overwhelmingly plausible to explain Fox's 'no' vote on the school budget by his belief that the proposed budget would raise taxes too much.

Now suppose that we had a total brain map of Fox's brain for a year during which he ran for the school board, voted against the school budget, gave interviews on TV denouncing the school budget for raising taxes too much, and so on. And suppose that we could pinpoint on the brain map each time at which Fox did something explainable by his belief that the school budget would raise taxes too much. His body moved in remarkably different ways on each of these different occasions. From the brain map, we could see all the ceaseless electrical and chemical activity that was going on in his brain prior to each of these actions.

My empirical conjecture is that with all this neurophysiological information, there would be no neurophysiologically salient property that was instantiated on each occasion and that could plausibly be identified as Fox's belief that taxes are too high. The various neural mechanisms would not contain a nonheterogeneous set of neural tokens that plausibly could be said to constitute Fox's belief that the budget would raise taxes too much. So, my conjecture is this: if neurophysiologists had a complete neurophysiological description of all the neural processes that controlled all the different kinds of bodily motions that constituted actions explainable by a particular belief that p, they would not find for each such neural process any particular state that could plausibly be identified in each case as the belief that p. If this is so, then T will not be confirmed by neuroscience if T is weaker than a type-identity theory, and 2.2322 is true. Since I have already argued that if T is a type-identity theory, then T will not be confirmed by neuroscience, it follows that T will not be confirmed by neuroscience at all.

Now we can work our way back up to the argument for premise 2 in the master argument, the claim that no noneliminativist theory according to which beliefs are brain states is true. Most recently, I argued that if T is weaker than a type-identity theory, T will not be confirmed by neuroscience (2.232) [This was based on my empirical conjecture.]; this 'empirical conjecture' argument followed an argument that if T is a type-identity theory, T will not be confirmed by neuroscience. So, we now have the conclusion 2.232 that T will not be confirmed by neuroscience. Since T will not be confirmed by neuroscience, we have the conclusion 2.23 that T is not contingently true (2.23). Adding that T is not contingently true to the earlier conclusion that T is not necessarily true (2.22), we have the conclusion that T is not true, which is 2.2 Since 2.1 is self-evident, and 2 follows from 2.1 and 2.2, we now have 2: No noneliminativist theory according to which beliefs are brain states is true.

We now need to consider premise 3 of the master argument - that eliminative materialism is not true. Before giving my argument against eliminative materialism, I want to criticize what I think is an unsound argument for eliminative materialism; then I want to present and defend a simple argument in favor of eliminative materialism. The unsound argument for eliminative materialism is this:

    a.   The brain is organized as a neural net.
    b.   If the brain is organized as a neural net, then connectionism is true.
    c.   If connectionism is true, then eliminative materialism is true.
∴ d.   Eliminative materialism is true.

I have no quarrel with a. and b. It seems likely that the brain is something like a neural net, and that some connectionist theory may well be true.[2] This seems to me to be purely an empirical question, to be settled by cognitive and neural scientists. But c., I think, is false. Elsewhere, I have criticized an influential article that contends that if connectionism is true, then so is eliminativism about the propositional attitudes.[3] But here I just want to point out that that conditional just presupposes the Standard View: For it assumes that if there were beliefs (or other propositional attitudes), then they would be brain states. Where eliminativists go wrong is to suppose that the brain is the place to look for beliefs in the first place. Let me emphasize what eliminative materialists overlook: Failure to find the relevant tokens or types of neural states with which to identify beliefs is not *ipso facto* confirmation of eliminative materialism. Failure to find the relevant neural states would confirm eliminative materialism, *only on the assumption that the Standard View is correct.* But if attributions of attitudes are not hypotheses about brain states in the first place, then no amount of brain research can confirm eliminative materialism. If, as we have seen, a noneliminative version of the Standard View were correct, then neuroscience *could* confirm the *non*eliminative version by identifying particular brain states with particular beliefs. But if - s now seems likely with the success of connectionism - the brain states recognized by neuroscience cannot plausibly be identified with particular beliefs, we cannot conclude that nobody ever had a belief. On the basis of neuroscience, we are only entitled to a disjunctive conclusion: either nobody has ever believed anything or beliefs should not be regarded as brain states. So, there is no non-question-begging argument directly from neuroscience to eliminativism.

---

[2] There are lots of controversies surrounding connectionism - Is it a theory of the mind? of the brain? is it an implementation theory? - but these issues do not matter to the point at hand. Let's assume that connectionism is a true theory of something; whatever it is a true theory of, c. is false.

[3] William Ramsey, Stephen Stich, and Joseph Garon, 'Connectionism, Eliminativism and the Future of Folk Psychology,' in *Philosophical Perspectives 4, Action Theory and Philosophy of Mind, 1990*, James E. Tomberlin, ed.: 499-533. I criticize this article in *Explaining Attitudes*, 75-77.

Now I think that eliminative materialism is false, but not because I think that eliminativists are wrong about the organization of the brain. On the contrary, I suspect that they are right about the organization of the brain. But it is plainly question-begging to infer from the fact that neuroscience does not find brain states that plausibly can be regarded as beliefs to the conclusion that no one ever had a belief. A non-question-begging argument for eliminativism would have to include a defense of the Standard View. The mere fact that the brain is organized in such a way that beliefs cannot be placed in one-to-one correspondence with brain states (if it is a fact) by itself lends no support to the view that no one has ever believed anything. To lend support to eliminative materialism, that fact would have to be supplemented by an argument to the effect that beliefs ought to be regarded as brain states in the first place. Now I share with the eliminativist the prediction that a completed neuroscience will not quantify over beliefs - that is my empirical conjecture - but, by rejecting the Standard View altogether, I need not conclude that no one has ever believed anything. If beliefs are not brain states in the first place, it is hardly surprising that a science of the brain is not a science of belief.

Having dispensed with this unsound argument for eliminative materialism, let me turn to the argument against eliminative materialism. Here is the argument for premise 3:

Argument for 3:
>   3.1   If eliminative materialism is true, then a description and explanation of all phenomena could be complete without entailing that anybody ever had believed anything (or ever had been in any state with propositional content).
>   3.2   A description and explanation of all phenomena could not be complete without entailing that anybody ever had believed anything.
>   ∴3.   Eliminative materialism is not true.

Although the controversial premise is 3.2, let me say a word about 3.1. 3.1 simply follows from what eliminative materialism is. Eliminative materialism is not just a view about belief. (Belief is just a stand-in for any attitude). Eliminative Materialism is about the status of propositional content and its legitimacy in psychological explanation. So, no one who rejected theories of belief (like Fodor's and Dretske's), but who accepted, say, plans and intentions as explaining behavior would be an eliminativist if the plans and intentions were individuated by propositional content. (An intention to do A differs from an intention to do B as A differs from B). Eliminative materialism is the view that a complete description and explanation of reality would not entail that anyone has ever had any propositional attitude. If eliminative materialism is correct, then, strictly speaking, no one ever believed or desired or intended to do anything.[4]

Now for 3.2: A complete description and explanation of all phenomena would entail that some beings had believed something. A description and explanation that did not entail that some beings had states with propositional content would leave out many if not most of the phenomena that we are familiar with, and hence would not be a complete description and explanation of all phenomena. Almost all ordinary behavior - inviting people to conferences, accepting invitations, studying philosophy, developing a new theory of motion - would be left out of any description and explanation that did not entail that anyone ever believed anything. Nothing would count as an invitation, an acceptance, pursuing a course of study, developing a new theory if no one had ever had a belief or other state with propositional content. There would be no such things as legislative or judicial phenomena. Nothing would count as debate on welfare reform in the U.S. Congress, nothing would count as a life sentence in prison, nothing would count as a world war if there were no states with propositional content. Nothing would count as being wealthy or impoverished, as being happy or being miserable, without propositional content. Nothing would count as being a felon, being a philosopher, or being governor of a state. There would be no economic phenomena, no artistic phenomena, no manufacturing, no 'information highway'. There would be no conferences, no scientific investigation; nothing would count as an experiment or an hypothesis if there were no propositional attitudes. The list of phenomena that would go unrecognized by a consistent eliminative materialism goes on and on.

A determined eliminative materialist could bite the bullet and say that what we think of as social and political phenomena, and all the rest that I've

---

[4] Paul M. Churchland, a noted eliminative materialist, speaks of assigning 'translational' content to aliens. 'We assign a specific content, p, to one of the alien's representations on the strength of whatever assurances we have that his representation plays the same abstract inferential role in his intellectual (computational) economy that the belief-that-p plays in ours. And what goes for aliens goes also for one's brothers and sisters.' ('Functionalism, Qualia and Intentionality,' in *A Neurocomputational Perspective: The Nature of Mind and the Structure of Science*: 42-43). This just seems confused. First, if eliminative materialism is true, there is no belief-that-p in my computational economy anyway. Second, if the alien's other attitudes are very different from mine, then it would be a mistake to assign p to the alien's representation that played the same role as some representation plays in my computational economy. Churchland's essay was first published in 1981. By 1989, he was speaking of 'vectorial' representation, as opposed to propositional representation. (It is unclear to me that Churchland is entitled to use the term 'representation' at all. He offers no naturalistic account of what makes a given activation vector represent a particular environmental feature).

mentioned, are not genuine phenomena at all. The only genuine phenomena, the eliminativist may insist, are those that can be described and explained without implying that anyone ever had any state with propositional content. This move would be blatantly ad hoc. Moreover, it would come at a significant cost. For, as I have argued elsewhere, accepting eliminative materialism would be a form of cognitive suicide.[5] If we really tried to understand the world without presupposing propositional content, nothing would make sense. Let me just give a few examples.

Far from being better explained without appeal to states with propositional content, behavior would become unintelligible in a world without attitudes. Here are some examples: (a) Our ability to predict behavior would be miraculous. Anthonie Meijers' fingers move across a keyboard; subsequently, my fingers move across a keyboard. He then predicts that I'll be in Holland in May. I in fact am in Holland in May. Amazing! How could Dr. Meijers predict such a thing? He could not have predicted my arrival unless he assumed that, e.g., I believed that I had been invited and I accepted the invitation; and usually when people accept invitations they intend to show up at the appointed time, and so on. (b) If no one had any propositional attitude, then behavior could never go wrong. In the absence of states with propositional content, no one could ever have done anything accidentally, involuntarily, or unintentionally; nor could anyone have done anything on purpose or deliberately. (c) People's explanations of their own behavior would be uniformly false. 'I fired because I thought my life was in danger' would always be false, as would 'I fired because I wanted her money.' (Legal and criminal proceedings would make no sense). (d) Moral judgments, which are parasitic on propositional attitudes, would make no sense. If there were no difference between believing that one was doing A and believing that one was doing B, then it would be altogether inappropriate to praise or blame a person for doing A.

Far from having a deeper understanding of ourselves if we eschewed propositional content, we would have no understanding of ourselves. Here are some further examples. (a) Without propositional attitudes, there would be no distinction between lying and an honest mistake. (b) Without propositional attitudes, nothing would ever have mattered to anybody. One cannot value something in the absence of beliefs, desires, and other contentful states. (Since regret requires memory, and memory requires content, if eliminative materialism were true, we would all live without regrets - no matter what we said). (c) Without propositional attitudes, there would be no deliberation. Our mental states would have no content at all. But there is no

---

[5] See my *Saving Belief: A Critique of Physicalism.*

way that Smith could be weighing the pros and cons of pursuing graduate study in philosophy, say, without having states with propositional content. (d) Without propositional attitudes, we would not be able to make sense of our own errors. If there are no states with propositional content, then not only has no one ever believed anything, but also it has never even seemed to anyone that she has believed anything. For seeming to believe is even more contentful than is belief. Indeed, the idea of understanding - understanding anything - would make no sense without propositional content. For to say what it is that one understands requires appeal to propositional content. (E.g., we understand *that* gravity is a fundamental force).

So, to be serious about eliminative materialism is to exchange an orderly, somewhat predictable world for one that makes no sense at all. (Indeed, without propositional attitudes, the concept of making sense makes no sense). It is not just the commonsense world of getting and spending, of being happy or miserable, of being well-off or impoverished, of being well-paid or unemployed that would be jeopardized by eliminative materialism; but also scientific inquiry itself would become unintelligible. Scientific inquiry requires proposing hypotheses, collecting data, setting up experiments - intentional activities all. One could not theorize at all without contentful states.

Eliminative materialists speak breezily of 'successor concepts' to the concepts that eliminativism would render unintelligible. These successor concepts are to be the materials for expressing whatever is true about commonsense and the practice of science. If eliminativism is correct, then the full truth of all these matters will be expressible without invoking propositional content. But no eliminativist has given any substantive indication of how the phenomena of behavior, self-understanding and scientific inquiry can be dealt with in a content-free way.[6] And I predict that it cannot be done. Eliminativism, consistently held, is the way of unintelligibility. (Of course, most eliminativists lead their lives as if eliminativism were false; otherwise, they could hardly get to work in the morning).

Since I do not think that we can make sense of ourselves, of each other, of the world or of our scientific research about the world without beliefs

---

[6] Paul M. Churchland has used connectionism to try to give an account of theories and explanation. Throughout, he conflates views on the nature of knowledge and views on the mechanisms that encode it. Connectionism, if true, may falsify sentences-in-the-brain models of internal mechanisms, but all that would follow is that propositions and propositional attitudes should not be understood in terms of sentences-in-the-brain. Throughout, the (plausible) claim that if connectionism is true, then sentences-in-the-brain models are false is elided with the distinct (and implausible) claim that if connectionism is true, then knowledge is nonpropositional. [This footnote is taken from my review of Churchland's *A Neurocomputational Perspective*. The review appeared in *The Philosophical Review* 101 (1992): 906-908.]

and other propositional attitudes, I would resist the ad hoc move of the determined eliminative materialist who refuses to acknowledge phenomena whose occurrence entails that some people have propositional attitudes. In that case, premise 3.2 stands, and the argument against eliminative materialism is sound.
Therefore,

3. Eliminative materialism is not true.

If 1 is true 'by definition' and 2 and 3 have been established, we should now conclude that

∴4.   No form of the Standard View is true.

This completes the line of reasoning that leads me to deny the Standard View and look elsewhere for an understanding of belief and other attitudes. Since the argument is valid, anyone who favors the Standard View - for whatever reason - must reject at least one of the premises. By laying out the arguments as I have, I am inviting those who disagree with the conclusion to identify the premise (or premises) that they find dubious.

3. Two Objections to Denial of the Standard View

One may be motivated to try to find a premise to reject by the suspicion that the price of denying the Standard View is too exhorbitant. I now want to respond to two potential grounds for such suspicion: First is the charge that to deny the Standard View is to reject the relevance of neuroscience to understanding behavior. Second is the charge that to deny the Standard View is to make it impossible that beliefs causally explain behavior.

I.   Some may charge that to deny the Standard View is to reject the relevance of neuroscience to understanding behavior. To that charge, I respond with an emphatic NO. My point is not that the brain is irrelevant to behavior, but rather that the relations between brain activity and propositional attitudes are much more complicated than the Standard View can allow. This, again, is my empirical conjecture. Of course, there are underlying mechanisms in the brain that 'subserve' our mental processes. But - if my empirical conjecture is correct - it is not the case that for every salient element of a mental process, there is a salient element of a neural process.

Of course, I agree that psychopharmacology, even before Prozac, was making strides in controlling moods. Everybody knows that changes in the brain (after ingesting LSD, say, or two liters of beer) make for changes in behavior. But even if neurophysiology and psychopharmacology could predict when someone will start having paranoid beliefs in general, I am doubtful that the difference between believing that one's neighbor is a space alien and believing that one is being followed by a federal agent can be detected by neurophysiology - and the difference in beliefs is important if we are trying to understand someone's behavior.

Let me try to fill this out a bit. I would expect neuroscience to tell us some things about our mental life, but not others. I would expect neuroscience to tell us about states of mind like paranoia, euphoria, dejection, and confusion. But that's different from telling us why you're dejected about your tenure review. As far as we know, we cannot tinker with brain states in order to produce beliefs about tenure in someone who has never heard of tenure. I doubt that at anytime in the future, I could go in for a 'brain state adjustment' and come out with the ability to speak Chinese or to write a symphony. Much of our mental life is relational and specific to culture - even though what is culture-specific takes place against a background of broader mental patterns like paranoia, euphoria, etc. I expect neuroscience to illuminate these broader mental patterns (like paranoia and depression); I am less sanguine about neuroscientific illumination of the vast portions of our mental life that are specific to culture.

Here is an analogy: Suppose that I am a fan of the Western television show, *Gunsmoke*, the longest-running television series in American TV. I now want to understand the relation between Matt Dillon, the protagonist, and the bartender, Miss Kitty. How far do I get by examining the wires and circuitry in the TV when I remove its back? Perhaps I understand why some days when I watch, Matt Dillon looks a little greenish; or perhaps I understand why some days the images flicker, and I have no sound. Perhaps I even understand the origin of the beams that give rise to what appears on the screen. But I do not understand why Miss Kitty waits for Matt Dillon for all those years. I can understand about color, sharpness and vertical hold by understanding the mechanisms inside the set; similarly, a neuroscientist can understand about mood, alertness, and sense of balance by understanding the mechanisms inside my head. But just as we would not expect to understand Miss Kitty and Matt Dillon by understanding the TV's 'insides,' so too we (or at any rate, I) should not expect to understand why Smith went to law school by looking at Smith's brain.

The reason that we do not understand why Smith went to law school by looking at Smith's brain is that the attitudes that causally explain Smith's going to law school are part of a pattern at a higher level of organization than patterns exhibited by Smith's brain states. And this is where I depart from the Standard View - if I am right, there is certainly no *requirement* that there be a one-to-one correlation between the elements of intentional patterns and the elements of nonintentional patterns. And my conjecture is that in general intentional patterns *in fact* are not isomorphic to nonintentional patterns.

In some cases, it is obvious that intentional patterns of action are not mirrored by nonintentional patterns of bodily motions. Suppose that a company's auditors are looking for an embezzler. They look for patterns of moving money around from different accounts, for patterns of withdrawals and so forth. It would be astonishing if these intentional patterns were mirrored by nonintentional patterns of the embezzler's bodily motions. Similarly, intentional mental patterns in, say, deliberation, need not be mirrored by nonintentional neural patterns detectable by neurophysiologists. Having certain kinds of brain events is necessary for deliberating, but it does not follow that we should regard each propositional attitude that is a step in the deliberation as just such a brain event.

The bearer of a mental life - the deliberator, the agent - is the person, not the brain; nevertheless, a person is constituted by a body. So, it is not surprising that bodily states - like low blood sugar, poor circulation, and even physical fitness - affect our mental life. And since the brain plays a crucial role in governing the body, it is not surprising that changes in the brain induced by drugs, legal and illegal, change moods and affect people's judgment. Indeed, neurophysiology could falsify particular explanations of actions in terms of beliefs - by the discovery, say, that the subject has a brain tumor, or Alzheimer's disease. But all of this is compatible with absence of correlation between beliefs and brain states. My point, again, is not that neurophysiology is irrelevant to understanding human activity, but rather that it does not have the relevance assumed by the Standard View.

II. Second are worries about causation. How is it possible that beliefs are causally explanatory if they are not brain states? This question has the form - How is it possible that p? - of an age-old philosophical question. In the Theaetetus, Plato has Socrates ask, 'How is it that we can have false belief?' Socrates admits to great perplexity in not being able to say how false belief arises in us.[7] It would have been ludicrous for Socrates, on finding himself unable to give a satisfactory account of false belief, to have concluded that there must be no such thing. Similarly, assuming that beliefs are not brain states, it would be ludicrous for us to suppose that we must give a satisfactory account of how these beliefs *could* be causally explanatory, in order to be justified in taking them to be causally explanatory.

---

[7] See Gareth B. Matthews, 'Perplexity in Plato, Aristotle, and Tarski,' *Philosophical Studies* 85 (1997): 213-228.

Our only access to causal efficacy is by means of successful causal explanation; and there is no doubt that our only reliable patterns of explanations of behavior invoke attitudes. We change people's behavior by changing their attitudes. Politicians spend millions trying to produce particular attitudes in the citizenry, and the attitudes causally explain the outcomes of elections. A job seeker tries to induce favorable attitudes in his interviewer. *Mens rea*, a matter of attitude, is an essential element in the criminal law. There is simply no doubt that attitudes are causally explanatory - whether beliefs are brain states or not. Beliefs have been used in successful causal explanations for millennia - long before anyone conceived of them as brain states. So, our knowledge that beliefs are causally explanatory does not depend on our ability to answer the question 'How is it possible that they are causally explanatory?'

Moreover, the question 'How is it possible that beliefs are causally explanatory?' is not necessarily answered by assuming that beliefs are brain states. The problem of mental causation was raised almost a decade ago in articles with names like 'Mind Matters' and 'Making Mind Matter More' and 'More on Making Mind Matter'.[8] These articles assumed that beliefs *were* brain states. The problem was this: How could the fact that a brain state was a belief be relevant to what that brain state caused? Wouldn't that brain state have had the same effects - caused another brain state or caused a bodily motion - if it had not been a belief? So, even if beliefs are brain states, there would still be the question of how beliefs qua beliefs could be causally relevant to behavior? So, construal of attitudes as brain states does not necessarily solve any questions about mental causation. If you are worried about mental causation, then token-identity of beliefs and brain states is too weak to help. And type-identity, or property-identity of beliefs and brain states is, I think, totally implausible. As I have already said, it seems highly unlikely that everyone who believes that the Cold War is over instantiates the same neurophysiological property.

Worries about mental causation, as they are usually expressed lead to an impasse. This suggests to me that we should reconsider the reasoning that led us to those worries. As I argued in *Explaining Attitudes* and in 'Metaphysics and Mental Causation,' worries about mental causation presuppose a faulty model of causation, one that does not fit actual successful explanatory practice. But not everyone agrees with my invoking pragmatic considerations in a metaphysical discussion. So, let me take another tack

---

[8] See Ernest LePore and Barry Loewer, 'Mind Matters,' *Journal of Philosophy* 84 (1987): 630-42; Jerry Fodor, 'Making Mind Matter More,' *Philosophical Topics* 17 (1989): 59-80; Ernest LePore and Barry Loewer, 'More on Making Mind Matter,' *Philosophical Topics* 17 (1989): 175-191.

here and tell a speculative story about how beliefs could be causally explanatory without being brain states.

To have a belief that p is to be ready to do, say or think various things in various circumstances. But if one is ready to do, say or think various things in various circumstances, then the brain too has a set of dispositions. Consider Jones, who wants to rise in the social world, and believes that becoming well known in the community is the best way to improve his social status. And suppose that associated with that belief are various counterfactuals like: If x were invited to speak at a men's club luncheon, then x would accept the invitation. If x had a chance to be a conspicuous contributor to a celebrity charity, then x would give a lot of money to that charity. And so on. Now if these counterfactuals are true of Jones, then Jones's brain must have it's own set of dispositions at yet a lower level. E.g., if in certain circumstances, Jones were to accept an invitation to speak at a men's club luncheon by saying 'yes', then his brain would have to be disposed to move his mouth in that way in those circumstances. And if in other circumstances, Jones were to give a lot of money to a charity by writing a check, then his brain would have to be disposed to move his hand in a check-writing way in those circumstances. When Jones does these things, his brain is moving his body in certain ways. For Jones's body to move in the appropriate ways, further counterfactuals are true - this time, not of Jones, but of Jones's brain: If Jones's brain received such-and-such sensory input, it would process it in certain ways (in speech centers - Broca's area and Wernike's area), and ultimately it would make the mouth move in certain ways. And if Jones's brain received sensory input of another kind, it would process it in another way, and ultimately it would make the hand move in certain ways.

My speculation is this: From a neurological perspective, there may be no salient similarity between Jones's giving a lot of money to a charity and Jones's accepting an invitation to speak at a men's club. But from the perspective of attitudes, the episodes are elements in a single pattern. The pattern is there. It is not just a matter of our interpretation. The episodes would not have occurred if Jones had not had the relevant beliefs (with the associated counterfactuals). But the pattern is invisible from the point of view of neurophysiology. That is my speculation. And whether the speculation is correct or not, I think that this fantasy shows how it is possible for beliefs to be causally explanatory if they are not themselves brain states.

Both the behavioral pattern and the elements in it are causally explainable by Jones's attitudes. Someone may object that since, on my view, it is logically necessary that attitudes are connected to actions by means of the associated counterfactuals, attitudes cannot causally explain actions. Of course, I agree that causes are not connected to their effects by logical necessity. However, a belief can still causally explain an action as long as the having of that belief does not depend on the performing of that action. For example, the belief that one could improve one's social status by becoming a community leader can causally explain one's accepting an invitation to speak at a men's club so long as there are counterfactuals sufficient for having that belief that make no reference to the action to be explained. For in that case, accepting the invitation would be logically independent of having the belief.

On this sketch, beliefs are causally explanatory, since if Jones had not had the belief that he could improve is social status by becoming well-known in the community, or that he could become well-known in the community by becoming a conspicuous contributor to a celebrity charity, then he would not have done the various things. His brain would not have had its dispositions to cause certain bodily motions in certain situations. But when his body moves in these various ways in various situations, it is altogether possible that entirely different brain states are engaged on different occasions. And - if there are no brain states in common to these episodes that can plausibly be identified as Jones's beliefs - then neurophysiological explanations of Jones's various attempts to gain social status will miss the causal pattern that belief-explanations capture.

Now I admit that there are huge empirical questions about how a brain acquires its various dispositions to move a body in ways that exhibit intentional patterns of action. What I think is really amazing is that the brain's dispositions to move the body in ways appropriate to belief in various circumstances are open-ended. In new situations, the brain moves the body in ways that continue the intentional pattern. How the brain accomplishes this, I do not think that anyone knows. But this is not a philosophical question. If anybody discovers the answer, it will be scientists, not philosophers.

But the important point is the distinction between causally explanatory properties (like believing that becoming well-known in the community is the best way to improve one's social status) and whatever underlying neural mechanisms produce bodily motions that constitute actions explainable by that belief. This distinction between causally explanatory properties and underlying (physical) mechanisms is taken for granted in other areas - e.g. in economics. We say that the decline in new housing starts was caused by the rise in the discount rate (the rate that the government charges banks to borrow money). And we can tell an intentional story in economic terms about the connection between the rise in the discount rate and the decline in new housing starts, but we do not know what nonintentional, physical underlying mechanisms sustain the connection. But nobody worries that we know of no nonintentional, physical underlying mechanisms, because there is a robust causal pattern exhibited by these economic phenomena. Moreover, I would be surprised if anyone thought that, in order for the rise in the discount rate to be causally explanatory, it had to be identified with some particular state of an underlying physical mechanism salient from the point of view of physics. For the same reason, beliefs need not be identified with brain states. So, I think that the distinction between causally explanatory properties and underlying mechanisms is useful for seeing how attitudes can be causally explanatory without being brain states.

This talk of different explanatory patterns will not sit well with those who take the task of philosophy to show how all phenomena fit into a single causal structure of microphysics - 'one size fits all'. There is, I believe, a deep methodological divide between many proponents of the Standard View and the proponents of what I've called Practical Realism. So, let me conclude with some remarks about philosophical method. To make the focus as sharp as possible, I'll baldly set out what I take to be methodological maxims of both positions. My formulation of these maxims is very crude and subject to correction and refinement. I'll call the two positions 'methodological physicalism' and 'methodological pragmatism'.

The methodological physicalist starts with a theoretical picture based on a philosophical idea of fundamental physics. He looks to see what general principles - like the causal closure of the physical and strong supervenience - that picture implies. Then, for any putative kind of phenomena, he checks to see how it fits the picture. If he cannot imagine how some putative phenomena fit in the microphysical world, then it is deemed unsuited for 'serious science'. And according to the methodological physicalist, nothing unsuited for serious science can play an ineliminable role in a complete description and explanation of all phenomena.

The methodological pragmatist, by contrast, starts with successful explanatory practice - in everyday life as well as in the sciences - without any a priori restrictions on what is or is not suited for science. The fact that something is indispensable for successful explanatory practice (e.g., attitudes) suffices to secure it ontological status. A methodological pragmatist thinks that one's theories and one's actions should be congruent - and would think it dishonest to deny in theory what he must manifest in action. No purely metaphysical reasoning (as opposed to empirical information about the circumstances) would make a pragmatist doubt that what she heard was caused by what the speaker said, where what the speaker said is identified by propositional content. What is right before our eyes takes precedence over metaphysical theories.[9]

---

[9] I would go so far as to take the fact that, e.g., the conjunction of strong supervenience and the causal closure of the physical has the consequence that all apparent macrocausation is

If we have overwhelming reason to hold that beliefs causally explain behavior, and good empirical reason not to identify beliefs with particular brain states, and, say, a theory of causation that requires beliefs to be brain states in order to be causally explanatory, then the methodological pragmatist says that the theory of causation should yield before successful explanatory practice. The methodological physicalist, by contrast, would hold on to the theory of causation that conforms to his metaphysical picture, and either argue that beliefs really are brain states (the noneliminativist Standard Viewer) or that beliefs do not really explain behavior (the eliminativist Standard Viewer). Both of these Standard-View strategies adjust the phenomena to his metaphysical picture; whereas the methodological pragmatist seeks to adjust his metaphysical picture to the phenomena.

It is this difference in strategy, I think, that makes the controversy over causation so difficult to settle. Both the physicalist and the pragmatist are rational, but neither is moved by the other's arguments. To the methodological physicalist, the pragmatist looks shallow and unprincipled; to the methodological pragmatist, the physicalist looks rigid and out of touch with reality. Hence, the impasse. Or at least this is the way that I see the difficulty right now. (I'd be interested to hear what others had to say about this). For these reasons, I do not believe that I am able to refute my metaphysical opponents, but I do hope at least to have opened the door to another position.

4. Conclusion

To sum up: I have presented a valid argument against the conception of the attitudes as brain states, and I have defended the premises and then defended the defenses of the premises. The Standard View of the attitudes as brain states, in both its eliminative and noneliminative versions, I argued, is false. Along the way, I criticized an unsound argument for eliminative materialism. A proponent of the Standard View, I admitted, might be motivated by either of two suspicions to find one of my premises to reject: First, one may suspect that if beliefs were not brain states, then neuroscience would be irrelevant to explaining behavior; second, one may worry about how beliefs could be causally explanatory if they were not brain states. I tried to allay both worries. In any event, if one takes such worries to be reasons to endorse the Standard View, then one will have to reject at least one of the premises in my argument against the Standard View. Finally, I contrasted two approaches to philosophy, which I dubbed methodological

---

illusory to be a *reductio ad absurdum* of the conjunction. See my 'Metaphysics and Mental Causation' in *Mental Causation*, John Heil and Alfred Mele, eds.: 75-95.

physicalism and methodological pragmatism. Needless to say, I find myself in the pragmatist camp. The sublime elegance of physicalism is seductive, but the rough-and-tumble of pragmatism seems closer to reality, as we all know it.[10]

References

Baker, L.R. 1987. Saving Belief: *A Critique of Physicalism*. Princeton: Princeton University Press.

Baker, L.R. 1992. Review of Churchland. P.M.. Review of *A Neurocomputational Perspective, The Philosophical Review*. 101: 906-908.

Baker, L.R. 1993. Metaphysics and Mental Causation. In *Mental Causation*, eds. John Heil and Alfred Mele, 75-95. Oxford: Oxford University Press.

Baker, L.R. 1995. *Explaining Attitudes*. Cambridge: Cambridge University Press.

Beckermann, A. 1992. Introduction: Reductive and Nonreductive Physicalism. In *Emergence or Reduction? Essays on the Prospects of Nonreductive Physicalism*. Eds. Ansgar Beckermann, Hans Flohr, Jaegwon Kim, Berlin: Walter de Gruyter.

Churchland, P.M. 1989. Functionalism, Qualia and Intentionality. In *A Neurocomputational Perspective: The Nature of Mind and the Structure of Science*. 42-43. Cambridge MA: MIT/Bradford.

Fodor, J. 1989. Making Mind Matter More. *Philosophical Topics* 17: 59-80.

Lepore, E. and Loewer, B. 1987. Mind Matters. *Journal of Philosophy* 84: 630-42.

Lepore, E. and Loewer, B. 1989. More on Making Mind Matter. *Philosophical Topics* 17: 175-191.

Matthews, G.B. 1997. Perplexity in Plato, Aristotle and Tarski. *Philosophical Studies* 85: 213-228.

Ramsey, W., Stich, S. and Garon, J. 1990. Connectionism, Eliminativism and the Future of Folk Psychology. In *Philosophical Perspectives 4, Action Theory and Philosophy of Mind*, ed. James E. Tomberlin, 499-533. Atascadero CA: Ridgeview Publishing Co.

---

[10] Many thanks to Katherine A. Sonderegger for her tireless help, and to Gareth Matthews for important comments.

3

Where is the Mind?*

FRED DRETSKE

Baker is a realist about the mind. We really do have thoughts, fears, hopes, and desires, but, contrary to contemporary (materialistic) orthodoxy, these mental states are not events in or states of the brain. The Standard View - a view that identifies beliefs, intentions, and desires with brain states - is as misconceived as would be a view that identified being flat broke or under arrest with states of the nervous system. Being flat broke and under arrest are, if you will, states of a person, but they are not states of that person's body, brain, or nervous system. Practical Realism (the name Baker gives her own view) asserts, instead, that the attitudes (a blanket term for the kind of mental states we normally invoke to explain behavior) are to be identified with facts expressed by conditionals that describe what people would do, say, and think in various circumstances. This isn't behaviorism (at least Baker denies it is: 1995, pp. 21, 155-56, 191); it nonetheless shares with behaviorism the idea that beliefs and desires are not, like bacteria, located inside people causing various observable symptoms. They are, rather, outside where the observable facts are, that are used to tell what people believe and desire.

---

* This essay is an expansion of a book review I wrote of *Explaining Attitudes* for *The American Journal of Psychology* 109.3 (1996), pp. 491-496. The first part is essentially that review (with a few stylistic changes); the remainder is a response to Baker's essay 'Are Beliefs Brain States?'

Explaining Beliefs: Lynne Rudder Baker and Her Critics.
Anthonie Meijers (ed.).

That is the main thesis of the book. There are a host of other objectives Baker tries to promote and a lot of trenchant criticism of other philosopher's views, but most of her positive proposals (e.g., that our common-sense conception of mentality requires no special validation by the sciences) depend on this one. If this doesn't wash, nothing else does either. Since Baker's discussion of this topic takes one to the very heart of contemporary philosophical debates about mind-body causation, I will concentrate here.

The Standard View, a view that Baker hopes to replace by Practical Realism, comes in different flavors. What they all have in common is that they are all forms of materialism and they all identify the attitudes with brain states. Type-identity theory says that every type of mental state (e.g., a belief that snow is white) is a type of brain state. If two people think snow is white, then there is some state of their brain that is the same. Thinking that snow is white is being in a brain state of *that* kind. Token-identity theory agrees that all beliefs are brain states, but denies that every instance (token) of a belief that snow is white must be a token of the same (type of) brain state. You and I could both believe that snow is white but be in quite different brain states. Functionalism (a version of token-identity theory) identifies beliefs with whatever brain states occupy (realize) an appropriate causal (functional) role. S_1 and S_2 have the same belief if there is some brain state (it needn't be the same type) in each of them that plays the right causal role. And so on. Even Eliminative Materialism - the doctrine that there are no beliefs at all - is a form of the Standard View since it holds that if there were any beliefs, they would be brain states. There just aren't any brain states of the right sort.

What is wrong with the Standard View? If there are beliefs, fears, expectations, and intentions, and we exclude (as Baker does) dualistic options, how could these attitudes not be states of the body? If beliefs are to causally explain what we say, do, and think (=behavior), how could they not be events in, or states of, the body of the person whose behavior they cause? Where (or what) else could they be?

Baker's answer is that beliefs are relational states of affairs, and relational states of affairs are not in people. They are not conditions or states of the body. I can be flat broke or disgraced, but being so is not a state of my body. They are (broadly speaking) conditions or situations I get into by coming to stand in certain relations to other things in the world. Beliefs are something like that. Just as two people could be in the same bodily state (think of them as exact twins) while one was, but the other was not, flat broke, so might physically identical bodies have different beliefs.

Baker is here embracing a philosophical view called *semantic externalism*. The semantic externalist maintains that the meaning or content (= semantics) of a person's mental state (what it is that person believes, desires, and intends) is a relational (hence, an external or extrinsic) property of the person. Another way of saying this is that what S believes, intends, and desires (=content) does not supervene on the physical stuff of which S is made. Physically identical bodies (having different histories and located in different circumstances, for instance) could have different beliefs. In this respect, psychological meaning or content (what S thinks) is like the meaning of words. The same sounds (in different languages, say, or in the same language at different times) can mean something quite different. Just so, the same brain activity in different heads (or the same head at different times) might be quite different beliefs. This may sound a little strange to the untutored ear, but according to semantic externalism it is no more surprising than a corresponding claim about the meaning or content of linguistic items. Meaning does not supervene on the intrinsic properties of the sounds and marks that have meaning. Semantics, the study of meaning, is one thing; physics and biology, the study of those things that have meaning, is another.

Semantic Externalism is the received doctrine in the philosophy of mind. Putman's (1975) and Burge's (1979) examples have convinced many that what people think - no less than what they say - fails to supervene on the vehicles of meaning (the sounds they make and the states of their brain). What one thinks is, in part at least, determined by one's relations to objects and conditions in one's environment. As Baker acknowledges (1995, pp. 11-12) the Standard View (in what Baker calls its relational construal) is compatible with Semantic Externalism. Token identity theorists, for instance, hold that token beliefs are identical with token brain states, but insist that what makes a token brain state the belief that snow is white (what gives it this content) are the relations it bears to external affairs. A different token of the same neural state type might be an altogether different belief. Functionalists maintain that what makes a brain state the belief that it is raining is the (relational) fact that it is apt to be caused by rain and apt to cause (in those who want to stay dry) rain-avoiding (e.g., umbrella carrying) behavior. Beliefs, the actual brain states that play these causal roles, are in the head, but the facts that make them beliefs (and the particular beliefs they are) reside in the causal relations these internal states bear tot external affairs.

Given the fact, then, that many standard theorists *are* typically externalists - functionalists of one stripe or another - it is surprising to hear Baker criticize standard theory for ignoring the relational, the extrinsic, the external, aspect of belief. I say this is surprising because a standard theorist (of the relational variety) would be happy to concede those facts that Baker uses to distinguish her view (Practical Realism) from the Standard View. She insists, again and again, that whether S believes p depends not on which brain states S has, but on S's relational properties (1995, 21, 22). There is nothing here that a standard theorist need disagree with. Why, then, should the fact that what makes a belief a belief is its relational properties mean that the belief does not reside within? What makes the paper in my pocket money are the conventions and practices constituting monetary exchange, and these conventions and practices are all outside my pocket. That doesn't mean the money isn't in my pocket.

Why, in other words, can't we locate the mind in the body (just as we keep our money in our pocket), but locate the facts that make mental states mental (e.g., the facts that give content to brain states and, thus, make them into beliefs) in that network of external - including historical - facts that exist (partially, at least) outside a person (at the time he has the belief)? This not only sounds like a tidier arrangement (it keeps my beliefs in me, yours in you), but it acknowledges what Baker takes to be of prime importance – the fact that what a person believes depends on her physical, social, and linguistic environment (1995, p. 158).

The Standard View (in its relational form) not only has these advantages, it boasts an added virtue that it is hard for the Practical Realist to match. Beliefs, remember, are not only states (of a person) having propositional content; they (together with other attitudes) are supposed to explain the (intentional) behavior of the person who has them. Clyde goes to the fridge because he thinks the beer is there. If he didn't think that, he wouldn't go there. So a thought with this content explains Clyde's trajectory through space. Give it a different content (the beer is in the basement) and Clyde goes elsewhere. It is hard to see how a belief with this content can determine the trajectory through space of a 200 pound person without the belief residing *inside* the person. How can the belief get Clyde going in this direction (toward the fridge) rather than that direction (toward the basement) if the belief is not a state of Clyde's nervous system? It is all well and good for Baker to remind us that there are states of a person that are not states of that person's body, but we can concede this while insisting that beliefs are relational states of a very special sort. Unlike being an uncle or flat broke, beliefs are states that *explain* the behavior of the person they are states of, and there is no way they can do this unless they exist in (or are states of) the motor control centers - the brain. Being an uncle needn't be a state of the body because *being* an uncle (to be carefully distinguished from *believed* to be an uncle) does not explain a person's behavior. Uncles do not acquire additional causal powers just in virtue of becoming uncles. Relational states of S do not have to be brain states *unless* they control (as beliefs are thought to control) bodily movements. Then you need them *inside* with their hand on the steering wheel. Or so I always thought.

Think about vending machines. Vending machines do things - e.g., they deliver soft drinks, candy bars, and potato chips - and we (normally) explain their behavior by describing the money we deposit (or fail to deposit) in them. I got a Coke, I say, because I deposited the required $. 75. The machine didn't give me a candy bar because I deposited only $. 65 (the bars costing $. 85). And so on. Although we cite monetary facts (the fact that I deposited $. 75) to explain the machine's behavior, we all (I assume) take the real causal explanation to consist in facts about the intrinsic properties of the internal objects (the coins) we place in these machines - the size, shape, density, etc. of the coins. The monetary value of these objects is causally irrelevant. Inserting slugs of the right size and shape would cause the machine to behave in exactly the same way. The machine is not sensitive to the historical-social-conventional-legal (i.e., extrinsic, relational) properties of the internal cause (the fact that the coins are worth, collectively, $. 75). Being worth $. 75, the fact we routinely mention in explaining the machine's behavior, therefore, cannot possibly explain why the machine behaves the way it does. In giving such explanations we take conversational shortcuts. We describe the cause (depositing $. 75) in terms of a property (the coins being worth $. 75) that are causally irrelevant. Depositing $. 75 causes the machine to dispense a coke, yes, but what it is about the cause that *explains* this result is not the fact that it was $. 75, but the fact that the $. 75 had certain intrinsic properties (shape, size, weight) that activated the control mechanisms of the machine.

Many standard theorists see beliefs in this way. Beliefs are, if you will, mental coins. Just like coins they have to be in the system whose behavior they cause even though (like coins) these internal objects have certain extrinsic properties (those that give them their content) which, though routinely mentioned in ordinary explanations of behavior, are not causally relevant to the behavior of the system in which they occur. That doesn't prevent us from invoking to them in our 'explanations' of behavior - anymore than the acknowledged irrelevance of monetary value prevents us from appealing to monetary value in our 'explanations' of machine behavior. If you want to know what makes vending machines dispense cokes and candy bars or what explains why they don't (when they don't), look to the intrinsic physical properties of the internal objects (including the coins we deposit in them). For exactly the same reason, if you want to know what makes people do the things they do, look not to relational properties (content = what we believe), but to the neurobiological (i.e., intrinsic) properties of the internal objects (the beliefs) that have that content. Look to the 'shape' and 'size' of our internal 'coins'. Such a view of the attitudes makes mental content explanatorily irrelevant to the behavior of persons (in the same way as the monetary value of coins is irrelevant to vending machine behavior) but it - of necessity - locates the cause of behavior (just like the coins in vending machines) inside the system whose behavior is being explained.

Critics (including Baker) are quick to point out that this view makes mental content epiphenomenal. What we believe (though not the belief itself) is causally irrelevant. This is true, but how disturbing one finds this result depends on what a materialist can reasonably expect of mental states. Is it enough that beliefs (brain states with content) cause behavior? If this is enough (Davidson obviously thinks it is), then the Standard View is in good shape. Brain states with content cause human behavior in the same way coins with monetary value cause candy bars to come tumbling out of vending machines. If, on the other hand, one is convinced that mental content is a causally relevant property (surely what we believe and desire makes a difference to what we do) one will look for the way that the relational properties underlying mental content figure in explanations of behavior. My own thinking (Dretske 1988) has gone in this direction.[1]

So Baker is right: a standard theorist of the relational sort has a problem. How is content - what we believe and desire - relevant to what we do? To bite the bullet and insist that it isn't relevant strikes me, as it does Baker, as a desperate option indeed. Frankly, I see little difference between eliminative materialism (denying we have beliefs) and the view that we have beliefs but that they (qua beliefs) don't do anything. What good is believing that the beer is in the fridge (rather than the basement) if believing this isn't relevant to where I go? One might as well not believe it for all the difference it makes.

So I'm on Baker's side in this matter. I not only want beliefs, I want them (qua beliefs) to *do* something, to (what else?) help explain the (intentional) things I do. Unlike Baker, though, I (a standard theorist) think the way to get this result is to locate beliefs (desires, intentions - the mental states that jointly explain behavior) inside the person whose behavior they explain. Only by putting them *inside* can I get them to cause the bodily (e.g., eyelid) movements associated with (but, as I see it, not identical to) intentional behavior (e.g., winking) we want to explain. But a Practical Realist like Baker does not think beliefs and desires are in us. There is *nothing* (nothing *mental*) inside causing the eyelids to move when we wink. In what sense, then, can a Practical Realist give an account of the causal relevance

---

1 See Baker's (1991, 1993) criticisms of my attempt to make relational properties causally relevant to behavior. I reply in Dretske (1991).

of belief? In what sense does Clyde go to the fridge *because* he thinks the beer is there. Why is my wanting to leave the party - the reason I wink at my wife - relevant to my winking? Standard theorists of Davidson's persuasion have an answer to these questions even if it doesn't satisfy people like Baker and me. Clyde's belief that the beer is in the fridge causes him to go to the fridge. My desire to leave the party causes my eyelid to move. This doesn't make *what* is believed and *what* is desired (i.e., content) relevant to what we do, but it does, at least, rescue beliefs and desires themselves (states having content) form epiphenomenal darkness. This may not be all we can ask, but it sure seems like a lot more than Practical Realism can deliver.

In her essay 'Are Beliefs Brain States?' Baker (briefly) addresses these issues. Doubtless feeling that a good offense is the best defense, though, she spends most of her time challenging standard theorists to say just what is wrong with her 'proof' that the Standard View is false. If standard theory is false, of course, then even if Practical Realism has no plausible account of the causal relevance of the mental, we would have to live with it anyway. We would have no choice. There would be no other game in town.

Before commenting on Baker's 'proof' that Practical Realism *is* the only game in town, though, let me comment on her attempt to address these explanatory problems in the last few pages of 'Are Beliefs Brain States?' Frankly, I have a problem understanding Baker's argument here. What I do understand, though, makes it seem as though she is caught in a tight little circle. Since she is going to have a chance to reply, let me describe the apparent circle. She will, I am sure, tell me why the appearances are deceiving.

Baker concedes that brain states explain the bodily movements associated with intentional acts:

> If in certain circumstances, Jones were to accept an invitation to speak at a men's club luncheon by saying 'yes', then his brain would have to be disposed to move his mouth in that way in those circumstances. ... if in other circumstances, Jones were to give a lot of money to a charity by writing a check, then his brain would have to be disposed to move his hand in a check-writing way in those circumstances. (34)

So the brain *moves* the body in the way the body must move if we are to do the things (say 'yes', sign a check) we do because of what we believe and desire. As I read this, Baker is admitting that if you want to know *why* the body moves the way it does when a person says 'yes' and signs a check, look at the brain. This being so, what explanatory role is left for the belief (that becoming well-known in the community is the best way to improve one's social status) and desire (to improve one's social status) - the reasons the person has for signing the check and saying 'yes' to the invitation?

According to Baker, the belief and desire have an explanatory role because there is a pattern in these actions (the actions undertaken to improve one's social status) that is invisible from the point of view of neurophysiology but visible from the standpoint of the attitudes. What is this pattern? We are not told, but it is difficult to see how the alleged pattern, the commonality, can lie in any place other than mental causes: both acts are done for the same reason - to improve social status.[2] Both acts are *attempts* to improve social status. What if a person did these acts for different reasons? He wrote the check for tax purposes and he accepted the invitation because his wife nagged him to (*she* was the social climber, not him). Would his actions *still* exhibit a common pattern? If they do, I don't see it.

If, as I suspect, common motivation is the pattern that Baker sees in these actions, then it turns out that the pattern we need the attitudes to explain is only a pattern that is created by the attitude explanation. This is no reason to introduce attitudes. It's like arguing that we need to introduce *love* as a mental construct in order to explain why puppies are so lovable. If there are genuine patterns that behavior exhibits, patterns that are only visible from the intentional stance, patterns not themselves created by the intentions attributed from that stance, we need to be told what they are. Baker says that the patterns are there. They are not, she assures us, just a matter of our interpretation. So what are they? Where are they? Until we are told, a skeptic (e.g., an eliminative materialist) will have no reason to acknowledge the need for anything in this explanatory game beyond the brain states everyone (including Baker) agrees explain the bodily movements and the external circumstances (pen in hand, ink in pen, pen making contact with check, etc, etc.) that convert check-writing bodily movements into the behaviors to be explained.

So, as far as I can see, we need to be told more about the objective patterns that are visible only from, and explicable only by, the intentional stance. An example would help.

Let me turn, though, to Baker's 'proof' that the standard view is false. She exhibits a curious blindspot throughout this discussion and it vitiates her 'proof' (I think the blindspot is also evident in the book, but I'll concentrate here on the essay). The first sign of trouble appears in the statement of the minimal commitment for all standard theories (theories which hold that mental states are brain states):

---

[2] It certainly doesn't seem to lie in the consequences of the acts since neither act need lead to improved social status.

(SV) For all persons S and propositions p, S believes that p only if there
is some neural token, n, such that (i) n has the content that p, or
means that p, and (ii) S token n.

The phrasing of this is puzzling. Since it is *types*, not tokens, that are
tokened, one is forced to read the first occurrence of the word 'token' as a
slip and interpret Baker as saying that all standard theories are committed to
their being (for every belief that p) some neural *type* which both means that
p and is tokened in everyone who believes that p. But this cannot be right
for this says (at least it can easily be interpreted as saying) that for every
type of mental state (e.g., a belief that snow is white) there is a *type* of brain
state (tokened in the believer) that means that snow is white. She cannot
mean this, of course, since this is type-identity theory and she has already
conceded that standard theorists (of the relational form) are *not* committed
to type identity theory. I am not. Functionalists are not. I conclude, therefore, that (SV) must be interpreted to read, simply, that for every belief that
p (for any p) there is some neural state or other in the believer (a token of
some neural state type) that means that p. It is a token (brain state), not a
type (of brain state) that means that p. *That* is what all standard theorists
(who are not eliminativists) are committed to, and *that* is what Baker has to
prove false.

I fuss about the exact wording (and interpretation) of (SV) because (for
me) so much depends on it. (SV) is supposed to express what I and every
other standard theorist is committed to. So, before we look at a 'proof' that
(SV) - and therefore my view - is false, I think it important to be clear about
exactly what (SV) says. Baker's way of stating things - suggesting, as it
does, a commitment to a form of type-identity theory - encourages exactly
the kind of mistake she goes on to make in her proof, the mistake of thinking that, according to standard theory, mental states are the proper study of
brain science - i.e., neurophysiology.

This mistake surfaces again and again. In her argument that no standard
theory is necessarily true, for example, she says (2.221) that if T (a
noneliminativist version of the standard theory) was necessarily true, it
would be necessary that human brains are organized in the way that T
claims. What makes her think that standard theories say *anything* about the
way brains are organized? As a matte ˆ fact, token identity theories are
committed to absolutely nothing abou. ᴊrain organization. According to
functionalism (and my own favorite - representationalism) there need not be
any 'salient' (as Baker likes to say) similarities in the nervous systems of
people who believe that snow is white. A believer that snow is white need
not even *have* a nervous system, much less one organized in a particular
way. Standard theorists (of the relational sort) can happily agree with
Baker's claim (2.222) that it is not necessary that human brains (or believ-

ers) be organized in any particular way. *Any* way will do. As long as the right relations hold between what is inside and what is outside, there can be jello inside.

The same mistake is repeated in Baker's argument that no (noneliminative) form of a standard theory (T) is contingently true. One of the premises used to support this conclusion is that if T is contingently true, then T will be confirmed by neuroscience (2.231). Why should one believe this? Why think *neuroscience* is the relevant science to identify beliefs? Why shouldn't evolutionary biology or the learning history of the organism be the relevant source to consult in determining whether any particular state of the creature is a belief that p? Only, I submit, if one thinks that a standard theorist (who holds that token beliefs are token brain states) also holds that a belief that p is always realized in (a token of) the same type of brain state. Baker must think that a standard theorist is committed to something like this since she asserts - without argument - that for particular neural tokens to be identified as constituting the same belief, 'the relevant neural tokens must have in common some property recognized by neurophysiologists'.[3] Why must they? This is exactly what standard theorists (who are not type-identity theorists) deny. Functionalists (and people like me) think token beliefs are token states of the brain, but we deny that such token brain states need have a common neurophysiological property, a property recognizable by *neuro*scientists. For an externalist about meaning, this is like saying that any sound that means *goodbye* must have a property recognizable by acoustic engineers.

Standard theorists have long been saying that to identify a neural state or mechanism as an edge (a bug, a movement, etc.) detector it isn't enough to look exclusively in the brain. You also have to look outside, at what it is that activates the detector and on what the detector does once it is activated. According to some, you also have to examine the *history* of the brain (or the evolutionary history of the species of which the organism having this brain is a member) to determine the kind of teleofunctions these brain states (or the mechanisms producing them) have. Bug (movement, edge) detectors are in the brain, of course, but what makes them detectors – not to mention bug (rather than edge or movement) detectors - is not in the brain. This isn't something that could be discovered by a *brain* map. There is no neurophysiological property that bug detectors have to have. If this is true of detectors, as standard theorists insist, why isn't it also true of beliefs? If O detectors need not have anything in common (besides occurring, or having

---

[3] She goes on to say 'even if there is not a single type of brain state shared by everyone who has a single type of belief'. But if the neural tokens have in common some property recognized by neuro-scientists, isn't this a single *type* of brain state?

the function of occurring, in the presence of Os) why must O beliefs have some salient *neurophysiological* feature in common?

I suspect that, without fully realizing it, Baker is under the false impression that although relational forms of the Standard View are not committed to there being a 'salient' neurophysiological property that *all* bug (movement, tax, etc.) beliefs have in common (my bug beliefs may be neurophysiologically much different from yours), still, any given person's bug beliefs (my belief that there is a bug in my soup on Monday and the same belief, about a different bug and different soup, on Saturday) must be brain states of the same neurophysiological type. She must think that the Standard View is committed to type-type identity for *individuals*.

Is the Standard View committed to this degree of type-type identity? Until we have an argument that it is, *and* an argument that no such identity exists, we will not have an argument against the Standard View even if we concede all of Baker's other premises.

References

Baker, L. 1991. Dretske on the Explanatory role of belief. *Philosophical Studies* 63:99-112.

Baker, L. 1993. What Beliefs are Not. In *Naturalism: A Critical Appraisal*. Steven J. Wagner and Richard Warner eds. Notre Dame: University of Notre Dame Press, pp. 321- 337.

Baker, L. 1995. *Explaining Attitudes*. Cambridge: Cambridge University Press.

Burge, T. 1979. Individualism and the Mental. In *Studies in Metaphysics*. Midwest Studies in Philosophy 4. Peter A. French, Theodore E. Uehling, and Howard K. Wettstein, eds. Minneapolis: University of Minnesota Press, pp. 73-122.

Dretske, F. 1988. *Explaining Behavior*. Cambridge, MA: MIT Press.

Dretske, F. 1991. How Beliefs Explain: Reply to Baker. *Philosophical Studies* 63: 113-117.

Putnam, H. 1975. The Meaning of 'Meaning'. In *Language, Mind and Knowledge*. Minnesota Studies in the Philosophy of Science, vol. 7. K. Gunderson, ed. Minneapolis: University of Minnesota Press.

4

The Real Reason for the Standard View

ANSGAR BECKERMANN

According to Lynne Baker, there are three main arguments for the 'standard view': an argument from metaphysics, an argument from science, and an argument from causal explanation - the last of these (the argument that mental states can have causal powers only if they are brain states) perhaps being the most important. This list, however, is incomplete since it leaves out what I regard to be the most effective argument for the 'standard view'- the argument from the implausibility of 'downward causation'. Put in a nutshell, this argument runs like this: If mental properties are causally efficacious and if they are not realized by neurophysiological or other physical properties of persons then there are neurophysiological (chemical, physical) events that cannot be accounted for by neurophysiology (chemistry, physics), i.e. then there are 'natural' effects that do not have 'natural' causes. Since this is very implausible and since mental properties seem to be causally efficacious, it seems to be very implausible to assume that mental properties are not realized by neurophysiological or other physical properties of persons.

1 Baker on the Arguments for the Standard View

In her recent book *Explaining Attitudes*, Lynne Baker pursues two main goals. On the one hand, she tries to undermine what she thinks to be the three main arguments for the Standard View, the view that mental states

Explaining Beliefs: Lynne Rudder Baker and Her Critics.
Anthonie Meijers (ed.).
Copyright © 2001, CSLI Publications.

are, or at least are constituted by, brain states. On the other hand, she develops an alternative to the Standard View - a view she calls Practical Realism. In this paper, I shall confine myself to the first part of her endeavor, arguing that Lynne Baker has ignored what to my mind is the most important argument in favor of the Standard View. This argument could be called the 'argument from the implausibility of downward causation'.[1] I shall start, however, by paying a short tribute to the three arguments for the Standard View that Baker addresses.[2]

The first, the *argument from metaphysics* rests on the fundamental premise that mental states are *internal* states. If we think of a person in the Cartesian way as composed of a soul and a body, this premise implies that mental states are either internal states of the soul, as Descartes thought, or internal states of the body. Hence, if we deny the existence of Cartesian souls, we have to conclude that mental states are internal states of the body. And since the organ on which our whole mental life depends is the brain, this seems to amount to the claim that mental states are brain states. The first argument, thus, can be summarized like this:

Argument from metaphysics
1   Mental states are internal states.
2   Therefore: Mental states are internal states of the soul or internal states of the body.
3   There are no Cartesian souls.
4   Therefore: Mental states are internal states of the body.
5   Therefore: Mental states are brain states.

The second argument, the *argument from science*, derives its force from recent research in cognitive science. Some people say that cognitive science has been very successful in explaining the cognitive capacities of human beings and other higher animals on the basis of the assumption that the brain works like a computer, i.e., that these capacities are grounded in certain processes of symbol manipulation which, though abstract in nature, have to be implemented in the brain in order to be effective. In the same vein it has been argued that having a certain belief comes down to having a certain mental representation tokened which is processed in a specific way. And representations, too, must be realized by brain states to fulfill the role

---

[1] This argument, of course, is not new. It has been forcefully put forward especially by J. Kim. Cf. e.g. Kim (1992).

[2] This tribute is not just a report of what Baker writes in her book, but rather an attempt to work out what to my mind forms the core of her arguments.

they are supposed to have. Therefore, according to these cognitive scientists, beliefs must be brain states.

There has recently been much criticism of such lines of argument. The critics of the computer metaphor, however, tend to place an even greater emphasis on the role the brain plays in cognition. They hold that it is not abstract algorithms, but concrete brain structures (neural networks, or what have you) that are responsible for cognitive behavior and cognitive capacities. Whatever else they criticize, these critics, therefore, do not take issue with the claim that beliefs and other intentional states have to be brain states if they are real at all. Hence, there are two versions of the argument from science:

Argument from science (1)
1   Cognitive capacities are grounded in certain processes of symbol manipulation which, though abstract in nature, have to be implemented in the brain to be effective.
2   Intentional states can play a role in this system of information processing only if they consist in having certain representations tokened which are processed in a specific way.
3   These representations must be realized by concrete brain states in order to be able to do what they are assumed to do.
4   Therefore: Mental states are brain states.

Argument from science (2)
1   Cognitive capacities are not grounded in abstract algorithms, but in concrete states and processes in the brain (neural networks, etc.).
2   Intentional states can play a role in the production of cognitive behavior only if they are part of this system of brain states.
3   Therefore: Mental states are brain states.
4   Whatever approach we prefer, science seems to tell us that intentional states must be brain states.

The last argument addressed by Baker is the *argument from causal explanation*. There are only few epiphenomenalists around these days. Most philosophers agree that mental states make a difference. People who believe that it will rain tomorrow behave differently from people who believe that the sun will shine. And people suffering from severe headaches behave differently from people who feel relaxed after having taken a soothing bath. The behavior of people, therefore, can often be causally explained by reference to their mental states. And this, in turn, implies that the mental states of persons indeed figure among the causes of their behavior. On the other hand, we know that physical events must have physical causes and that our behavior is, in the end, caused by what is going on in our brains. Mental states, therefore, can be among the causes of our behavior only if they are states of our brains. That is, unless mental states are brain states they cannot be causally relevant to our actions. Put in a nutshell, the *argument from causal explanation*, thus, proceeds like this:

Argument from causal explanation
1   The mental states of a person are causally relevant for his/her behavior.
2   The mental states of a person cannot be causally relevant for his/her behavior unless they are brain states.
3   Therefore: Mental states are brain states.

In what follows, I shall sketch a fourth argument in favor of the Standard View that, although it is - in a way - related to the argument from causal explanation, enables us to look at the problem of the causal relevance of mental states from a different angle.

Before taking up my argument, I would like to stress two points in which Baker's and my views concur. Let me stress that I wholeheartedly agree with Baker that there is not the slightest reason to believe that mental states are brain states *if* brain states are construed as 'spatially and temporally locatable inside a spatiotemporal entity like an organism' (Baker, 1995: 14). In my view, it would be pure nonsense to assume that internal states have the ontological status of physical *particulars* which are part of other physical particulars. Believing something, desiring something, fearing something and all other mental states no doubt have the ontological status of *properties*. This classification marks the second point on which Baker and I are in full agreement. However, I do not see why proponents of the Standard View should be committed to denying this or why they should be committed to the view that mental states are brain states *in the sense mentioned*. Think, for example, of Fodor's Representational Theory of Mind. Fodor is *not* claiming that a belief is, in the end, nothing but a mental representation, i.e. a 'spatially and temporally locatable' state of the brain. What he does claim is this: A belief is, in the end, a relational property of an organism, a property the organism has if it stands in a certain relation to a certain mental representation. This brings me to a first point of disagreement - the question of what exactly it is that proponents of the Standard View claim.

2 What the Standard View Really Amounts to

To my mind, the formula 'Mental states are brain states'[3] simply is far too vague to be a good candidate for an adequate answer to this question. But what more precise formula would be better suited to this purpose? If we keep in mind what e.g. proponents of Logical Behaviorism or the Identity Theory did in fact say and if we also bear in mind that what is being asked for is an account of mental *properties*, perhaps the following formula would do a better job: 'Mental properties are either identical with or reducible to physical properties'. Indeed, this is my preferred reading of what the Standard View comprises. But even this formula is still too vague - at least as long as we do not have a more precise idea of what 'identical with' and 'reducible to' could mean in this context. I would, therefore, like to start with an answer to this last question.[4]

In my view, the most sophisticated account of the concepts of identity and reducibility rests on a distinction which was first drawn by C.D. Broad some seventy years ago, the distinction between *mechanically explainable* and *emergent* properties.[5] Broad developed this distinction in the context of the debate concerning the problem of Vitalism. With regard to this problem, two factions opposed each other: the *Mechanists*, who claimed that the properties characteristic of living organisms (metabolism, perception, goal-directed behavior, procreation, morphogenesis) could be explained mechanically in the same way in which the behavior of a clock can be explained by the properties and the arrangement of its cogs, springs and weights, and the *Vitalists*, who held the contrary view, namely that an explanation as envisaged by the mechanists was impossible and that one had to postulate a special substance in order to explain life - an entelechy or an *élan vital*. In his theory of emergent properties Broad attempted to create room for a third position mediating between these two extremes.

Broad's first step was to point out that the problem of Vitalism is only a special case of a much more general problem - the problem of how the *macroproperties* of a complex system are related to its *microstructure*, i.e., of how the macroproperties are related to the *properties of the parts* which make up the system and their *arrangement*. With regard to this relation there is the possibility (which amounts to a vitalistic position) that a macroproperty F of a system cannot be explained by means of its microstructure, but only by postulating an additional substance. However, if we disregard

---

[3] Cf., e.g., Baker (1995, pp. 6-7); and also Baker's contribution to this volume.

[4] For the following see also Beckermann (1992a; 1992b; 1996; 1997a; 1997b).

[5] Cf. especially Broad 1925.

this possibility, we are not left with *one* further possibility (mechanism), but - Broad argues - with *two*: the property *F* can be *mechanically explainable*, but it can also be *emergent*. Broad explains the difference between these two positions as follows:

> Put in abstract terms the emergent theory asserts that there are certain wholes, composed (say) of constituents A, B, and C in a relation R to each other; that all wholes composed of constituents of the same kind as A, B, and C in relations of the same kind as R have certain characteristic properties; that A, B, and C are capable of occurring in other kinds of complex where the relation is not of the same kind as R; and that the characteristic properties of the whole R(A, B, C) cannot, even in theory, be deduced from the most complete knowledge of the properties of A, B, and C in isolation or in other wholes which are not of the form R(A, B, C). The mechanistic theory rejects the last clause of this assertion. (Broad 1925, 61)

Broad thus stresses two points:

1. Both mechanically explainable and emergent properties depend nomologically on corresponding microstructures. That is to say, if a system *S* with the microstructure $[C_1, ..., C_n; R]$[6] possesses a macroproperty *F*, the sentence 'For all *x*: if *x* has the microstructure $[C_1, ..., C_n; R]$, then *x* possesses the macroproperty *F*' is a true law of nature, regardless of whether *F* is mechanically explainable or emergent.

2. Mechanically explainable properties differ from emergent properties in that the former can, at least in principle, be deduced 'from the most complete knowledge of the properties of [the components $C_1, ..., C_n$] in isolation or in other wholes' while this cannot be done for the latter.

Thus, emergent properties are characterized by two features: (a) Like mechanically explainable properties they depend on corresponding microstructural properties; but (b) in contrast to mechanically explainable properties they cannot even in principle be deduced 'from the most complete knowledge of the properties of [the components $C_1, ..., C_n$] in isolation or in other wholes'.

I think that this yields a very illuminating first step towards drawing the distinction in question. But why does Broad use the complicated clause 'from the most complete knowledge of the properties of [the components $C_1, ..., C_n$] in isolation or in other wholes'? And what does he mean by

---

[6] 'System *S* has the microstructure $[C_1, ..., C_n; R]$' is a shorthand for '*S* consists of the parts $C_1, ..., C_n$ which stand in the (spatial) relation *R* to each other'.

saying that certain properties of a system can be 'deduced' from the complete knowledge of the properties of its parts while others cannot?

With regard to the first question, what Broad seems to have had in mind is precisely what Hempel and Oppenheim some twenty years after the first publication of *The Mind and Its Place in Nature* phrased thus:

> If a characteristic of a whole is counted as emergent simply if its occurrence cannot be inferred from a knowledge of all the properties of its parts, then, as Grelling has pointed out, no whole can have any emergent characteristics. Thus ... the properties of hydrogen include that of forming, if suitably combined with oxygen, a compound which is liquid, transparent, etc. Hence the liquidity, transparency, etc. of water *can* be inferred from certain properties of its chemical constituents. (Hempel/Oppenheim 1948, 260)

In order to avoid rendering the concept of emergence vacuous, inferences of this kind must be blocked. Broad's formula serves precisely this purpose, since it is obviously designed to guarantee that we cannot have recourse to properties like those mentioned by Hempel and Oppenheim when we attempt to deduce a macroproperty F of a complex system from the properties of its parts and their structure. However, the question remains as to whether this purpose could have been accomplished with a simpler and more lucid formulation. This much seems clear: It is crucial that in our attempts to deduce some macroproperty F of a complex object from the properties of its parts and their structural relations, we are not allowed to use 'ad hoc'-properties such as the property that certain components, if arranged in a specific way, form a complex object which has the property F. The question, therefore, is how we can guarantee this without at the same time excluding properties which we may legitimately refer to in such an attempt.

It may be possible to find an answer to this question if we consider which laws we may use in deductions of this type. For here we encounter another possible source of trivializing the concept of emergence. If we could utilize the law mentioned above, i.e. the law 'For all x: if x has the microstructure $[C_1, ..., C_n; R]$, then x possesses the macroproperty F', there would not be any emergent properties, either. After all, Hempel and Oppenheim could have formulated their point thus:

> It is a true law of nature that, if suitably combined with oxygen, hydrogen forms a compound which is liquid, transparent, etc. Hence the liquidity, transparency, etc. of water *can* be derived by means of the laws of nature.

Broad, thus, must rule out recourse to laws of this type as well. That he, indeed, sought to do so can be seen from the following passage discussing the properties of clocks.

> We know perfectly well that the behavior of a clock can be deduced from
> the particular arrangement of springs, wheels, pendulum, etc., in it, and
> from *general laws of mechanics and physics which apply just as much to
> material systems which are not clocks.* (Broad 1925, 60 - italics mine)

Obviously, Broad holds that if we attempt to deduce some macroproperty F of a complex object from the properties and arrangement of its parts,
we may only use *general laws* which are valid for the parts of a complex
system independent of the specific configurations of these parts. Hence, the
most straightforward answer to the question 'which properties of a system's
parts may we refer to in such a deduction?' is apparently this: 'to those
properties which are mentioned in these general laws of nature.' I would
therefore like to suggest that we replace Broad's clause with the formula 'if
F can be deduced by means of the general laws of nature which are true of
the components C_1, ..., C_n from the properties of the components mentioned in these laws.'[7]

Even after this point has been clarified, the question remains what
Broad meant with 'deduction' in this context. Broad himself does not offer
any precise answer. However, it may be possible to reconstruct the missing
answer with a little additional consideration. Properties are normally characterized by a set of features:

- something has the property of being a bachelor if it is a man and un-
  married.
- something has the property of being magnetic if it attracts iron filings,
  if it induces electricity in circular conductors and if it shows all the
  other characteristics which are typical for being magnetic.
- something has a temperature of 300 K if upon touch it induces a certain
  sensation of warmth, if the mercury column of a thermometer with
  which it has been thermally balanced reaches the mark 26.85 C, and if
  it has all the other causes and effects which are characteristic of this
  temperature.

If we wish to deduce the macroproperty F of a system from the system's
microstructure, it, therefore, is crucial that we succeed in showing that it
follows from the general laws of nature that each system which has this
microstructure also possesses all features which are characteristic of F. On
the whole, I take it that Broad's considerations concerning the distinction

---

[7] In the last consequence, this improved version of Broad's formula renders superfluous any
reference to admissible properties; if we specify which laws can figure in the derivations in
question, we have implicitly determined which properties may play a role in the derivations
mentioned.

between mechanically explainable and emergent properties can best be summarized in the following two definitions:

(ME)   A macroproperty F of a complex system S with the microstructure $[C_1, ..., C_n; R]$ is *mechanically explainable* if and only if the following is true:
   (a) The statement 'For all x: if x has the microstructure $[C_1, ..., C_n; R]$ then x has the macroproperty F' is a true law of nature, and
   (b) it follows from the general laws of nature applying to the components $C_1, ..., C_n$ that S possesses all features which are characteristic of the property F.

(E)   A macroproperty F of a complex system S with the microstructure $[C_1, ..., C_n; R]$ is *emergent* if and only if the following is true:
   (a) on the one hand the statement 'For all x: if x has the microstructure $[C_1, ..., C_n; R]$ then x has the macroproperty F' is a true law of nature, on the other hand, however,
   (b) it does not follow from the general laws of nature applying to the components $C_1, ..., C_n$ that S possesses all features which are characteristic of the property F.

A great merit of these two definitions resides in the fact that Broad's distinction between mechanically explainable and emergent properties far better captures the intuitive difference between reducible properties and properties that cannot be reduced to more fundamental properties than all other accounts have been able to, including the ones offered by Logical Behaviorism and the Identity Theory. That is to say, from the definition (ME) we can immediately derive a definition of the concepts of reducibility or realization that is much more in accord with our intuitive preconceptions than any other definition proposed.

(R)   A macroproperty F of a system S is at t *reducible to* a microstructure $[C_1, ..., C_n; R]$ (is at t *realized by* a microstructure $[C_1, ..., C_n; R]$) if and only if S at t has the microstructure $[C_1, ..., C_n; R]$) and if it follows from the general laws of nature applying to the components $C_1, ..., C_n$ that S at t possesses all features which are characteristic of the property F.

This definition may also serve as a starting point for a better understanding of what 'identity' can mean in this context. For that F is identical with a certain microstructure $[C_1, ..., C_n; R]$ seems to amount to no more than that

F is, for whatever reasons, *always* realized by the same microstructure $[C_1, ..., C_n; R]$. A simple and adequate definition of 'identity', thus, can be given in this way:

(I) A macroproperty *F* is 'identical' to a certain microstructure $[C_1, ..., C_n; R]$ if and only if any object *x* has *F* if and only if *x* has the microstructure $[C_1, ..., C_n; R]$ and if it follows from the general laws of nature applying to the components $C_1, ..., C_n$ that *x*, if it has the microstructure $[C_1, ..., C_n; R]$, possesses all features which are characteristic of the property *F*.[8]

Perhaps an example may help us to understand better what these definitions - and especially definition (R) - amount to. Take for instance the property of being liquid. Presumably everyone would agree that the liquidity of water is reducible to its microstructure. But why is this? In general, liquids differ from gases in that their volume is (almost) incompressible. They differ from solids in that their shape is changeable and moulds itself to the receptacle holding them. This is the case because in liquids - as opposed to gases - the molecules are as tightly packed as possible. They cannot get any closer to each other (or rather, they can do so only under very great pressure), because the repulsive forces between the molecules do not permit this. On the other hand, the molecules of liquids can move relative to each other, they can - so to speak - roll over each other freely, while the molecules of solids are prevented from such motion by the forces which hold them in their relative positions. Therefore, the molecules of solids can only move together: the whole object moves, while the relative position of its molecules remains the same, thereby keeping the object's form constant. Now, almost all scientists would agree that the forces which water molecules exercise on each other under certain conditions follow from the natural laws that are generally true of them. Hence, it also follows from these natural laws that the repulsive forces between the molecules are such that they do not permit them to get any closer to each other, and that the attractive forces are great enough to minimize the distance between the molecules, but not so great as to fix them in their relative positions.

Even this simple example demonstrates clearly that definition (R) encounters a problem concerning interlevel connections. For, obviously, from the general laws of nature applying to the components of a system it only follows how these *components* behave under certain conditions. Thus, the

---

[8] The term 'identical' here is put in quotes because 'identity' in the sense of definition (I) indeed is very different from the strict identity of logic.

question remains of how we can infer from the properties of a system's components which properties the system possesses as a whole. Broad does not offer an answer to this question, and perhaps no general answer can be given. Nevertheless, if we consider concrete examples, it can be seen how this problem may be solved in individual cases. In the example just cited, for instance, the inference from the behavior of the system's components to the behavior of the system as a whole is based on a simple principle: If we know which forces the molecules of an object exert on each other, we also know how easily these molecules can move relative to each other. And if we know the latter, we also know whether the object is solid or liquid. Another principle which is very important in a range of similar cases is this: If we know how all constituent parts of an object move, we also know how the whole object moves. This principle is applied in the following case.

Among the characteristic features of the property of being magnetic counts the fact that magnetic objects attract iron filings in their proximity. Does this follow from the general laws applying to the parts of magnetic objects? Consider, for instance, a permanent magnet, e.g. a piece of iron which is permanently magnetic. A permanent magnet, as physics informs us, consists of many tiny elementary magnets, which all point in the same direction. The iron filings in its proximity also consist of small elementary magnets, albeit unordered ones. From the general laws which apply to elementary magnets it follows: If the elementary magnets in some piece of iron are directionally aligned, they generate a relatively strong magnetic field around this piece. This magnetic field causes the - previously unordered - elementary magnets in the iron filings to align themselves in such a way that they point towards the permanent magnet with that pole which is opposed to the closest pole of the permanent magnet. This has the following consequence: on all elementary magnets in the iron filings a force is exerted in the same direction, namely the direction towards the permanent magnet. Since this force is not counteracted by any other force, the elementary magnets begin to move in that direction. And if all constituent parts of an object move in a certain direction, the object itself also moves in that direction.

The principles which have so far been illustrated by just two examples do not allow us to deal with all cases, but they may give an impression of how the problem of interlevel connections associated with the definitions (R) and (I) may be solved in individual cases.[9]

---

[9] In Beckermann (1992b) the author discusses an example in which the color of a liquid is explained by the chemical structure of the liquid. Obviously, in this example the following principle is used: If we know photons of which wavelength are absorbed by the molecules of a liquid, we also know which color that liquid has.

3   The Real Reason for the Standard View

Having thus elaborated the main thesis of the Standard View, viz. the claim that mental properties are either identical with, or reducible to, physical properties, we can proceed to the question of what arguments can be offered to establish the truth of this thesis. Well, I do not think that the thesis can be given an *a priori* proof. But there are some arguments which indeed lend it a high *prima facie* plausibility. As already mentioned, in what follows I shall concentrate on one of these arguments, since I believe that it supports the Standard View in a very strong way.

In order to understand the argument, it may be reasonable to begin by asking what would follow if the Standard View were false. On the basis of the definitions (R) and (I), there is a plain answer to this question: If the Standard View were false, mental properties would at least be emergent, i.e., they would be properties that, even in principle, could not be deduced from the properties of the parts of the organisms that are their bearers. This is why we should try and be as clear as possible about what it would mean if mental properties were emergent, i.e. what it would mean to claim that at least some macroproperties of physical systems are not realized by their microstructures. Let us ask, for example, what would be the case if it turned out that the property of being magnetic was an emergent property.

We have already seen that the property of being magnetic is (at least in part) characterized by the fact that magnetic things behave in a particular way:

-   Magnetic objects attract iron filings in their proximity;
-   the needle of a compass near a magnetic object tends to point in its direction;
-   magnetic objects induce an electrical current in coils which they pass through;
-   magnetic objects tend to magnetize non magnetic pieces of iron in their vicinity; etc.

Being magnetic, thus, makes a difference especially to the behavior of certain objects in the neighborhood of magnetic things. These behavioral differences, however, do not only concern these objects themselves but also their parts. If a magnetic object induces electrical current in a coil which it passes through, for example, this is so because the magnetic object causes the electrons in the coil to behave differently. And even in the case where a magnetic object causes a nearby compass needle to point in its direction, this can happen only in virtue of the atoms which the needle consists of being caused to move in a specific way.

Now, think of an arbitrary magnetic object S. If being magnetic is emergent, then, by definition, S's being magnetic is not realized by its microstructure. And that, in turn, implies that it does not follow from the general laws of nature applying to the parts of S that S (and the objects in S's neighborhood) behave the way they actually do. In other words, if being magnetic is emergent (a) the fact that electrical current is induced in a coil which S passes through cannot be explained by the general laws of nature applying to the parts of S. And, by the same token, if being magnetic is emergent (b) the fact that a nearby compass needle moves to point in S's direction cannot be accounted for by these same laws. But that is not yet the whole story. What is even more important is this: Since a flow of current consists of certain movements of the electrons in the coil and since the movement of the compass needle occurs in virtue of certain movements of the atoms which make up this needle, it follows from (a) and (b) that, if being magnetic is emergent, not even the movements of the electrons in the coil and the movements of the atoms which the compass needle consists of can be explained by the *general* laws of nature applying to the parts of S, i.e. applying to the atoms which make up S.

The irritating consequence, then, is this: if being magnetic is emergent, then nuclear physics is incomplete in a disturbing way. Each time the movements of certain atoms are caused by a certain object's being magnetic, these movements *cannot* be accounted for by the relevant general laws of this part of science. Or, to put it another way, since movements are always caused by corresponding forces, the emergent character of being magnetic would imply that atoms are sometimes moved by forces the existence of which cannot be derived from the general laws of nuclear physics.

And this, of course, can be generalized. *Each emergent property which is at least in part characterized by the fact that objects having this property move in a certain way leads to a gap in nuclear physics, i.e. leads to the assumption that atoms are sometimes moved by forces that cannot be explained by means of the general laws of this science.* The only proviso that should be added is perhaps that this conclusion can be drawn only if the macrobehavior characteristic of the emergent property in question can take place only if the atoms which the corresponding macrosystems consist of themselves move in specific ways.

Some might think, however, that there is a way to bypass this consequence. Broad himself admitted that emergent properties are nomologically dependent on microstructural properties. That is, according to Broad's account, for each emergent macroproperty F there exists a set of microstructures M such that the following holds:

1. A system x can possess F only if it has one of the microstructures belonging to M.
2. For each member M_i of M: if x has M_i, then x has F.

Even if being magnetic is emergent, our system S, therefore, can have this property only if it has one of the corresponding microstructures, i.e., if it consists of certain atoms arranged in a specific manner R. In order to explain the movement of the electrons in the coil or the movement of the atoms of the compass needle we thus need not leave the level of atoms. For, instead of accounting for these movements by reference to S's being magnetic, we can explain these movements just as well by tracing them back to the fact that the atoms S consists of are arranged in the manner R. Thus, in contrast to what has been claimed so far, all effects of emergent properties can be accounted for at the level of atoms.

This objection, however, would miss a decisive point. For the most intriguing upshot of the argument is not that the existence of emergent properties would imply the existence of effects at the atomic level that cannot be explained at this very level, but that the existence of emergent properties would imply the existence of effects at the atomic level that cannot be accounted for by the *general laws* of nuclear physics, but only by what might be called *special laws*, i.e. laws that tell us nothing but that certain (unexpected) effects E_1, ..., E_m occur if particles of kind C_1, ..., C_n are arranged in the manner R. According to Broad's account of emergent properties, the movement of the electrons in the coil or the movement of the atoms of the compass needle can, of course, be explained by the fact that S consists of certain atoms arranged in a certain manner. But if being magnetic is indeed emergent, the law which tells us that atoms of this kind, arranged in this way, cause these kind of movements *itself* cannot in any way be derived from the laws that generally hold for particles of this kind. For if it could, it would follow from these general laws that objects that consist of atoms of this kind arranged in this way would have all features that are characteristic of being magnetic. And this in turn would imply that being magnetic is not emergent.

Thus, a better way to make the essential point of the argument would be to say that the existence of emergent properties would destroy the *homogeneity* of nuclear physics. It would make nuclear physics a science with some general laws and a whole bunch of exceptions, i.e., it would make physics what may justly be called a *weird* science. To take a simple example, in classical mechanics, the law of gravitation

$$F = \frac{m_1 \cdot m_2}{r^2}$$

is thought to hold quite generally for all masses m_1 and m_2 and all distances r. It would strike us as very strange if it turned out that there were some masses and distances for which the force exerted on the two bodies would not conform to this law. Say, if it turned out that for $m_1=1$ and $m_2=10$ and $r=1$ the force exerted would amount to 5 instead of 10 N. Or, to take another example, we are all fairly convinced that the principle of the parallelogram of forces applies to all bodies and all forces whatsoever. Thus again, it would be very strange indeed if it turned out that for certain pairs of forces F_1 and F_2 the resulting force did not equal the vector sum of F_1 and F_2.

The assumption that there are emergent properties, however, would yield exactly this result. It would imply that the general laws of physics have quite a number of exceptions. For emergent properties, at least if they are in part characterized by the fact that objects having this property move in a certain way, cause the parts of the systems whose properties they are to move in ways that cannot be accounted for by the general laws of the relevant sciences. Each such case, therefore, constitutes an exception to these laws; which is why we need a special law to account for it.

Returning to the Standard View, we only have to apply the result of the foregoing considerations. For it is one of Baker's main claims that mental properties make a difference, that more often than not we are able to causally explain the behavior of persons by reference to their intentional attitudes. And there can be no doubt that when I raise my arm because I want to call someone's attention this can happen only if the muscles, cells and atoms which make up my arm move in a certain way. Thus, if the Standard View is false, i.e. if at least some mental properties are emergent, then there are movements of the muscles, cells and atoms which make up the limbs of persons that cannot be explained by the general laws of neurophysiology, biochemistry or physics. The falseness of the Standard View, thus, would imply that all these sciences are weird sciences in the sense explained.

Just to make this quite plain, I am not maintaining that this is impossible, that there is an *a priori* proof that at least physics is not a weird science. (Empirical research *may* show that indeed it is.) But I do think that, for all we know, this is a highly implausible idea. Therefore, I *do* claim, that there is a high *prima facie* plausibility to the position that the Standard View is true.

Perhaps Baker would answer that only someone who is already in the grip of what she calls 'methodological physicalism' is prone to think so.

> The methodological physicalist starts with a theoretical picture based on a philosophical idea of fundamental physics. He looks to see what general principles - like the closure of the physical and strong supervenience - that picture implies. Then, for any putative kind of phenomena, he checks to

see how it fits the picture. If he cannot imagine how some putative phenomena fit the microphysical world, then it is deemed unsuited for 'serious science'. And according to the methodological physicalist, nothing
unsuited for serious science can play an ineliminable role in a complete
description and explanation of all phenomena. (This volume, p. 23f.)

But this is not quite the truth. The 'argument from the implausibility of
downward causation' does not rest on 'a *theoretical* picture based on a
philosophical idea of fundamental physics'. Just like the argument against
the Standard View put forward in Baker's contribution to this volume, it
rather rests on 'an empirical conjecture about the future of neuroscience'
(this volume, p. 19) or, in the end, about the future physics. The argument
does *not* run: According to my theoretical picture, complete physics will
have such and such features; therefore downward causation is impossible;
therefore there are no emergent properties. Instead its main premise is empirical: For all we know, it seems plausible to assume that within complete
physics all microphysical phenomena will be explainable by means of a
certain set of fundamental laws.

Thus, in the end there seems to be a clash of empirical conjectures concerning the future of certain sciences. Baker thinks that 'neuroscientists in
the long run will *not* be able to identify particular neural tokens as tokens of
the belief that *p* (for any belief that *p*)' (this volume, p. 24). And she argues
that this, together with her other arguments, shows that the Standard View
is false. Defenders of the 'argument from the implausibility of downward
causation' on the other hand think that within complete physics all microphysical phenomena will be explainable by means of a certain set of fundamental laws. And they argue that this implies that there are no emergent
properties, i.e., that the Standard View is true (if there are any mental properties at all). Do we have to acknowledge a stalemate? Or is there any
means of resolving this difficulty?

There is. For, in my view, defenders of the Standard View are not
committed to the thesis that for each token of a mental state there is a corresponding neural token to which it is identical or by which it is realized.[10]
Defenders of the Standard View only have to claim that mental properties
are not emergent. Whether, e.g., a certain belief is emergent or not, however, does not depend on whether there is a corresponding neural token, but
only on whether it follows from the fundamental laws of nature that a person who is made up of such and such cells arranged in such and such a
manner possesses all features which are characteristic of someone who has
this belief. That is, if a belief is realized at all it may well be realized not by

---

[10] The talk of 'types' and 'tokens' in this context has aptly been criticized in Andreas Kemmerling (1997).

a *particular neural* state, but by the *overall state of the person's body*. I am not sure whether Baker would also claim that scientists in the long run will *not* be able to show that a person who is made up of such and such cells arranged in such and such a manner possesses all features which are characteristic of someone who has a certain belief. Maybe she would. But I feel that such a claim would be hard to substantiate.

4 References

Baker, L.R. 1995. *Explaining Attitudes.* Cambridge: Cambridge University Press.

Beckermann, A. 1992a. Introduction: Reductive and Nonreductive Physicalism. In *Emergence or Reduction?* A. Beckermann, H. Flohr, J. Kim, eds. Berlin: Walter de Gruyter: 1-21.

Beckermann, A. 1992b. Supervenience, Emergence, and Reduction. In *Emergence or Reduction?* A. Beckermann, H. Flohr, J. Kim, eds. Berlin: Walter de Gruyter: 94-118.

Beckermann, A. 1996. Eigenschafts-Physikalismus. In *Zeitschrift für Philosophische Forschung* 50: 3-25.

Beckermann, A. 1997a. Property Physicalism, Reduction and Realization. In *Mindscapes. Philosophy, Science, and the Mind*, M. Carrier, P. Machamer eds. Konstanz: Universitätsverlag / Pittsburgh: Pittsburgh University Press: 303-321.

Beckermann, A. 1997b. Was macht Bewußtsein für Philosophen zum Problem? In *Logos* 4: 1-19.

Broad, C.D. 1925 *The Mind and Its Place In Nature.* London: Routledge and Kegan Paul.

Hempel, C.G., Oppenheim, P. 1965. Studies in the Logic of Explanation. In *Philosophy of Science* 15 (1948): 135-175. Reprinted in: C.G. Hempel, *Aspects of Scientific Explanation and Other Essays in the Philosophy of Science.* New York: The Free Press: 245-290.

Kemmerling, A. 1997. Überzeugungen für Naturalisten. In *Analyomen 2, Vol. III*, G. Meggle (Hg.). Berlin: Walter de Gruyter, 59-83.

Kim, J. 1992. Downward Causation. In *Emergence or Reduction?* A. Beckermann, H. Flohr, J. Kim, eds. Berlin: Walter de Gruyter: 119-138.

5

Brain States, with Attitudes

Louise Antony

Lynne Rudder Baker has been laboring mightily over the last decade or so to discredit what she calls the 'Standard View' in the philosophy of mind: the view, simply put, that beliefs and other propositional attitude states 'are' (in some sense of 'are') brain states. Her strategy is two-pronged: on the one hand, she offers arguments directly against the Standard View, and on the other, she argues against it indirectly by trying to undercut arguments that its supporters have offered in its favor. But I do not think Baker has made her case: I think the general reasons for accepting some version of the Standard View still stand, and I think that at least one version of the Standard View, a position I'll call 'non-emergentist non-reductive materialism' (NENR materialism) survives her direct challenge.

Overall, I think that the shortcomings in Baker's critique have two sources: first, failure to appreciate the significance of differences among various Standard View theories, and second, confusion about the significance of semantic and psychological externalism. (Baker is hardly alone, by the way, in fallaciously drawing from externalism unduly pessimistic conclusions about the prospects for a reductive explanation of mental phenomena). I'll defend my diagnosis in the course of analyzing three of Baker's arguments, beginning with an indirect argument and moving on to two direct arguments. The first two arguments are found in her book, *Explaining Attitudes* (Baker 1995; 'EA' hereafter), and the third comes from her essay 'Are Beliefs Brain States?' (Baker 2001 this volume; 'ABBS' hereafter).

Explaining Beliefs: Lynne Rudder Baker and Her Critics.
Anthonie Meijers (ed.).

1 A Typology of Materialist Theories

To begin, let's get clear about the relationship between what Baker calls the 'Standard View,' and *reductionism* in its various forms. According to one standard philosophical taxonomy, there are two types of reductionism: strong, or type-reductionism, which holds that every mental property can be identified with some physical property; and weak, or token-reductionism, which denies that mental properties can be identified with physical properties, but still maintains that every token instance of a mental property is either identical with, or is constituted by some token instance of some physical property. It is easy to see how views of both types could be regarded as versions of the view that 'beliefs are brain states,' although strong and weak reductionists would have to mean different things by the slogan. Type-reductionists would mean 'to be a belief is to be a brain state of type X' while token-reductionists would mean 'every individual belief is identical with, or is constituted by some individual brain state or other.'

But the distinction between strong and weak reductionism does not provide either a full or an adequate taxonomy of non-dualistic theories of mind. For one thing, the distinction says nothing about some very important differences among monistic theories regarding the relationship between mental and physical phenomena: for example, it lumps together as forms of weak reductionism views as dissimilar as Donald Davidson's and Jerry Fodor's. A second problem is that it leaves no room for Baker's view, which rejects both dualism *and* the Standard View. A more adequate taxonomy is suggested by some recent work of Jaegwon Kim's (Kim, forthcoming). He has argued that the notion of 'reduction' involves, intuitively, three kinds of demand: first, for *ontological* economy, second, for a basis for inter-level prediction, and third, for a basis for inter-level explanation. We might, then, try to classify non-dualistic theories of the mental according to how they fare *vis á vis* these desiderata. Strong reductionist theories clearly satisfy all three demands, since according to them, mental entities, states, and events are *nothing but* entities, states and events of a certain physical type. But once we turn to theories that reject the strong reductionist claim that mental kinds can be identified with physical kinds - and this includes both weak reductionism and Baker's 'pragmatic realism' - the picture gets more complicated.

Do theories of this sort satisfy the ontological demand? While theories in this group effect some ontological economy by rejecting *substance* dualism, they still maintain an ontological distinction between mental and non-mental *properties*. Such theories, then, while they should be counted as materialist, are arguably not fully reductionist: a situation we can capture by designating these theories versions of 'non-reductive materialism.' Baker's own view falls within this category. But now, to complete the taxonomy suggested by Kim's analysis, we now have to inquire into the predictive and explanatory aspects of reduction. This is where we discover the differences among non-reductive materialists that are obscured by the standard taxonomy.

Any materialist who rejects type-reductionism is going to hold that mental properties are ineliminable in principle as well as in practice; that is just what it is to reject type-reductionism. To be a non-reductive materialist is just to hold that something would be lost if we were not able to invoke mental properties in descriptions, predictions, and explanations. Thus, *all* non-reductive materialists will reject what Baker has called the 'replaceability thesis:' the thesis that explanations in terms of belief can be *replaced* by explanations in terms of brain states. Still, non-reductive materialists are going to differ on the question of the relation between the truth-conditions of mentalistic claims and phenomena at lower levels of description. Some non-reductive materialists believe that the truth of mentalistic claims, especially the truth of mentalistic explanations, requires the existence of some sort of systematic nomic connection between mental and non-mental phenomena. Other non-reductive materialists, however, believe that there either are not or need not be any such systematic connections between the mental and the non-mental. I am in the first camp; Baker is in the second.

Roughly, those of us in the first group are committed to what Baker calls the 'brain-explain' thesis: the claim that '[u]nless beliefs were brain states they could not causally explain behavior.'[1] We hold that all mentalistic facts, including mentalistic explanatory facts, require explanation in terms of lower-level mechanisms, and that the existence of such mechanisms requires systematic, nomic connections between mental phenomena and the phenomena at the lower-level that constitute the mental. Since an understanding of such mechanisms could, in principle, provide predictions about mentalistic phenomena, as well as explanations of regularities observed at the mentalistic level, these versions of non-reductive materialism do, in a sense and to an extent, satisfy Kim's second and third desiderata. But non-reductive materialists of Baker's ilk *reject* the 'brain-explain' thesis, on the grounds that mentalistic explanations stand on their own metaphysically, and require no 'vindication' from lower-level sciences. They also deny the possibility, in principle, of 'bottom-up' predictions of mental phenomena - predictions from facts described in physicalistic terms to events described mentalistically. Thus, these non-reductive materialists would reject Kim's second and third desiderata.

---

[1] Although see discussion below for an important caveat.

Kim does not believe that any form of non-reductive materialism is viable; the first form, he believes, will collapse into strong reductionism, and the second will turn out to be equivalent to an unacceptable form of emergentism. This is not the place to argue against Kim on the first point,[2] nor to offer my support for his position on the second. But I'll borrow his terms: I'll distinguish the two groups of non-reductive materialism, tendentiously, by calling the first group 'non-emergentist non-reductive (NENR) materialists' and the second, 'emergentist non-reductivist (ENR) materialists'.

The difference between emergentist and the non-emergentist strains of non-reductive materialists, is explained, I suspect, by the different reasons we each have for rejecting strong reductionism. We non-emergentists are motivated mainly by considerations of multiple realizability. Because we believe that mental properties are functional or structural properties of physical systems, we also believe that there are a variety of distinct physical systems that can instantiate mental properties, and thus that no physical property can be necessarily co-extensive with any mental property. Emergentists, on the other hand, tend to reject strong reductionism because they think there is some sort of 'incommensurability' between the mental and the physical - some feature of our mental categories that makes it impossible for them to ever mesh smoothly with the categories of the natural sciences. Donald Davidson, for example, has argued, notoriously, that the essential 'normativity' of the mental prevents there being any strict laws linking the physical and the psychological.[3] Baker, as we'll see, also has an 'in-principle' argument against even the limited sort of reductive account favored by us non-emergentists.

Altogether, the taxonomy I propose looks like this:

---

[2] But see Antony & Levine, 1997.

[3] Notice, however, that Davidson considers himself a token-reductionist. (Indeed, Davidson takes the principle of the anomalism of the mental to be a premise in his argument for token-reductionism). He would thus have to be counted as a proponent of the Standard View by Baker's accounting, although he would certainly reject the Brain Explain Thesis. This doesn't seem right - by my reckoning, Davidson has much more in common with Baker than with me. Davidson's presentation of the theory of anomalous monism is in Davidson 1980.

Materialist Theories of Mind

Can mental properties be reduced to physical properties?

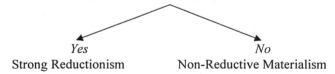

Yes	*No*
Strong Reductionism	Non-Reductive Materialism

Can mental properties be explained/predicted in terms of physical properties?

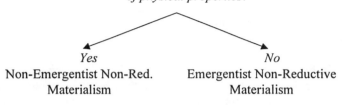

Yes	*No*
Non-Emergentist Non-Red. Materialism	Emergentist Non-Reductive Materialism

Now, how do theories thus classified stand on the Standard View? My sense is that the theories that Baker is really after are all the theories *except* ENM theories.[4] The thesis that defines the Standard View, in its full-dress version, clearly includes Non-emergentist non-reductivist accounts: 'What Standard View theories have in common is the thesis that each instance of each belief is identical with, or is constituted by, an instance of a particular brain state' (EA, 12). But when Baker involves the Standard View thesis in arguments, she tends to use the abbreviated version, 'Beliefs are brain states,' a formulation that obscures the differences between strong reductive accounts and non-reductive accounts. This would be all right if nothing in the arguments depended on the difference; but as we shall see, *everything* depends on the difference.

---

[4] I say this, noting as I did above, that Davidson's anomalous monism ought to be counted a Standard View theory in virtue of its being a token-identity theory.

2   Explaining 'Brain Explain'

Let's turn to the arguments. I'll start with one of Baker's indirect attacks on the Standard View. This argument of Baker's is meant to counter one of the arguments frequently made in favor of the Standard View, an argument Baker calls the 'argument from causal explanation.' Her reconstruction of the pro-SV argument looks like this:

(IIIa)   Unless beliefs were brain states they could not causally explain behavior. (The 'brain explain' thesis)

(IIIb)   Beliefs can causally explain behavior

(IIIc)   Beliefs are brain states. (EA, 17)

The argument is clearly valid, and Baker accepts premise (IIIb). Her objection is to the first premise, the 'brain explain' thesis. The argument against it depends on two further premises:

(C1)   No belief explanation is replaceable by brain-state explanations.

(P3)   If the 'brain explain' thesis is true, then belief explanations are replaceable by brain-state explanations of the same phenomena. (EA, 138)

As a defender of NENR materialism, I'm clearly committed to premise (IIIb), the claim that beliefs can causally explain behavior. And since mine is a non-reductive account, committed to the autonomy of the mental, I want also to endorse (C1). But what about premise (P3)? Why should I or anyone but a *type*-reductionist believe that belief explanations can be replaced by brain-state explanations, whether or not the 'brain-explain' thesis is true? On the face of it, it would seem that the denial of this conditional is virtually the defining tenet of non-reductive materialism. Baker, however, insists that, whatever we want to believe, commitment to the brain explain thesis really does commit us to the replacement thesis as well. So we need to look at her defense of (P3).

Baker offers two arguments: the first depends on a general principle about levels of explanation,[5] for which Baker admits she has 'no

---

[5] EA, 140. The principle is this: 'Let E be a causal explanation that cites property P to explain some phenomenon F. Then, the causal explanatoriness of P depends on the relation of P to some lower-level property P^* only if E is replaceable by an explanation E^*, where E^* cites P^*.' It seems to me that this principle simply begs the question whether the brain explain thesis entails the replaceability thesis.

argument...other than intuition.' Aware that others may not share her intuition (I, for one, do not), she offers a second argument. This one, she promises, is directed precisely against someone like myself, a non-reductive materialist who thinks that 'the "brain explain" thesis is true *even if* belief explanations are not replaceable by brain-state explanations.' (EA, 138).

The argument is this: The claim that beliefs are constituted by brain states is meant by its advocates to be a contingent, rather than a conceptual claim. Thus, even according to advocates of the brain explain thesis, it could have turned out that the world was (e.g.) Aristotelian, in which case brain states would not have constituted beliefs. In such a world, all *superficial* sensory phenomena would be just as they are in the actual world: 'If the sensible and social world were the same as our world, we would have had the same range of explanations, deployed in the same ways and with the same degree of success, that we actually have.' (EA, 141). Hence, beliefs in the Aristotelian world, although not brain states, would still causally explain behavior. And this shows that even if beliefs *are* brain states in the actual world, the properties in virtue of which they are explanatory are not their neurological properties.

> Thus, since the explanatoriness of belief is compatible with the world's being Aristotelian, but beliefs' being brain states is not compatible with the world's being Aristotelian, it follows that the explanatoriness of the attitudes does not require that attitudes be identical to or constituted by brain states. (EA, 142)

But there is something very puzzling about this argument. What is its conclusion? From the passage quoted above, it looks like the conclusion is this: 'the explanatoriness of the attitudes does not require that attitudes be identical to or constituted by brain states.' But *this* claim is virtually equivalent to the negation of the brain-explain thesis, and *that* wasn't meant to be the conclusion. The conclusion was *supposed* to be (P3) - a claim that a certain conditional relationship held between the brain-explain thesis and the replaceability thesis (brain-state explanations can replace belief explanations). But not only does this argument fail to demonstrate the truth of that conditional - it actually demonstrates that it's *false*, since it shows that belief states' *actually* being brain states is compatible with their having their explanatory force in virtue of their mentalistic properties! Baker's idea seems to have been this: if it can be shown that beliefs would continue to explain behavior even in a world in which beliefs had no neurological basis whatsoever, then it follows trivially that, in such a world, belief explanations cannot be replaced by brain-state explanations. And indeed it does; quite so. Indeed, it shows, quite generally, that the explanatory value of beliefs *does not depend on their mode of realization*. *Ipso facto*, belief explanations can *never* be replaced by brain-state explanations *even if* they are realized as brain states.

Essentially, what Baker has done is to produce an argument for the autonomy of intentional explanation - a point on which she and her non-reductive materialist antagonists can agree. What she has *not* done is show that commitment to the Standard View leads a non-reductive materialist into embarrassment; that is, she has not shown that commitment to the idea that beliefs are, in fact, realized as brain states requires one to give up the autonomy of intentional explanation.

Now it's possible that Baker had something else in mind here: perhaps she means for the argument above to tell directly against premise (IIIa) - the claim that 'unless beliefs were brain states they could not causally explain behavior.' This interpretation is supported by the following passage, in which Baker spells out what she takes to be the significance of her formulation of premise (IIIa).

> Premise (IIIa) is an extremely rich philosophical thesis. It is a modal claim.... If the premise were merely a truth-functional conditional, then, on the assumptions that beliefs do causally explain behavior, and beliefs are in fact brain states, (IIIa) would be true - even if there were no connection between the causal explanatoriness of belief and beliefs' being brain states. So, (IIIa) must support counterfactuals: In nearby worlds in which beliefs causally explain behavior, they are brain states (*or, more generally, physically realized internal states*). Thus, the conclusion of the argument against (IIIa) in Chapter 5 is that even if beliefs are brain states in the actual world, they need not be brain states in order to be causally explanatory. (EA, 17-18) [my emphasis]

But now the non-reductive materialist can rightly object that there's equivocation afoot. How exactly is Premise (IIIa) to be understood? Let's distinguish a *strong* and a *weak* reading:

(IIIa - strong)   In any possible world in which beliefs are explanatory, beliefs are brain states.

(IIIa - weak)   In any possible world in which beliefs are explanatory, beliefs are physically realized internal states, and in this world those states are brain states.

Baker seems to say, in the passage cited above, that she intends the weak reading. And well she should, for no one who believes in multiple realizability would accept the strong reading. And (IIIa), recall, was supposed to be a premise in an argument that was accepted by all (non-eliminativist) partisans of the Standard View. But the problem for Baker is that her thought experiment doesn't refute the *weak* version of (IIIa) - it does not show that beliefs could be explanatory even if they failed to be physically realized *at all*.[6]

Talk of realization brings us back to the problem about the inadequacy of Baker's taxonomy. Baker frequently cautions us that when she uses the slogan 'beliefs are brain states,' she means it to be understood in such a way as to cover not only type- and token-identity theories, but theories that posit a potentially weaker relation than even token-identity, like 'realization' or 'constitution.' Now again, if we take the slogan simply and literally, then we can see how Baker's thought experiment might be taken to provide a refutation, since it shows, *inter alia*, that beliefs can *exist* without being brain states, and thus that beliefs cannot be literally *identified* with brain states. I find this inference less than sure; evaluating it fully would require discussion of topics beyond the scope of this paper.[7] But it doesn't matter, since once again, it is clear that the argument does not show that brain states do not *constitute* or *realize* beliefs in the actual world.

I think what we can see from all of this is that Baker never properly grasped the argument from causal explanation. I was willing to accept her formulation of the argument provisionally, on the understanding that (IIIa) would be understood in the weak sense. But the following would have been a better, and my by lights safer, formulation:

1   Unless beliefs were realized by some kind of physical states, they could not causally explain behavior.
2   Beliefs causally explain behavior.
∴ 2.5   Beliefs are *realized by some kind of physical states*.
2.75   The physical states that realize beliefs in human beings in the actual world are brain states.
∴ 3'   Beliefs in humans *in the actual world* are (realized by) brain states.

---

[6] Baker doesn't provide any details about the microstructure, or even the biology, of her imagined Aristotelian world. But she does make it clear that the thought experiment is not supposed to rest on the possibility of beliefs' being *immaterial*: 'To say that the *explanatoriness* of beliefs...is independent of their being brain states (or computer states) is not to say that beliefs or investments are in some sense "immaterial". They could not be immaterial - any more than our practice could be.' (EA, 143)

[7] We would have to settle at least the following question: even if it's true that something could be a belief without being a brain state, does it follow that some *particular* belief, which in the actual world is constituted by a brain state, could exist without being a brain state? Compare: something can be a statue without being a lump of marble; but can something be Michaelangelo's David without being marble? And if not, couldn't it then be the case that all *actual* beliefs are identical with brain states?

This, I contend, is the 'argument from causal explanation' that proponents of NENR versions of the Standard View have in mind. Formulated this way, the argument is immune from Baker's objections. It is clear that the conceivability of an Aristotelian world has no bearing whatsoever on premise (1), which replaces Baker's (IIIa). Also, while respecting Baker's point above, this version of the argument separates the modal claim about the requirements for beliefs' being causally explanatory, from the simple, non-modal claim that it is brain states that are the actual realizers of beliefs in human beings. Finally, it makes clear that the relation posited by proponents of this argument between mental states and their physical realizing states is a relation potentially weaker than identity.

There's one more point I want to make in connection with this argument, and that concerns Premise (P3) - the claim that if the Brain Explain Thesis is correct, then so is the Replaceability Thesis. Why does Baker think this is true? My suspicion is that she is committing a subtle equivocation on 'requires': that she is conflating the *metaphysical* requirements for a causal explanation to be *true*, with the *epistemological* requirements for a causal explanation to be *acceptable*. The Brain Explain Thesis, as she first states it, and as I understand it, states the metaphysical preconditions of its being true that beliefs causally explain actions, viz., that beliefs be physically realized. But as Baker reads it, I suspect, it is a statement about what must be presumed to be true in order for us to be warranted in accepting the citation of a belief *as a causal explanation*. In this sense, the thesis would assert that in order for us to be warranted in accepting belief explanations as causal explanations, we would have to *know that* beliefs were physically realized as brain states. But this claim I categorically reject. *Knowledge of* the metaphysical preconditions for constituting a cause is never a prerequisite for finding acceptable a proffered causal explanation.

On my view, as on Baker's, what generally suffices to warrant the acceptance of a causal explanation is inductive evidence of the usual sort, evidence that the explanation passes what Baker calls the 'Control Test.' As she says, '...we know that we have an adequate causal explanation when it affords control over the phenomena of the type explained' (EA, 122). Knowledge that we have hold of a controlling property - one that figures in nomic, counterfactual-supporting regularities - is all we need, epistemologically, to justify a claim to having a causal explanation. It is thus not necessary - indeed, how could it be? - that we know anything about the mechanisms by which the regularities in question are sustained, in order to causally explain behavior.[8] Without knowing any chemistry - or indeed, without knowing even that there's such a thing as chemistry - we can be warranted in citing the application of heat to a pot of water as the cause of its boiling. So too we can cite your anxious mood as the cause of your snappishness without having any idea how the brain realizes a mood, or even that it does. In both cases the 'explanatoriness' derives, as Baker insists, from the belief that we have a causally or nomically relevant property, and this belief can be justified in a number of ways.[9]

Everything I've just conceded, however, about the epistemology of explanation is perfectly consistent with the *metaphysical* thesis that in order to be a genuine cause of behavior a belief must be (either identical to or) realized in a brain state. The citation of beliefs is explanatory (roughly) because it works; intentional explanations afford the sort of control that Baker is talking about. But a further question is certainly legitimate: *how* do they afford such control? What sustains the relevant regularities? If we are physicalists, in the sense that we endorse the principle that all basic causal powers are fundamental properties of physics, then these questions take on a more determinate form. How do physical interactions constitute mental events? What physical mechanisms sustain psychological regularities?

---

[8] See Antony 1991 and 1995.

[9] I do differ from Baker, however, in this: I believe that even highly warranted upper-level generalizations may be defeated by new findings about the micro-level. I just believe very firmly that they won't be. Interestingly, at (at least) one point Baker seems to recognize this distinction between the metaphysics and epistemology of explanation:

'In general, we should distinguish between having an adequate causal explanation and knowing the physical conditions that in fact obtain when the explanatory properties are instantiated. Knowing physical conditions for the instantiation of explanatory properties may be irrelevant to assessing the putative explanation...knowing the physics of television broadcast transmission may be irrelevant to understanding the influence of television on children who watch it...[though it] may be just what you need if you want to sabotage Saturday morning cartoons...'

Quite so. However, she then continues:

'But we should not conclude that the adequacy of an intentional explanation depends on any particular relation between the intentional properties and physical properties.' (EA, 136)

I can perhaps agree with this last claim so long as 'adequate causal explanation' and 'depends on any particular relation...' are read epistemologically. But if by 'having an adequate causal explanation' one means that the properties in the explanans are in fact causally relevant to the production of the explanandum, and if by 'depends on' one means the relation of metaphysical necessitation, then, I contend, it *is* the case that having an adequate causal explanation depends on there being the right relation between the intentional properties and the physical properties.

Ironically, Baker's own example illustrates the point. Recall that she appeals to the epistemological possibility that the world could have been Aristotelian in its physics. She claims that while the difference between an Aristotelian physical world and ours would make a tremendous difference to the truth of the thesis that beliefs are brain states, it would make no difference to our ability to explain behavior by appeal to beliefs. Certainly. But the same could be said for the explanation of a pot of water's boiling by appeal to the application of sufficient heat. In an Aristotelian world, where 'water' (the phenomenological analogue of water) is a simple substance, the way in which applying heat to 'water' would make it boil is presumably going to have to be very different from the way in which heat causes boiling in the actual world. Nonetheless, we would be just as able to explain why 'water' boiled by citing the application of sufficient heat as we are in the actual world. In both this case and the actual case, we can be justified in believing that we have hold of a genuine regularity. It is up to further investigation to determine what precisely are the mechanisms, if any, that sustain the regularity, but our ability to explain events by appeal to accessible surface properties do not await the outcome of these investigations. And of course, none of this has any bearing on the claim that in *this* world, water is H_2O.

3   Where's the Belief?

What's Baker got against the Standard View, anyway? Why does she think beliefs are not brain states? Her objections to SV theories fall into two categories: objections that any non-reductivist would make, and that I therefore endorse, and objections that only emergentist non-reductivists would make. I'll focus on the latter. In particular, I'll look at two argument threads meant to apply to theories in the category that's supposed to include functionalism, one drawn from ABBS, and the other from EA.

The argument in ABBS is a sort of progressive pruning of a decision tree of possible SV theories of mind. Since I agree with Baker about eliminativist theories - they're wrong, for just the reasons she gives, let me begin with her general argument against non-eliminativist theories. Baker's first move is to show that all viable non-eliminativist theories must be contingent.

The argument runs like this:

2.21   If T [where 'T' can be replaced by any non-eliminativist theory] is true, then T is either necessarily true or contingently true.

2.22   T is not necessarily true.

2.23   T is not contingently true.

∴.2.2   T is not true.

Now how should a NENR theory be classified - as necessary or as contingent? I'm inclined to say that if it's true, then it's necessarily true: non-emergentist non-reductive materialism is a theory about the nature of mental states, and theories about natures of things are, if true, necessarily true. But Baker thinks that no SV theory *could* be necessarily true, for the following reason:

> Since T is a noneliminative theory of beliefs as brain states, T includes an account of how the human brain is organized. So, if it is necessary that T is true, and according to T, the brain is organized in a certain way, then it is necessary that the brain is organized in that way....But however the brain is organized, it is not necessary that it is organized that way....So even if the human brain is in fact organized in the way that T claims, it is not necessary that the brain is so organized. (ABBS, 20)

But this argument harbors a confusion. It must be remembered that for any theory, like functionalism, that holds mental states to be multiply realizable, the claim 'beliefs are brain states' must be interpreted as a *contingent* claim about what physical states realize mental states *in this world*, and how, given their physical characteristics, they are able to realize mental states. The other part of the theory, however - the part that specifies the kind of functional organization required for a physical system to realize a mind - is necessary, if true at all. But this part does not entail that the brain must be organized in any particular way. It does entail that *in order to be a mind* the brain must be organized in some particular way, but to assert that we can imagine counterexamples to *this* claim would be simply to beg the question.

However, I'm willing to set this objection aside, and suppose, along with Baker, that the 'standard' non-eliminativist theory is contingent. The relevant argument, then, is this one:

2.231   If T is contingently true, then T will be confirmed by neuroscience.

2.232   T will not be confirmed by neuroscience.

∴.2.23   T is not contingently true.

Let me record, but not belabor one quick objection to premise 2.231 - it conflates the metaphysical issue of a theory's truth with epistemological issues about whether and how the theory will be confirmed. Baker has things to say in response to this objection, and I have rejoinders, but let it all pass. The more interesting objection comes in regard to the defense of premise 2.232. Skipping Baker's attack on type-identity theories, we get to the following argument, which should apply to non-emergentist non-reductionist theories:

> 2.23221   If T is not a type-identity theory, then T will be confirmed by neuroscience only if neuroscientists in the long run are able to identify particular neural tokens of the belief that p....
>
> 2.23222   It is false that: neuroscientists in the long run are able to identify particular neural tokens as tokens of the belief that p.... (*Empirical Conjecture*)
>
> ∴ 2.23221   If T is not a type-identity theory, then T will not be confirmed by neuroscience.

My first objection to this argument is that its first premise, 2.23221 is far too strong. We all have excellent reason to believe that all chairs are composed of atoms. Our excellent reason is that the broad outlines of atomic physics are extremely well-confirmed, and atomic physics tells us that all physical objects, including chairs, are composed of atoms. Nonetheless, I seriously doubt that any physicist *could*, even should she take the odd notion into her head to try to do it, identity particular complexes of atoms as token chairs. We can have, in other words, well-confirmed theories about the constitution of complex macro objects without having or hoping to have specific theories about the composition of any given one.[10]

My second objection concerns Baker's defense of her 'Empirical Conjecture' (2.23222). She argues that:

> In order for particular neural tokens to be identified as constituting tokens of a belief that p, the relevant neural tokens must have in common some property recognized by neurophysiologists....If the brain states in question were completely heterogeneous, there would be no reason to suppose that their tokens all constituted tokens of the same belief-type. (ABBS, 23)

---

[10] Another question for Baker that I will not take up: is it wrong to say that 'beliefs are *molecular* states?' If so, then beliefs would seem to be non-material things. But if it's OK, why doesn't the argument that's supposed to show that they aren't brain states going to serve equally well to show that they aren't molecular states, either?

But, she thinks, there will not turn out to be any salient neurophysi-ological property that fills the bill, that is, no such property that:

> (1) ... is exhibited on each occasion on which a person manifests a belief of a certain type, and (2) ... would warrant calling particular tokens of dif-ferent types each a 'realization' of that belief. (Baker 1988, 8)

There are two problems with this argument. The first is that the re-quirement that the particular neural assemblages that are candidates for re-alizing some belief have some *neurological* property in common is gratui-tous. Functionalists hold that beliefs are functional states; hence the indi-viduation conditions for belief realizers may very well advert to functional or abstract structural properties of neuronal assemblages, properties that may not be taxonomic for neurobiology, but that would be of great signifi-cance to *neuropsychology*. Carburetors are made of metal; but the particular metal assemblages that constitute carburetors are of no more interest to mettalurgy than any other assemblage. It is generally true about the relation of higher-level and higher-order sciences to lower-level sciences that groupings that are principled and salient at the higher level are utterly arbi-trary at the lower level. Baker misses the point of NENR theories, which is precisely to assert the inadequacy of any lower-level or lower-order theo-retical taxonomy for capturing the regularities in which mental phenomena participate. She is effectively requiring non-reductivist theories to accept a condition of empirical adequacy that could only be satisfied if strong re-ductionism were true - a clearly illegitimate demand.[11]

It may be, however, that the reference to 'neurophysiologically salient' properties is idle. That is, it may be the main thing Baker is skeptical about is that there should turn out to be *anything* neurophysiological that instances of a belief state type should have in common, whether or not the property is one that is taxonomic for neurophysiology. This interpretation is supported by the example Baker offers to defend her pessimism: she asks us to con-sider the *variety* of circumstances in which it might be true that an individ-

---

[11] I am somewhat baffled why Baker thinks this is an argument that would move anyone *but* a strong reductionist. Perhaps what she's thinking is that someone who believes in multiple realizability is, in effect, a *relativized* type reductionist: someone who thinks that 'pain' is the property of being C-fibers firing in humans, D-glot zappings in Martians, E-circuit glowings in robots, etc., so that relative to each pain-capable creature, there is a type-type relation be-tween the higher-order and the lower-order realizing property. But although non-reductivist views leave this picture open, they do not require it. Particularly with respect to psychological attitude properties, which on a representationalist view will always involve relations to mental representations, which may be 'spelled' differently in different individuals, it's more plausi-ble that the characterization of a given belief at the psychological level will have to abstract over many individual differences in physical realization.

ual acted from a particular belief. Suppose, she suggests, we have a 'brain map' of this individual throughout an entire year:

> And suppose we could pinpoint on the brain map each time at which Fox did something explainable by his belief that the school budget would raise taxes too much. His body moved in remarkably different ways on each of these different occasions....
>
> My empirical conjecture is that with all this neurophysiological information, there would be no neurophysiologically salient property that was instantiated on each occasion and that could plausibly be identified as Fox's belief that taxes are too high. (ABBS, 24)

But even ignoring the reference to 'neurologically salient' properties, there is a serious problem with the argument: it appears that Baker is simply begging the question against her NENR opponent. Representationalists like me believe that the best account of how beliefs cause actions is one that posits mental representations: neural assemblages that are type-identified by their structural (or syntactic) properties, and which properties in turn mirror their semantic properties. Instances of representation types can serve to realize either beliefs, desires, or wonderings, depending on the functional environment in which the tokening occurs. Intentional behavior, we contend, is the result of the causal interaction of a belief and a desire. Thus, representationalism is indeed committed to there being, on every occasion of Fox's doing something because he thought taxes were too high, some instance of the mental representation type 'taxes are too high,' and thus that there must turn out to be *some* kind of repeated pattern on the brain map. But Baker gives no *reason* for thinking this won't or can't happen; she just 'conjectures' that it won't.

The missing reason - or at least one reason - for Baker's pessimism on this point is supplied in the second direct argument against the Standard View that I will consider. In Chapter 6 of EA, Baker contends that there is the following insuperable problem for the brain state theorist, even one of the non-reductivist variety: Brain states are internal states, intrinsic to the subject, but psychological states are not. The confirmation of attitude ascriptions - indeed, the confirmation of ascriptions of any property involving intentionality - requires us to look not only at the individual to whom the belief is ascribed, but also to the social environment in which the individual is embedded. This shows how beliefs differ, not only from natural substance kinds, like water, but also from physical dispositional kinds, like fragility:

> The property mentioned in the consequent of the counterfactual associated with fragility - O's breaking - supervenes on O's microstructure; but it is not the case that the property mentioned in the consequent of the counterfactual associated with the belief - the property of working on a journal article - supervenes on Jones's neural properties or on any other of her in-

trinsic properties. If the property of working on a journal article supervenes on anything, it supervenes on the properties of Jones's physical, social, and linguistic environment together with her intrinsic properties.
(EA, 181)

Now it's clear that the fact, if it is one, that beliefs and other attitudes
are 'wide' properties, constitutes a difficulty for a strong reductionist, who
wants to claim that to be a belief is to be a brain state. But does the fact that
intentional properties supervene partly on circumstances outside the head of
the believer, show that they cannot be *properties of* brain states? Does this
fact really constitute an argument against the view that beliefs are *realized*
by brain states?

Baker claims that the wideness of intentional properties creates a dilemma for advocates of this thesis that beliefs are 'realized' by brain states.
This thesis, she contends, is ambiguous: on one reading, it says that being a
belief state *supervenes* on being a (certain kind of) brain state. On this
reading, the thesis is false, because of the considerations marshaled above.
On the second reading, the thesis says only that beliefs are 'constituted' out
of brain states, in the way that a contract may be constituted out of the set of
molecules that make up the paper on which it's written. Read in this way,
Baker is willing to allow that the thesis is true, but now, she contends, the
thesis becomes uninteresting. The thesis thus understood tells us nothing
about the *nature* of belief states.

> [It] fails to have epistemological or explanatory import. Unlike superven-
> ience - which although theoretically interesting, does not hold between
> beliefs and brain states - constitution is simply not a theoretically inter-
> esting relation for most intentional phenomena. The fact that a contract is
> constituted by a piece of paper reveals nothing about the nature of con-
> tracts. This point holds for intentional phenomena in general: Even when
> there is an undisputed relation of constitution between an intentionally
> identified object and material elements that constitute it, the constituting
> elements shed no explanatory light on the constituted object as intention-
> ally identified. (EA, 183)

Baker's ultimate complaint, then, against NENR theories is that they are
either false, or that they fail to tell us what it is that makes a belief *intentional*. And if they fail to tell us that, then they fail to provide any explanation of how the intentional properties of intentional objects figure in the
phenomena in which they participate.

But Baker's dilemma is false; she has both disjuncts wrong. In the first
place, the thesis that beliefs are realized by brain states does not entail that
beliefs supervene on intrinsic states of the individual, and in the second
place, the thesis that beliefs are constituted by brain states has a great deal
of explanatory import - it explains how beliefs can be causes. Let me make
each point in turn.

To understand properly what NENR theories say about the relation between beliefs and brain states, we need to appeal to a distinction of Sydney Shoemaker's. Shoemaker points out that there are two different sorts of lower-level properties that could with justice be viewed as the realizers (or in his own terms, 'realizations') of some second-order functional property.

Let **T** be a theory that functionally specifies some mental property, say, the property of being in pain. Ramsifying **T**, we get a functional predicate of the form

$$\exists F_1...\exists F_n \left[\mathbf{T}(....F_j...) \text{ and } x \text{ has } F_j \right]$$

where F_1 - F_n range over physicalistic (or at least non-mentalistic) predicates. The predicate variable F_j represents the physicalistic predicate that will replace the mentalistic predicate that is receiving a functional definition, in this case, the mentalistic predicate 'is in pain.' In human beings, we may suppose, F_j will be replaced by the predicate 'has C-fibers firing.' Since, for human beings, having one's C-fibers fire will be necessary and sufficient for being in pain, it seems correct to say that 'has C-fibers firing' is the first-order property that realizes the second-order property 'is in pain,' and thus that it is substituends of F_j that should be regarded as the first-order realizer properties of the second-order property of being in pain. Shoemaker calls these properties *core realizations*.

However, as Shoemaker points out, core realizer properties are only *contingently* the realizers of any particular second-order property. The F_j property only realizes pain if the creature has the functional organization specified by **T**, that is, only if the *complex* physical predicate '$\exists F_1...\exists F_n$ [$\mathbf{T}(....F_j...)$ and x has F_j]' is satisfied by that creature. If we instantiate the predicate with a particular sequence of physical predicates, we get the complex predicate '$\mathbf{T}(...P_j...)$ & $P_j x$' or, abbreviating, '$\mathbf{T}x$ & $P_j x$'. (Shoemaker suggests that we think of $\mathbf{T}x$ as expressing the property: 'being physically constituted in such a way that P_j plays the causal role definitive of pain').

This *conjunctive* property constitutes what Shoemaker calls the *total realization* of the second-order, functionally defined property. (Shoemaker 1981, 264-265)

By appeal to this distinction, an NENR can easily accommodate the intuition that beliefs are broad. The core realization of the belief that publications are necessary for tenure will be simply the tokening of the appropriate neural state in the subject; but the total realization of that belief will include both the tokening of the neural state, and whatever other conditions - whether internal or external to the subject - necessary for that neural state to be endowed with the content that publications are necessary for tenure. The slogan, 'beliefs are brain states,' in the mouth of an NENR theorist must be interpreted as saying that brain states are the *core* realizers of beliefs in humans, and this does not entail that beliefs supervene on brain states.

What about the second horn of Baker's supposed dilemma? Recall that an NENR theory has two aspects: a general theory of the nature of mental states, and a particular theory of how mental states are realized in a given case. The realization theory is not meant to illuminate the intentionality of mental states; it is meant rather to illuminate the causal mechanisms whereby particular mental systems instantiate the functional organization distinctive of mental phenomena. And this information is crucial if we are to understand how intentionality *works* in a physical world. It is true that we do not look to the molecular structure of paper to understand why a signed contract is valid. But if we want to understand how documents do the things they do - how they certify ownership, establish credentials, etc., we are going to have to appeal to facts about the way that a valid contract is created, preserved, and recognized, and this will involve stories relating the perceptual mechanisms of human animals to the appearance and feel of paper. Similarly, if we want to understand how beliefs cause behavior, we are going to have to understand how the stuff that composes beliefs - brain states - interacts with the neuromuscular bases of behavior.

Notice that both total and core realizations play an important role in the account of the mechanisms by which mental states cause behavior (or stimuli cause mental states, or mental states cause each other). If we want to know what mechanisms sustain the nomological relation among, say, the belief that drinking water quenches thirst, the desire to quench one's thirst, and the intention to drink some water, we have to know how to realize the belief, desire, and intention in question. But the realization of a belief that drinking water quenches thirst involves more than the instantiation of a certain brain state. The total realization of this belief state will involve being in a brain state that maintains certain nomological relations with other internal states, with water in the larger environment, and with the kitchen sink, for all we know now. Clearly if we want to explain all the regularities that are exhibited in our environment by creatures that have beliefs about *water*, we'll need to have a theory of the total realization.

On the other hand, a theory of the total realization entails a theory of the core realization since the core realizer is just that state/property whose relations to everything else are at issue. The core realization, the brain state, is the one whose tokening or not constitutes - given the background conditions determined by the total realization - coming to have the belief or not. It is the core realization that actually gets the body to move, and therefore must be located within the subject. Michael Jordan could not be a *basketball* player, and thus could not shoot *baskets* but that he was embedded in a certain complex social environment. Nonetheless, coaches who want their players to emulate that winning technique will focus on Jordan's individual body and individual mind.

4 Safe from Science?

I conclude with a diagnosis. Baker's Pragmatic Realism is an attempt to shelter our folk psychology from the possibility of empirical refutation. Because she is essentially convinced by the premise in the eliminativists' argument that says that there can be no systematic connections between the categories of folk psychology and those of neuroscience, she concludes that the truth of folk psychology must be shown not to depend on the existence of such connections. She thinks she has demonstrated this by refuting the argument from causal explanation. But as I've shown, her 'refutation' fails, because it depends on misinterpreting NENR theories.

Does the truth of folk psychology then depend on the existence of systematic psycho-physical connections, of the kind that would satisfy the explanatory and predictive demands of reduction? Yes. Does it depend on the *discovery* of such connections? No. And that's the good news that Baker has not yet grasped: the truth-conditions of a claim need not be identical with its acceptability-conditions. But anyone who believes that there are such things as hidden essences ought to have grasped this point. According to the best biological theories, to be a human being is to be an organism with a certain phylogenetic history, or at least to have a genome of a certain sort. Yet the vast majority of us identify beings as human without knowing the details of these theories, much less being in a position to confirm them in any particular case. We are epistemically warranted in using superficial indicators to judge that a being is human - the theory of the human essence tells us, *inter alia*, *why* those indicators work. The non-emergentist non-reductivist does concede that folk psychology is at empirical risk - risk that it will turn out that intentional kinds do not map onto non-intentional kinds in the right way. But the risk is not great. It is the very reliability of our psychological explanations and predictions - so emphasized by Baker - that should provide confidence that the appropriate inter-level connections exist.[12]

[12] I would like to thank Joe Levine for his help with this essay; several of the arguments presented here were first developed together with him and are borrowed from Antony & Levine, 1997. I would also like to thank Lynne Baker for many hours of stimulating conversation on the topics treated here.

References

Antony, Louise M. 1991. The Causal Relevance of the Mental: More on the Mattering of Minds. *Mind and Language* 6, no. 4.

Antony, Louise M. and Joseph Levine 1997. Reduction with Autonomy. In *Philosophical Perspectives* 11, ed. James E. Tomberlin. Malden, MA and Oxford: Blackwell Publishers: 83-105.

Baker, Lynne Rudder 1995. *Explaining Attitudes: A Practical Approach to the Mind*. Cambridge: Cambridge University Press.

Baker, Lynne Rudder 2001. Are Beliefs Brain States? In this volume.

Davidson, Donald 1980. Mental Events. In *Essays on Actions and Events*. Oxford: Oxford University Press: 207-24.

Kim, Jaegwon (forthcoming). *Making Sense of Emergence*.

Shoemaker, Sydney 1981. Some Varieties of Functionalism. In *Identity, Cause, and Mind*: Cambridge, Cambridge University Press.

Tomberling, James ed. 1995. Law and Order in Psychology. *Philosophical Perspectives* 9: Malden, MA and Oxford: Blackwell Publishers: 83-105.

Wedgewood, Ralph 2000. The Price of Non-Reductive Materialism. *Noûs*, Vol. 34, No. 3: 400-21

6

Brain States, Causal Explanation, and the Attitudes

REINALDO ELUGARDO

Lynne Rudder Baker has criticized what she calls 'the Standard View' of the attitudes, which is the view that the propositional attitudes are states of certain material or immaterial parts of a person.[1] All physicalistic versions of the Standard View minimally entail the following claim:

> (SV) For all persons S and propositions p, S believes that p only if there is some neural token, n, such that (i) n has the content that p, or means that p, and (ii) S tokens n. (ABBS, p.18)[2]

---

[1] Baker 1995. That work continues Baker's project, begun in Baker 1987, of restoring the propositional attitudes to what she thinks is their proper place in the philosophy of mind.

[2] See Baker's leading essay in this volume, 'Are Beliefs Brain-States?'. References to her essay will be indicated in the text by the symbols, 'ABBS', followed by a page number. As Baker rightly notes, (ABBS, p.18), anyone who holds (SV) can be an externalist or an internalist about belief-content. She also points out that one can endorse (SV) and either hold or deny the Language of Thought hypothesis. Thus, the Standard View, understood in its most minimal form, cuts across a wide spectrum of philosophical views about the mind. For her part, Baker rejects (SV). In that respect, she is in the same company with Norman Malcolm, Gilbert Ryle, and Ludwig Wittgenstein. On the other hand, she parts company with them on two important points. First, according to Baker, attitude terms are genuine referring terms that refer to global states of persons. Second, she holds that belief-reports are descriptive factual reports that are either objectively true or false; they are not semantically equivalent to open

(continued)

Explaining Beliefs: Lynne Rudder Baker and Her Critics.
Anthonie Meijers (ed.).
Copyright © 2001, CSLI Publications.

In her leading essay, 'Are Beliefs Brain-States?', Baker develops her critique by defending two important theses: first, *SV* is false, and second, beliefs would still be causally explanatory even if they were neither brain states nor constituted by them. In this chapter, I will discuss both of her claims and try to show that her arguments for them are problematic.

The text consists of two major parts. In the first part, I examine her case against token-identity and token-constitution theories of belief. I will try to show that her subargument contains a dubious premise, namely, the claim that such theories are true only if they will be confirmed by neuroscience. The premise is false on any reasonable interpretation of 'confirmed'. In the second part, I turn to Baker's arguments for her second thesis, namely, the claim that beliefs are causally explanatory even if *SV* is false. I will also try to show that her defense of that claim is also open to doubt. The main reason is that her various counterfactual analyses (or tests) of causal explanation, which she presents in Baker 1995 and hints at in *ABBS*, fail to provide a sufficient condition for an explanation's being a causal explanation. If these skeptical conclusions are correct, then Baker has not succeeded in refuting the Standard View.

1   Baker's First Thesis

Let *T* be the claim that, for each token of the belief that *P*, there is some neural token with which it is identical or by which it is constituted (for any proposition *P*). *T* entails *SV* but not conversely. Still, if *T* is false, then one cannot reasonably conclude that *SV* is true on the basis of any set of premises that includes *T*. Rather than presenting Baker's detailed argument against *T*, I will present instead her two-step subargument for the statement that *T* is not *contingently* true. [3]

One of the premises of Baker's subargument is (2.231):

---

behavioral hypotheticals that lack mental terms. For Baker's positive view, what she calls 'Practical Realism', and her defense of these two points, see Baker 1995.

[3] Baker notes that T is true only if it is contingently true or necessarily true (ABBS, p.20). Since T is not a necessary truth, she tries to show why T is not contingently true either (ABBS, p.21). The reason that T is not necessarily true is that, if it were, it would entail that our brains had to have been organized in the way they actually are. Since our brains might have been organized in some other way (and still be human brains) if our environment or our evolutionary history had been different, the entailed claim is at best contingently true. And, if a true statement entails a contingent truth, then the entailing statement must be contingently true.

(2.231) If T is contingently true, then T will be confirmed by neuroscience. (*ABBS,* p.21)[4]

Baker offers two reasons for its acceptance. First, if T will never be confirmed by neuroscience, then no one 'should believe T'. Second, T is 'subject to confirmation or disconfirmation by the relevant science, which in this case is neuroscience' - as she puts it, 'we expect, rightly, that empirical theories be confirmed' (*ibid*).

However, (2.231) is not true and Baker's reasons for accepting it are not compelling. Before I defend both of those claims, I will first present her reasons for accepting the second premise of her subargument against the contingency of T:

(2.232) T will not be confirmed by neuroscience. (*ABBS*, p.21)

My strategy is this: by examining Baker's defense of (2.232), I will be able to construct the argument I need to question (2.231). For, Baker's second premise is plausible only on the standard positive instance reading of 'confirmation' whereas premise (2.231) is not.

1.1 Baker's Argument for Why T Will Not Be Scientifically Confirmed

According to Baker, a necessary condition for confirming T is that there be lots of positive instances of T:

> Confirmation of a noneliminative version of the Standard View that is weaker than type-identity would consist of neuroscientists identifying particular neural tokens (of *different* neural types) as tokens of a particular type of belief. The behavioral evidence would tell the neuroscientists what type of belief is in question, and the neuroscientists would look for the neural tokens that could be said to be identical to, or to constitute tokens of that belief-type. I do not see how anything less than actual discovery of relevant brain states to regard as beliefs would confirm T. (*ABBS*, pp. 7-8)

Furthermore, 'in order for particular neural tokens to be identified as constituting tokens of a belief that p, the relevant neural tokens must have in common some property recognized by neurophysiologists - even if there is not a single type of brain state shared by everyone who has a single type of belief' (*ABBS*, p.23). Thus, on her view, if neuroscientists are to empirically confirm T, they must at least specify some neurophysiological property common to many different kinds of neural tokens.

---

[4] I adopt Baker's numerical ordering.

But not just any recognizable, commonly shared, neurophysiological property will do. It must be one that 'is exhibited on each occasion on which a person manifests a belief of a certain type' and that 'would warrant calling particular neural tokens of different types each a "realization" of that belief' (ibid). The relevant property must be, then, nomologically necessary and sufficient for a neural token to be a belief-token of some particular intentional kind. If one can independently specify such a property, then one would be warranted in identifying its tokens as tokens of the belief that P, which in turn would confirm T.

Baker is skeptical of the whole idea, however (*ABBS*, p.24).[5] According to her, neuroscientists can confirm T only by identifying a salient neurophysiological property the instantiation of which is both nomically necessary and sufficient for any neural token that has it to be a token of some particular belief-type or other.[6] However, no neurophysiological

---

[5] Since salience is a second-order epistemic property that is relative to particular observers, contexts, and theories, it is at best an open question as to which neural properties, if any, will be counted as salient for applying a belief-predicate of the form, 'x believes that P', to subjects who exemplify them. That will depend on other factors including, among others, whether the internal states of the subject play a causal role in the subject's inferential and noninferential behavior, whether they causally interact with the subject's perceptual states and to what degree they do, etc. To be sure, we do not appeal to, and do not need to appeal to, any internal state in ascribing mental attributes to ourselves or to one another (even if we could). But it does not follow that no internal state could be identified, for scientific theoretical purposes, as being a token of the ascribed mental attribute.

[6] Some noneliminative versions of the Standard View that are not versions of the type-identity theory are functionalist theories. With regard to our example, functionalists will deny that N1-events and N2-events must have a salient neurophysiological property in common if they are to be confirmed as being the occupants of a causal functional role definitive of, say, the belief that icy sidewalks are dangerous. Baker contends, however, that 'if the brain states in question were totally heterogeneous, there would be no reason to suppose that their tokens all constituted tokens of the same belief-type' (ABBS, p.23). But suppose that T is a correct functionalist theory of belief and that T is true of you and me. Then, to confirm that my N1 brain-event and your N2 brain-event are tokens of that belief-type it is enough to show two things. First, they share in both of us the same wide functional property that T identifies as the property of believing that icy sidewalks are dangerous. Second, they each have the neural properties that make it possible for them to have this functional role for us. If we can confirm that both brain events have the same belief-determining functional property, then we will have confirmed that they are distinct tokens of the same belief-type even if they are neurophysiologically heterogeneous. Therefore, if some wide functionalist account of beliefs is correct, then Baker's premise (2.231) is false given her condition on confirmation.

Baker will counter that, if T is a functionalist theory of beliefs, then for T to be confirmed, my N1 brain-event and your N2 brain-event must have some salient functional property in common which would make them tokens of the same psychological type. She could then restate her argument to show that the instantiation of such a property by both brain

(continued)

property will likely meet this constraint even if 'neurophysiologists had a complete neurophysiological description of all the neural processes that controlled all the different kinds of bodily motions that constituted actions explainable by a particular belief that *p*' (ibid). One reason is that many neural tokens will differ in many neurophysiological ways across a given population of psychological subjects. The other reason is that, of the many neurophysiological properties that a group of neural tokens do share, none will stand out as being *the* property that is necessary and sufficient for being a token of a particular type of belief (*ABBS*, pp. 22, 23-24).[7]

Baker doubts that any such property will ever be identified (*ABBS*, pp.23, 37).[8] In order to identify any such neurophysiological property, one must first type-individuate the relevant neural tokens in some principled way. Beliefs are type-individuated, *qua* intentional kinds, in terms of their propositional content, which in turn is partly fixed by the believer's historical and causal connections to his or her external environment.[9]

---

events is very unlikely. For, relative to different descriptions, they will have many different functional roles no one of which will sufficiently stand out as being the belief-conferring property. Hence, no functionalist theory of belief-tokens will be scientifically confirmed either if Baker is right.

[7] It is extremely difficult to localize a certain area of a human brain to a specific psychological function given that its complexity and multi-layered processing mechanisms. To be sure, studies have been done on animal brains in which subcortical areas, such as the hippocampus and the amygdala, are linked to spatial learning and to the emotions. Different studies are sometimes done on brain area, like lesions, electrophysiology, drug injection, etc., to localize a psychological function. According to Baker, it is one thing to experimentally correlate some brain area/function(s) with some general type of psychological function (e.g., memory, language processing, perception, etc.), it is quite another thing to identify a specific brain event with the brain's having a specific intentional mental state. She accepts the former but not the latter, cf. ABBS, pp. 32-34. My guess is that most, if not all, neuroscientists would agree with her if only to avoid the risk of anthropomorphizing the brain in their empirical studies. For a general survey of the work that has been done in the neurosciences on the brain, with an eliminativist slant, see Churchland 1986.

[8] The reason why I think Baker makes this claim is that she is an externalist about belief-content. On her view, beliefs are type-individuated by their contents, and intentional actions are type-individuated by the intentional attitude-contents they presuppose. Belief-contents cannot in turn be wholly fixed by the believer's internal states, e.g., her neurophysiological states, for well-known Burge-type and Putnam-type reasons. Thus, adverting only to the subject's neurophysiological states could never help confirm what belief-contents the subject has, and that just means that it could never help in confirming what her beliefs are. I present this argument in the next subsection. Baker defends an anti-individualistic view of content-individuation and action-individuation in both Baker 1987 and Baker 1995.

[9] The classic sources for this externalist claim are Burge 1979 and Putnam 1975.

Neural tokens are type-individuated, *qua* neural kinds, independently of the believer's (or his or her brain's) historical or causal relations to the external environment. The type-individuation conditions of neural kinds and intentional kinds are essentially different and are therefore orthogonal to one another. At best, there will be many-to-many correlations between neurophysiological kinds and belief-kinds. But, then, no single neurophysiological property can be scientifically identified as being *the* property that is both nomically necessary and sufficient for having a specific belief-type. That is why, according to Baker, *T* will never be empirically confirmed.

1.2 Some Objections (and Replies) to Baker's Argument for (2.232)

One might object that tokens of complex, disjunctive, neurophysiological properties are confirming instances of *T* provided that Baker relaxes her constraint on confirmation. For, there will always be wildly disjunctive, neurophysiological properties whose instantiations are both experimentally confirmable and sufficient for their instantiations to be belief-tokens of a particular intentional kind.

To use Baker's own example, suppose I form the thought that walking on icy sidewalks can be dangerous, and as I do, a neural event that has a neurophysiological property *N1* occurs in my brain. Suppose that my brain is such that, *ceteris paribus*, whenever that property is instantiated in my brain, I form that particular thought. Suppose you form the same thought, and, as you do, some neural event that has neurophysiological property *N2* occurs in your brain. Again, imagine that whenever that property is instantiated in your brain, you form the same thought under the same input/output conditions. By hypothesis, *N1* and *N2* are different neurophysiological properties. There is no level of neurophysiological description of our brains according to which *N1*-events and *N2*-events are neurophysiologically type-identical events.

Let φ be the disjunctive neurophysiological property of instantiating *N1* or *N2*, under specified input/output conditions (which will also likely be a wildly disjunctive set). When some neural event in my brain instantiates *N1*, it must also instantiate φ. Similarly, when some neural event in your brain instantiates *N2*, it must also instantiate φ. Since my brain's instantiation of *N1* suffices for my thinking that walking on icy sidewalks can be dangerous, and since your brain's instantiation of *N2* suffices for your thinking the same thought, our brains' instantiations of φ must therefore suffice for our thinking that thought. Hence, there will always be a neurophysiological property common to both of our neural tokens which, under the appropriate input/output conditions, suffices for our thinking that walking on icy sidewalks can be dangerous, namely, the disjunctive neurophysiological property φ.

Let us assume, for the sake of argument, that each property-constituent of φ can in principle be empirically correlated with the corresponding thought-property in each individual case. It follows, then, that neural tokens of this common, disjunctive, neurophysiological property can be identified as being, or as constituting, tokens of the same correlated thought-property. The same argument can be repeated in many other cases involving thoughts. One may conclude, then, that Baker's argument for her second premise - (2.232) - fails.

The above objection, however, conflicts with another aspect of Baker's view of empirical confirmation:

> In order for neuroscientists to *confirm* a noneliminative version of the standard view, the neural tokens that are supposed to constitute tokens of a particular type of belief cannot be a complete motley. They must be nonheterogeneous: The relevant neural tokens must have something in common other than the fact that they are all said to constitute tokens of a particular type of belief. (*ABBS*, p.23)

The bottom-line is this: disjunctive neural properties are just too heterogeneous to serve any interesting role in the empirical confirmation of T. Hence, one is justified in dismissing them as positive data for T.

Unfortunately, Baker's condition on experimental confirmation is far too stringent even for actual scientific practice.[10] For example, the class of

---

[10] Barry Loewer reports, in private correspondence, that one may have reason to think, and one may even come to confirm, that an F-event is token-identical with a G-event, assuming a Davidsonian conception of events. And yet, there may be no nomic generalization that connects Fs and Gs. For example, I might have a good reason to think that the bombing of Hiroshima is the event that led to Japan's unconditional surrender in World War II. I may have some good reason to believe this without knowing a generalization that connects atomic bombings to unconditional surrenders. In fact, there is no nomic generalization that connects the two. In which case, there is no common salient property shared by all tokens of the first property that lawfully makes them tokens of the second property. Still, I can confirm, in this instance, that the bombing of Hiroshima is token-identical with the event that led to Japan's unconditional surrender in World War II.

By analogy, then, suppose I were to discover that a certain neural event caused your mouth to move. If I were to independently discover that a certain intention on your part caused the same bodily movement, then I would have some reason to think that either that neural event was identical to or a part of that same mental event, assuming that this is not a case of causal overdetermination. Yet, there need not be any generalization that nomically connects neural tokens to intention-tokens. Following Donald Davidson's suggestion, we can confirm token-identities if we can confirm, other things being equal, that the event-tokens in question have the same causes and the same effects. Acceptance of Davidson's metaphysical view is not really germane to the main issue. The general point is that one is not forced to

(continued)

neural tokens that are also DNA tokens in a given species of organisms is quite heterogeneous. Some DNA-tokens that constitute a gene are contiguous with one another, but others are not. A single stretch of DNA can code for a number of different genes. The transcription process going from DNA to RNA to proteins can read noncontinuous stretches of the DNA, and different transcription processes will read different bits of the same long DNA sequence. There is, then, a one-to-many correlation between stretches of DNA and genes.[11] Not all chunks of DNA, then, 'must have something in common other than the fact that they are all said to constitute tokens of a particular type of gene'.

What determines whether any particular stretch of DNA constitutes a particular kind of gene is its role as the mechanism of trait-inheritance for successive generations of a reproductive species. Searching for a salient neurophysiological property common to all and only genes will not likely result in the confirmation of the claim that all genes are portions of DNA material. But biologists have experimentally confirmed that hypothesis. Consequently, Baker's condition on the confirmation of token-identity and token-constitution claims does not therefore fit actual scientific practice.

Baker will likely dismiss the DNA/gene example as not being relevantly analogous to the neural/belief case, which is a point that she implicitly makes in the following passage:

> If the brain states in question were totally heterogeneous, there would be *no reason to suppose* that their tokens all constituted tokens of the same belief-type. The claim of token-identity (or token-constitution) would be purely *ad hoc*. (*ABBS*, p.23. Italics added)

---

accept the view that empirical confirmation of token-identities must involve the independent specification of nomic property-correlations. See Davidson 1967 and Davidson 1969.

Baker could agree with the general point just made but would likely offer the following reply. The intention example given above begs the question. You would have a reason to think that the intention that caused someone to move her mouth is identical with, or contains as a part, the neural event that caused the mouth to move only if you already had some reason to think that T is true. But, until one can explain how having certain neural properties could make a neural event be an intention with a certain content, one has no reason for thinking that T is true.

[11] There can also be hunks of 'junk' DNA scattered around. These do not code anything and the transcription process ignores them. A single stretch of DNA whose segments includes a junk sequence may code for one or more proteins, and since the junk sequence is ignored anyway, it will code for the same protein(s). Thus, the relation between genes and DNA sequences is really many-to-many. I am grateful to Wayne Riggs and Stephen Stich for this information.

In other words, if T is to be experimentally confirmed, then any confirming neurophysiological property must figure in an explanation of why the neural tokens that have it constitute belief-tokens of the same intentional type. Having some kind of DNA property or other and a certain biological functional role may help explain why a disparate group of DNA molecules are tokens of a particular kind of gene. But neither having a certain complex, disjunctive, neurophysiological property nor having a functional role (or both) can explain why any neural token that has either (or both) is a belief-token of a particular intentional type.[12] My neural token's being either *N1 or N2* does not help explain, in any obvious way, why it is also, e.g., my thought *that walking on icy sidewalks can be dangerous* (rather than, say, my thought *that dogs have fleas*), especially if other neural tokens of the same disjunctive property are tokens of other thought-types. Indeed, my neural token's having *N1* (rather than some other neural property) does not explain why it is a token of that thought-content rather than some other thought-content.

Baker's reply to the 'too stringent' objection depends on a crucial assumption. Suppose that a branch, B, of science confirms that Fs are Gs - where G is some high-level property and F is some low-level property. Then, an F's being a G is explainable in terms of F's lawfully having certain theoretical properties postulated by B, where the explanation is formulated in terms of concepts used in B to type-individuate/type-identify Fs. That general claim is plausible given some well-known examples of scientifically confirmed identity-claims and constitution-claims, e.g., genes and DNA molecules, etc. However, if the claim is true, then neuroscience will be unable to confirm the hypothesis that certain neural tokens are belief-tokens. For, neuroscientists cannot explain how a neural event can be a particular intentional kind of belief by appealing only to its neurophysiological properties. Again, the reason is that intentional kinds are type-individuated widely rather than narrowly, whereas neural kinds are type-individuated narrowly for scientific explanatory purposes.[13] For my purposes, I will grant Baker's assumption and her reasons for accepting

---

[12] Teleofunctional semanticists who appeal to widely individuated causal, historical, functional roles of brain states in type-individuating mental content will object to this claim. See Millikan 1989 and Papineau 1987. So would some co-variation semanticists, e.g., Dretske 1986. I will defer here to Baker's criticisms of teleofunctional and co-variation semantics in Baker 1995 and elsewhere.

[13] But see Wilson 1995 for arguments in support of the claim that, for scientific taxonomic purposes and for explanatory purposes, neural states qua computational states are best type-individuated widely.

premise (2.232). I will now argue that her arguments in support of (2.232) can be used to undermine premise (2.231).

1.3 Objections to Premise (2.231)

Baker's argument against T depends on the assumption that to confirm T is to have positive instances of its generalization. That is how she uses 'confirm' in her arguments to show that T will never be confirmed by neuroscience. Charity requires that we understand her to mean the same thing by 'confirmed' in (2.231):

(2.231) If T is contingently true, then T will be confirmed by neuroscience.

So understood, (2.231) is certainly not a conceptual truth, which Baker concedes: 'it is logically possible that T be a true empirical theory that is never confirmed by neuroscience' (*ABBS*, p.21). Indeed, her comment can be generalized across the sciences. To cite one example from physics, many physicists believe that the magnetic monopole must exist if only to make the classical equations of electromagnetism, i.e., Maxwell's equations, symmetric with respect to electricity and magnetism. But it has never been observed. Imagine, then, that all attempts to observe the magnetic monopole fail. The hypothesis that postulates its existence will then never be experimentally confirmed since no direct positive instances of the hypothesis will be forthcoming. Still, for all we know, the hypothesis may be true. Similarly, T can be contingently true even though it will never be (experimentally) confirmed by neuroscience for the reasons that Baker gives.[14] Consequently, the confirmation of T by neuroscience, if it should ever come to pass, is not a logically necessary condition for its contingent truth.

But if (2.231) is not a conceptual truth, then why should we accept it all? Baker gives two reasons. First, no one 'should believe T' if T is never confirmed by neuroscience, (*ABBS*, p.21). Under a *broad* interpretation of 'confirm', Baker's first answer to our question is virtually analytic. After all, given scientific norms of justification, no scientist is justified in accepting a theoretical hypothesis unless it has either been experimentally confirmed to some high degree or other, shown to have some explanatory

---

[14] Indeed, Baker must hold it to be a priori true that no technology could ever possibly be developed that would confirm T. The reason is that, on her view, belief-tokens are just not the sorts of things that could be said to be identical with or constituted by neural tokens. We will later see why she is committed to that last claim.

power, or shown to fit remarkably well with other accepted, explanatorily powerful, theories. If some empirical scientific hypothesis will forever be *completely* unconfirmed in every sense of the term, then no one is ever justified in believing it. But if we accept (2.231) on this broad interpretation of 'confirmed', then Baker's master argument suffers from an equivocation. For, the rest of her argument involves the *narrow*, experimental, sense of 'confirmed'.

Moreover, Baker's first reason for accepting (2.231) is incorrect on the narrow interpretation. One may be warranted in believing an empirically true theory that will in fact never be experimentally confirmed if one has other, epistemically strong, nondefeating reasons for its acceptance.[15] For instance, in physics, Wolfgang Pauli put forth the neutrino hypothesis in the 1930s. Physicists at that time accepted the hypothesis since the alternative would have been to deny the conservation of energy. The hypothesis was not empirically confirmed until the 1950s. Nonetheless, even if the hypothesis had never been experimentally confirmed, physicists in the 1930s would still have been justified in accepting the hypothesis partly because of its explanatory power and partly because of its systematic connections to the rest of physics.

To sum up this part of my argument, Baker's first reason for accepting premise (2.231), namely, that no one should believe T if T is never confirmed by neuroscience, can be understood in two different ways depending on how 'confirmed' is interpreted. It may be interpreted broadly to mean an explanationist coherentist form of epistemic justification; in which case, Baker's premise is correct - but then her two-step subargument against the contingent truth of T is invalid because it suffers from an equivocation on 'confirmed'. Premise (2.231) may also be interpreted narrowly to mean direct experimental confirmation; in which case, Baker's premise is incorrect. Either way, Baker's first argument for (2.231) does not show that neuroscience *will* confirm T if T is contingently true. Hence, even if no one is ever justified in accepting a completely unconfirmed empirical

---

[15] The argument that is implicit in my discussion of my example is simply this. Suppose that the world had ended five minutes before the actual confirmation of a true scientific hypothesis took place. Then, of course, the hypothesis would not have been confirmed after that. Even so, scientists who accepted the hypothesis on theoretical explanatory grounds would still have been justified in accepting it five minutes ago, ten years ago, or whatever period of time, before the Cataclysmic Event took place. Their epistemic reasons for accepting the hypothesis in the counterfactual case are the same, we may suppose, and would have provided them with the same degree justification as in actual case in which the hypothesis is eventually confirmed.

theory, the (contingent) *truth* of the theory is logically independent of its being actually confirmed in the future.

Baker's second reason for accepting (2.231) is that T is 'subject to confirmation or disconfirmation by the relevant science, which in this case is neuroscience' (*ABBS,* p.21*)*. As she puts it, 'we expect, rightly, that empirical theories be confirmed'. Both claims are true but they do not entail that our best explanatory theories *will* be confirmed, at least not in any direct way, if they are contingently true. Moreover, the mere fact that we expect and hope that our best theories will be confirmed someday does not show that their (eventual) confirmation is necessary for their truth. If the property of being true (contingent or necessary) is a conceptually nonepistemic property of statements, theories, etc., then premise (2.231) is false. At the very least, Baker has to show that contingent truth really is an epistemic property, which is not an easy thing to show.

Perhaps Baker has this more modest interpretation of (2.231): If T is contingently true, then we have some reason to believe that T will eventually be confirmed under epistemically optimal conditions, all things being equal. In other words, we have good reason to think that, given enough time and ingenuity, neuroscientists will someday experimentally confirm T if it is contingently true - provided that the technology needed for testing T exists or will be developed, adequate funding for testing T continues, scientists continue to perform their experiments correctly, and so forth. This modest reading makes (2.231) plausible.

However, (2.231) is false even on the more charitable reading. Given Baker's arguments for the claim that neuroscience will never confirm T, i.e, that premise (2.232) is true, we really do not have, and never will have, any good reason to think that T will be confirmed by future neuroscience even under the best of circumstances. And yet, T might still be contingently true.

Consider the following analogy. We really have no good reason to believe that physicists will someday confirm that, e.g., *this marble statue* is or constitutes *a Gothic statue*. Being a Gothic statue is a property fixed by factors that are not intrinsic to the statue's material properties, such as its historical and social properties, among others. No physicalistic account of the marble's compositional structure could therefore explain why the statue the marble composes is a Gothic statue rather than, say, a Roman statue. And yet, this same marble Gothic statue *is* physically constituted by *this* collection of physical particles.[16] Although the collection of particles might

---

[16] Baker herself defends this view of the relationship between artifacts and the material stuff that composes them. See Baker 2000.

not have constituted a Gothic statue, this particular marble statue would not have existed *qua marble* statue unless it was composed of marble, even though it need not have been composed by exactly the same particles.

Similarly, although *T* will never be confirmed by neuroscience even under epistemically optimal conditions, and we have no reason to suppose it ever will for the reasons that Baker gives, it does not follow that no belief-token is constituted by a brain-state that tokens it. For, unless beliefs are essentially mental properties of purely immaterial mental substances, it may be that no belief can be a tokened unless its instantiation is structurally composed of some brain-event or other, although not necessarily the same brain-event. Any noneliminative Standard Theorist, who rejects Substance Dualism, is committed to that minimal claim. In conclusion, Baker has not shown that no noneliminative version of the Standard View is contingently true. The reason is that premise (2.231) is false. In which case, her master argument against the Standard View, which embeds her subargument against *T*, is unsuccessful.

In spite of what I have argued, Baker does not really need premise (2.231) to make her case. A more plausible premise she could use is this: If *T* is true, then either there are no beliefs or the intentional content of a belief-type or belief-token is wholly fixed by the subject's internal physical properties or by the brain's causal/historical naturalistic relations to its external environment. Baker has criticized eliminativist conceptions of belief in *ABBS* and elsewhere. She has argued in various places that belief-content cannot be fixed by a person's intrinsic physical properties (Baker 1995:180-184). She has also argued against naturalized, reductive, accounts of belief-content (ibid, pp. 56-62). Assuming that her critiques of eliminativism, internalism, and content-naturalism are successful, she can use the new premise to deduce that *T* is false.

I will now turn to Baker's discussion of the explanatory power of beliefs. For, if she can explain how beliefs can be causally explanatory without being brain states, then she will have taken away a powerful reason for accepting the Standard View even if she has not refuted it.

2   Baker's Second Thesis

According to Baker, many philosophers accept the Standard View because they hold what she calls *'the "Brain Explain" Thesis'*:

(*BET*) ' . . . unless beliefs were (either identical to or constituted by) brain states, they could not causally explain behavior.' (Baker 1995:137)[17]

Not surprisingly, she rejects *The 'Brain Explain' Thesis*. In fact, her second thesis in *ABBS* is that beliefs can causally explain behavior without being brain states. Her second thesis follows if no noneliminativist form of the Standard View is true and if beliefs are causally explanatory. For, suppose that they do causally explain behavior. Then, if *The 'Brain Explain' Thesis* is true, beliefs are either identical with or constituted by brain states, contrary to what Baker holds. Thus, it is important for her to show that *The 'Brain Explain' Thesis* is false given that she thinks that beliefs and other propositional attitudes are causally explanatory.

Baker advances two separate arguments against the view. The first is what I shall call, 'The Replacement Argument'. The second is her Aristotelian Argument. She also sketches an account of how beliefs could be causally explanatory if they are neither brain-states nor constituted by brain-states. I will now consider each component of her critique of *The 'Brain Explain' Thesis* in turn.

2.1 Baker's Replacement Argument

According to Baker, *The 'Brain Explain' Thesis* entails what I will call '*The Replacement Thesis*':

(*RT*)   All belief explanations are replaceable by brain-state explanations of the same phenomena.[18]

She rejects *The Replacement Thesis* for two reasons (Baker 1995:138-139). First, no intentional explanation can be replaced by a physical explanation

---

[17] Jerry Fodor presents a version of the 'Causal Power' Argument in support of the 'Brain Explain' Thesis. See Fodor 1987. He gives a modal version of the same argument in Fodor 1991. Baker criticizes Fodor's modal version in Baker 1995: 42-55. Other critics of Fodor's 'Causal Power' Argument are Robert van Gulick and Robert Wilson. See Van Gulick 1989 and Wilson 1995.

[18] The expression 'same phenomena' can have two different readings. It could be taken to be referring to the event (process, state) that falls under different event-descriptions. Or, it could be taken to be referring to the explanandum of some explanation, where the explanandum may be construed as an ordered pair consisting of an event and some contextually determined explanationist predicate that is true of the event. The Replacement Thesis may be true on the first reading. But since brain-explanations and belief-explanations have different explananda, they do not explain the same phenomena (in the second sense of 'the same phenomena'), even if The 'Brain Explain' Thesis is true. Thus, I will argue that the former is false on the second reading, which is the relevant reading for Baker's purposes.

of the constituents of the explained intentional phenomenon. Second, belief explanations are intentional explanations. Notice that if *The 'Brain Explain' Thesis* entails *The Replacement Thesis*, and if the latter is false, then the former is also false even if beliefs had brain states as constituents.

But does *The 'Brain Explain' Thesis* entail *The Replacement Thesis*? Or, to put it another way, is what I call, *'Baker's Premise'*, a necessary truth?

> *Baker's Premise*: If beliefs cannot causally explain behavior unless they are either identical with or constituted by brain states, then belief explanations are replaceable by brain-state explanations of the same phenomena.

Baker thinks so since she says it follows from a plausible general principle - but a principle for which she has no defense 'other than intuition', (Baker 1995:141). Here is what she says:

> Let E be a causal explanation that cites property P to explain some phenomenon F. Then, the causal explanatoriness of P depends on the relation of P to some lower-level property $P*$ only if E is replaceable by an explanation $E*$, where $E*$ cites $P*$. Since E is replaceable by $E*$ just in case either $E*$ is a deeper explanation of the same phenomenon than E, or $E*$ supersedes E, [*Baker's Premise*] follows as an instance of the general principle. (Baker 1995:140-141. Bracketed remark added)

The 'general principle' that Baker is referring to is this:

> The causal explanatoriness of P depends on the relation of P to some lower-level property $P*$ only if E is replaceable by an explanation $E*$, where $E*$ cites $P*$.

The 'relation' that P must have a to a lower-level property $P*$ if it is to have causal explanatory power may be identity, constitution, or having a functional proxy. Either way, as I will now argue, neither *Baker's Premise* nor the 'general principle' from which it is derived is true.

2.1.1 Is *Baker's Premise* True?

Both *Baker's Premise* and Baker's 'general principle' are questionable given that, on her own view, *all* explanations are pragmatic.[19] On the pragmatic view of explanations, an explanation may explain the same phenomena under one description but not under another. What counts as 'the same phenomena' will depend, for explanatory purposes, on certain

---

[19] For a defense of the pragmatic theory of explanation, see Van Fraassen, 1980.

contextual factors, such as the inquirer's explanatory goals and interests. Whether or not some 'deeper explanation' actually explains the same event that is explained by some higher-level explanation will depend (on Baker's view) on several pragmatic factors, including the context of inquiry and on how the relevant explanations are to be individuated with respect to their explananda/explanans relative to those contexts.

If explanations are essentially pragmatic, then belief-explanations are not replaceable by brain-state explanations even if brain-states compose beliefs. To see why, consider the following example. One might ask, 'Why did Smith suddenly leave the room?' and we might answer, 'Because he thought he was late for his doctor's appointment'. Smith's *sudden* departure is the phenomenon to be explained and it is causally explained, at a certain level of description, by the fact that he *thought* he was late for his doctor's appointment. Assume, for the sake of argument, that *The 'Brain Explain' Thesis* is true. Assume also that the mental explanation of Smith's sudden departure depends on a deeper explanation of his bodily movements, one that appeals to certain neurochemical facts about his body, his brain, and their causal properties. This dependence relation may be put counterfactually: if *Smith's departure* had not been constituted by *this particular collection of neurophysiological events*, and if *his brain* had not been constituted by *these neural parts*, then, given the relevant molecular causal laws, his thinking that he was late for a medical appointment would not have explained why his departure was *sudden*.[20]

Given the aforementioned assumptions, which Baker would reject in any case, does *The Replacement Thesis* follow? No, not if explanations are context-sensitive. Let '$N1$' be some neurophysiological description of the event, $e1$, that is Smith's sudden departure, and let '$N2$' be some neurophysiological description of the event, $e2$, that is Smith's thinking that he is late for his doctor's appointment. By hypothesis, there is a neurophysiological explanation that explains the occurrence of $e1$ in terms of the occurrence of $e2$ and its lawful causal properties, under descriptions $N1$ and $N2$, respectively. Given that the position represented by 'x' in the schema, 'Explanation E explains why x happened', is an intensional context, it does not follow that the same molecular explanation explains $e1$

---

[20] Of course, Baker rejects the counterfactual claim. However, the issue here is not whether the counterfactual is true, but whether it logically implies that the mental explanation of Smith's sudden departure can be replaced with the corresponding neurophysiological explanation of Smith's bodily movements without any loss of explanatory or descriptive power. Baker thinks that the counterfactual claim does imply that. I am arguing that it does not even if we grant that the counterfactual is false.

under the description, 'Smith's sudden departure' even though that description is (by hypothesis) extensionally equivalent with $N1$.[21] For, any explanation that explains $e1$ under the first description will entail that *Smith* exists, that he *departed*, and that his departure was *sudden* (which is the phenomenon to be explained). No neurophysiological explanation of $e1$ will entail any of those things. Nor will it entail them in conjunction with some bridge law since no strict projectible law nomically connects neurophysiological facts with specific individuals or with their sudden departures.

Consequently, no neurophysiological explanation of any neural event that is or that constitutes Smith's departure can supercede any higher-level mental explanation of Smith's sudden departure: they apply to two different domains of inquiry. Given Baker's definition of explanation reduction, no lower-level explanation of Smith's bodily movements can therefore replace our higher-level mental explanation of his sudden departure without some loss in explanatory and descriptive power. And yet, the mental explanation is, by hypothesis, counterfactually dependent on the neurophysiological explanation for its causal explanatory properties *if The 'Brain Explain' Thesis* is true. Hence, *The 'Brain Explain' Thesis* does not entail *The Replacement Thesis*. Refuting the latter does not, therefore, show that the former is false.

2.2 Baker's Aristotelian Argument

Baker concedes that the Standard View Theorist 'may claim that if beliefs are actually constituted by brain states, then the 'brain explain' thesis is true, regardless of whether or not belief explanations are replaceable by brain-state explanations' (Baker 1995:141)[22] For that reason, she presents a second, more direct, argument against The '*Brain Explain' Thesis*:

> But, if we assume the 'constitution' version of the Standard View to be contingent, the causal explanatoriness of belief does not require that be-liefs be constituted by brain states (even if in fact they were so consti-tuted). Suppose that the universe had turned out to have been Aristotelian. How would that have affected assumptions about the attitudes' being brain states? A lot: An Aristotelian would not construe beliefs as brain states. How would a supposed Aristotelian universe have affected our ex-

---

[21] A number of philosophers have made the general point that explanation-contexts are non-extensional. For a defense of this view, see Achinstein1983.

[22] I am indebted to my colleague, Hugh Benson, for his remarks on the issues discussed in this subsection.

planations of intentional phenomena? Not one whit: If the sensible and social world were the same as our world, we would have had the same range of explanations, deployed in the same ways and with the same degree of success, that we actually have. In an Aristotelian universe, we would still have explanations in terms of beliefs, as well as explanations in terms of making bad investments. Thus, since the explanatoriness of belief is compatible with the world's being Aristotelian, it follows that the explanatoriness of the attitudes does not require that the attitudes be identical to or constituted by brain states. (Baker 1995:142-143)

An example might be helpful here. Suppose we observe Smith laughing for no apparent reason. We ask him why he is laughing and he answers: 'Because I just remembered a funny joke I heard yesterday on the way to work.' Call Smith's response to our question, '(E)', and the context in which we observed him laughing, 'C'. Suppose that, relative to that context, (E) is a true causal explanation that sufficiently explains why Smith was laughing.

Imagine that the scenario just presented also obtains in a world just like the actual world except that it is Aristotelian with respect to the mental. In that world, Smith's memory-state is then neither token-identical with nor constituted by any brain-state that he is in. But, as in the actual world, (E) causally explains his laughter. Thus, his memory has a causal explanatory role, but for that to be so, it cannot be a requirement that his memory be composed of some brain process or other. For, Smith's memory would still have retained its causal explanatory role even if the world had been Aristotelian. Even if his memory were actually constituted by certain kinds of brain events, that is inessential to its having the causal explanatory role that it has. Consequently, *The 'Brain Explain' Thesis* is false.

2.2.1 An Objection to the Aristotelian Argument

Although Baker's Aristotelian Argument is very persuasive, it has some problems.[23] Presumably, mental states are causally explanatory of certain

---

[23] Louise Antony and Joseph Levine argue that Baker's Aristotelian Argument is also unsound (Ántony and Levine 1997). According to them, it suffers from an equivocation on 'require'. Specifically, they charge her with conflating 'the metaphysical requirements for a causal explanation to be true, with the epistemological requirements for a causal explanation to be acceptable' (p.95). Understood in the first, metaphysical, sense of 'required', her conclusion does not follow from the premises of the argument and it begs the question against someone who holds The 'Brain Explain' Thesis. Understood in the second, epistemological, sense of 'required', her conclusion does follow from her premises but it is logically compatible with The 'Brain Explain' Thesis, since the latter is a thesis on the metaphysical requirements of belief causal-explanations and not on their epistemic requirements. Although I am

(continued)

behavioral effects only if they are causes of those effects or are causally relevant to the production of those effects. But, short of accepting some form of dualism, it is difficult to see how any mental state could cause anything (or be causally relevant to the production of any physical behavioral effect) if it is neither a brain-state nor constituted by any brain-state. I will now offer a familiar argument in support of that last claim.[24]

Consider our earlier example about Smith. In the Aristotelian world, the same mental event, namely, Smith's remembering a funny joke, *causally explains* the fact he was laughing only if it *causes* his laughter (or is causally relevant to his laughter). Let us suppose, for the sake of argument, that Smith's memory caused him to laugh in the Aristotelian world. Then, it must have caused him to undergo a series of muscular facial movements since certain muscular movements would have had to physically constitute his laughter. Certain neurochemical processes occurred in Smith's brain that causally produced certain kinds of facial movements. So, either the mental event of Smith's remembering a joke is a causal relatum in this series of neurochemical causes/effects or it itself causally initiated the series. The first option must be ruled out since, in the Aristotelian world, the memory-event is neither identical with any neurochemical event nor is constituted by any such event (or by any collection of neurochemical events). Furthermore, every relatum in the causal chain that leads from Smith's brain to his facial movements is either a neurophysiological event or is constituted by one. That leaves us with the second option, namely, that the

---

sympathetic with their criticism, there is hardly any textual evidence in Baker 1995, which is the work that they discuss, to support their charge against Baker. If anything, the evidence in that book strongly suggests that she consistently separates the metaphysical requirements for causal explanations from the epistemological requirements—indeed, Antony and Levine come close to admitting as much in the last footnote of their paper. Baker argues, in Baker 1995, that there are no deep metaphysical requirements for the truth of any causal explanation. Ironically, it is in ABBS where I think Baker explicitly tries, unsuccessfully I believe, to connect the metaphysical and epistemological issues in some essential way, e.g., premise (2.231).

[24] The argument that I am about to present should sound familiar - it is a version of The Exclusion Argument, which Jaegwon Kim gives in many of his writings on mental causation (see Kim 1995). Given the present context, the Exclusion Argument will undoubtedly appear to be question-begging since it seems to assume The 'Brain Explain' Thesis. But we can grant that The 'Brain Explain' Thesis is false, and still use the Exclusion Argument to raise the question of how beliefs can cause physical behavioral effects (or be causally relevant), as oppose to being causally explanatory, if they are neither brain-states nor constituted by brain-states and if (as Baker assumes) Cartesian Interaction Dualism is false. For other discussions on the Exclusion Argument, see Fodor 1989, Lepore and Loewer 1987, Marras 1994, McLaughlin 1989, Sosa 1984, and Yablo 1992.

memory-event itself causally initiated the entire chain of neurochemical events directly. However, the second option raises the age-old problem of how some event, which is neither identical with nor is constituted by anything neurophysiological, can causally initiate a series of neural events if the causal initiation is itself not physically implemented in any neurochemical way. Baker will certainly want to avoid that problem.

In the Aristotelian world, Smith's memory therefore plays no causal role in the physical production of the muscular facial movements that constitute Smith's laughter. It causally contributes nothing over and above what the underlying physical processes already causally contribute. He could not have laughed unless his facial muscles moved in a certain way, and they could not have moved in the particular way that they did unless they were caused to move in that particular way by certain brain events that are causally sufficient for the movement. Thus, Smith could not have laughed unless certain brain events sufficient to produce his laughter occurred. Baker will no doubt agree with all of this. But, then, Smith's memory causally contributes nothing to the process that begins with certain neurochemical events in Smith's brain and ends with the facial movements that constitute his laughter. For, by hypothesis, his memory is not constituted by anything neurophysiological in the Aristotelian world, and only things that are so constituted can causally contribute to the facial movements that constitute Smith's laughter. Or so, it would seem.

Smith's memory is thus causally inert with respect to all of his bodily movements (in the Aristotelian world). If so, then it is also causally inert with respect to the bodily movements that constitute his laughter (in that world). Presumably, his memory of the joke cannot cause his laughter without also causing the facial movements that constitute his laughter. In which case, it doesn't even cause his laughter. But if it doesn't, then (E) - Smith's saying, 'Because I just remembered a funny joke I heard yesterday on the way to work' - does not causally explain, in the Aristotelian world, his laughter. By hypothesis, (E) does causally explain his laughter in the actual world. And so, contrary to what Baker contends, we do not have the same causal explanations once we shift from the actual world to the Aristotelian world.

2.2.2 Replies, Concessions, and Rejoinders

One might reply that, in both worlds, Smith's memory causes his laughter, but his internal brain processes cause instead the facial movements that constitute his laughter - the two causal processes are causally and metaphysically independent of each other but operate in parallel. But it would seem that once the facial movements are caused, so is the laughter they constitute. There seems to be no need to posit a separate, nonphysical, mental cause of the laughter given that its compositional elements have their own neurophysiological causes; otherwise, causal overdetermination is actually far more ubiquitous than we care to admit.

One could also deny that mental events cause actions that are constituted by bodily changes only if either they are members of physical causal chains that culminate in such changes or they directly causally initiate the chains but are not links in the chain. One could deny both alternatives and still hold that mental events really do cause the *actions* that are constituted by bodily movements even though no mental event is identical with nor constituted by any brain process. Mental causes are what make certain bodily events *actions* by virtue of their intentional content-properties. That is Baker's view and, for all I have argued, she may be right. In which case, my objections to her Aristotelian Argument don't actually refute it. They at best pose a challenge: explain how mental events can be genuine causes of physically constituted actions while avoiding rampant causal overdetermination and the traditional problems of Cartesian Interactionism. I have no doubt that Baker can and will rise to the challenge.

Another possible countermove that Baker could make against my objections is to deny my assumption that nothing causally explains anything unless it causes something or causally contributes something to the production of an effect. She could argue that there is a perfectly respectable notion of causal explanation that is neutral to any notion of causation or causal relations. If she can show that, then she can deny that she is committed to the ubiquity of casual overdetermination. In the next sub-section, I will explore this option and argue that, if there is such a notion, Baker has not yet presented it.

2.3 Baker on the Causal Explanatory Power of Beliefs

In *ABBS*, Baker explains how beliefs can be causally explanatory without being brain states. Suppose that S performs action A and also believes that P. According to Baker, for S's belief to causally explain S's doing A, there must be true, nonvacuous, noncircular, counterfactuals that connect the belief with the action (*ABBS*, p.35). In particular, they must be true of S only if S's brain is disposed to cause certain bodily movements in S that constitute A, (*ABBS*, p. 36). In other words, S's believing that P causally explains S's doing A only if that explanationist fact requires that S's brain be in certain causal dispositional states that result in, in the right contexts, bodily movements that constitute A (*ABBS*, pp. 37).

So far, we are told what must follow if beliefs causally explain actions, namely, that our brains will have acquired certain causal dispositions that they would otherwise not have had. But that does not explain what it means to say that beliefs can causally explain actions. Our brains could still have the causal dispositions they have even if our beliefs and actions were not counterfactually connected in the ways that they actually are.

Suppose, for example, that I have not slept for the last two days. Imagine that I am waiting for you at the bus station and that I have consumed a lot of coffee. As I wait, I think about an old friend of mine who had recently told me that he would be coming into town for a visit. Your bus arrives and I see you get off. I come to think that the person I see there is you. I then wave to you. In this example, my waving is the relevant action and my belief that the person I see there is you is the causally relevant explanatory belief.

In what sense, then, does my belief causally explain my action assuming that my belief is not constituted by any of my brain-states? Baker's answer seems to be this: if my belief were not counterfactually connected to my action in the ways that it is, my brain would not have been disposed to causally activate the afferent nerves responsible for my arm motion that constitutes my wave. But that is incorrect. Suppose I had come to believe that the person I see at the (same) bus station, who is in fact you, is my old childhood friend. (You resemble my friend in some striking ways.) I come to believe that partly because I remembered what my friend said, and partly because I perceptually mistook you to be him. As in the actual situation, I have not slept in several days, and I have consumed a lot of caffeine. My perceptual error was the result of my fatigue and of my other beliefs about my friend. As before, I wave. Thus, in some of closest-to-the-actual worlds in which the same antecedent conditions hold, my brain is disposed to respond in just the way it actually did. That is so even if, contrary to fact, my actual belief about you (namely, that the person I see getting off the bus is you rather than my friend) had not led to my action given that, in the relevant counterfactual situation, I do not have that particular belief about you. Still, in the actual situation, my belief about you causally explains why I waved to you.

Baker might insist that, in the example, my actual belief really doesn't causally explain my action if we can sever the relevant counterfactual connections between the two. For that reply to work, it must be that a belief's having some counterfactual dependence relation to the explained action is *constitutive* of a belief-explanation's being a *causal* explanation of that action I will now examine that idea more fully.

2.4 Baker on Causal Explanations

In Baker 1995, Baker presents two ways of showing how our beliefs might be said to causally explain things. First, she gives a (pre-theoretic) set of sufficient conditions for any explanation to be a causal explanation:

> . . . I understand a causal explanation (1) to give information about why a particular phenomenon occurred, and (2) to mention explanatory proper-ties that are instantiated before the occurrence of the phenomenon and that are not definitionally linked to the phenomena to be explained, and (3) to support relevant counterfactuals about the phenomenon. (Baker 1995:99)

Nonpsychological intentional explanations, which are explanations that 'presuppose that there are psychological attitudes, without explicitly mentioning them,' pass her test (ibid, p.98). Here is one of her examples: 'Al's application for a gun permit was turned down. The causal explanation is that Al is a convicted felon. If he had not been a convicted felon, he would have received the gun permit' (ibid, p.100). The property of being a convicted felon cannot be instantiated in a world in which there are no intentional states. Nor is there a strict physical law or physical property with which the property of being a convicted felon and the property of having one's gun permit application form rejected are jointly projected. But, according to Baker, the adduced explanation of Al's action is a causally adequate explanation if her conditions (1)-(3), presented above, are jointly sufficient for causal explanation.

However, they are insufficient. Consider the following example. It is customary for each adult member in my family to host a large family Thanksgiving dinner at least once. Each host is selected on a rotational basis. It was my turn to host it in 1996, which I did. Thus, if you were to ask why the annual Elugardo Thanksgiving feast was held at my house in 1996, my explanation would be this: 'The Elugardo Thanksgiving feast was held at my house in 1996 because it was my turn to host it then.' The statement is true even though it does not provide a causal explanation of why the feast was held at my house in 1996. Being my turn to host the 1996 event, which is the explanans, did not causally bring it about that the event would take place at the particular location where it actually occurred. The location of the event was instead causally fixed by something else - my residence in 1996. Indeed, the explanans did not cause the Thanksgiving feast that took place in my house in 1996, although it explains (given the relevant background context and specific information) why it took place there and at that particular time.

Baker's conditions, (1), (2), and (3), are met in my example. First, as I said, the fact that it was my turn to host the festivities in 1996 explains, given the context, why the event occurred at my place that year. Second, once the rotation was set-up, I acquired the property of being the person responsible for hosting the dinner in 1996, which is a property that I acquired long before I actually hosted the event. Furthermore, one can know that it was my turn to host on Thanksgiving Day 1996 without knowing that I actually did host it that day, and vice versa. Knowing what the explanans-statement means is insufficient for knowing that the explanandum-statement is true, and conversely. So, there is no definitional link between the two in my example. Third, if it had not been my turn to host the traditional Thanksgiving family dinner in 1996, the dinner would not have been held at my house that year — either some other family member would have hosted it instead or it would not have been held at all. But we have no causal explanation here because the explanans did not cause anything. Baker's three conditions fail, then, to exclude noncausal explanations.

Baker presents a second test for determining when an explanation is a causal explanation. She calls it, 'the Control Thesis' (Baker 1995:122). The basic idea is this: If we can produce or prevent a certain type of phenomena at will, then an explanation of how either one was done would have to be a causal explanation. Let F and G be two temporally distinct types of events such that, in circumstances C, one can produce/prevent a G-event by producing/preventing an F-event. Then, Baker's Control Thesis is this:

> An occurrence of F in C causally explains an occurrence of G if:(i) if an F had not occurred in C, then a G would not have occurred in C;and (ii) given that F did occur in C, an occurrence of G was inevitable. (ibid, p.122)

Again, many nonpsychological intentional explanations, psychological explanations, and physical explanations satisfy conditions (i) and (ii). All of them are therefore causal explanations if the Control Thesis holds.

But conditions (i) and (ii) are jointly insufficient if circumstances C is highly unusual or special in certain respects. Suppose that my brother and I live in the same apartment. He is blind but he can hear; I am deaf but I am sighted. To help us know when someone is at the door, the apartment is electrically wired in such a way that our doorbell will ring when and only when the light bulb in our doorway, which is always on, glows dim and bright in an alternating pattern. Because of the internal circuitry, the correlation between the doorbell ringing and the light bulb glowing holds as a matter of law. Consequently, you cannot cause the light bulb to alternate between dim light and bright light by pressing the doorbell button without also bringing about a situation in which my brother's eardrums vibrate (when he is home, within earshot, etc.) For, as a matter of law, doing the first is nomically correlated in this context with causing the doorbell to ring, which in turn normally causes my brother's eardrums to vibrate. We may suppose that the doorbell ringing is the only cause of the vibrations in this context. Therefore, given the facts of the case, if the light bulb had not dimmed and then glow brightly, my brother's eardrums would not have vibrated. And, given that the light bulb did glow in this pattern, the vibration of my brother's eardrums was inevitable.

Conditions (i) and (ii) of Baker's *Control Thesis* are met. However, causing the light to alternate between dimness and brightness does not causally explain why my brother's eardrums vibrate in that context. For, there is no causal path that traces the second kind of event back to the first without bypassing the causal connection between the sound of the doorbell ringing and my brother's eardrums vibrating. It is the latter connection that explains this event given the causal laws that subsume sound waves and eardrum vibrations. Baker's *Control Thesis* does not, then, provide a sufficient condition for causal explanation.[25]

2.5   The Final Upshot

The following moral may be drawn from my discussion of Baker's view of causal explanation: No counterfactual analysis of the sort that she envisages is likely to provide a sufficient condition for an explanation's being a causal explanation. Furthermore, we do not yet have an account of how our explanatory practices can constitute a causal connection between our attitudes and our actions.[26] We need such an account. After all, our brains remain causally connected with the bodily movements that make up our actions, independently of our social and linguistic practices.[27] So, we need an explanation of how our linguistic and institutional practices can literally create causal connections in a physical world that impact on such

---

[25] One could add a clause to Baker's Control Thesis that excludes any property that screens off the putative causal explanatory property. However, such a move would be a concession to the Standard View Theorist since it means that higher-level properties are not causally explanatory properties. That runs counter to Baker's program to show that intentional explanations, both psychological and nonpsychological, are autonomous causal explanations.

[26] I am here in agreement with Antony and Levine. See Antony and Levine 1997.

[27] For a nice discussion on the tension that arises when one holds, on the one hand, that psychological explanations rationalize the actions they causally explain, and also holds, on the other hand, that mental properties are anomalous and thus irreducible, see Antony 1989.

metaphysically independent causal relations.[28] Otherwise, we cannot explain how our mental attitudes can causally explain anything if they are neither constituted by nor implemented by our brain-states.

3 Conclusion

In this chapter, I defended two claims. First, Baker's subargument against noneliminative versions of the Standard View fails. It involves the questionable premise that such a theory of beliefs is true only if it will be confirmed by neuroscience someday. I suggested that she really does not need that premise anyway and offered a plausible alternative on her behalf. Second, her various counterfactual accounts of how beliefs can be causally explanatory, even if they are not brain states, fail to provide a sufficient condition for a belief-explanation to be a causal explanation.

In spite of these concerns, Baker's work is a major contribution to the philosophical literature on the mind. No one who writes on the topics she discusses can ill-afford to ignore her arguments - in particular, the Standard Theorists. Although Baker accepts their slogan, 'No brains, no attitudes', she clearly rejects their ideology. According to her, there are no brains that have an attitude. Those who think otherwise will have to change their minds if Baker is right.[29]

References

Achinstein, P. 1983. *The Nature of Explanation*. New York: Oxford University Press.

Antony, L. 1989. Anomalous Monism and the Problem of Explanatory Force. *Philosophical Review* 98: 153-87.

Antony, L. and Levine, J. 1997. Reduction With Autonomy. *Philosophical Perspectives: Mind, Causation, World* II, ed. J. Tomberlin, 83-105. Boston: Blackwell.

Baker, L.R.1987. *Saving Belief: A Critique of Physicalism*. Princeton: Princeton University Press.

---

[28] Baker's counterfactual account is therefore compatible with the view that beliefs, and the other attitudes, are global epiphenomenal properties of persons.

[29] I am indebted to Hugh Benson, Monte Cook, and Wayne Riggs for their helpful comments on an earlier draft of this paper. I would also like to thank the contributor of this volume who read my paper and the editorial referee for their helpful comments. The second section of my paper is a revised version of a portion of my review of Baker 1995 (Elugardo 1999). I would like to thank Ernest Sosa, the editor of the journal in which my review appears, for granting me permission to use some of the material from my review.

Baker, L.R.1995. *Explaining Attitudes: A Practical Approach to the Mind*. Cambridge: Cambridge University Press.

Baker, L.R. 2000. *Persons and Bodies*. Cambridge: Cambridge University Press.

Burge, T. 1979. Individualism and the Mental. *Midwest Studies in Philosophy* 4: 73-121.

Churchland, P. 1986. *Neurophilosophy*. Cambridge: MIT Press.

Davidson, D. 1967. Causal Relations. *The Journal of Philosophy* 64:691-03.

Davidson, D. 1969. The Individuation of Events. *Essays in Honor of Carl Hempel*, ed. N. Rescher, 216-34. Dordrecht: D. Reidel Publishing Company.

Dretske, F. 1986. Misrepresentation. *Form, Content, and Function*, ed. R.J. Bodgan, 17-36. Oxford: Clarendon Press.

Elugardo, R. 1999. Review of Explaining Attitudes, by L.R. Baker. *Philosophy and Phenomenological Research* 59:513-24.

Fodor, J. 1987. *Psychosemantics*. Cambridge: MIT Press.

Fodor, J. 1989. Making Mind Matter More. *Philosophical Topics* 17:59-79.

Fodor, J. 1991. A Modal Argument for Narrow Content. *Journal of Philosophy* 87:5-26.

Kim, J. 1995. *Supervenience and Mind*. Cambridge: Cambridge University Press.

Lepore, E. and Loewer, B. 1987. Mind Matters. *Journal of Philosophy* 84:630-42.

Marras, A. 1994. Nonreductive Materialism and Mental Causation. *Canadian Journal of Philosophy* 24:465-94.

McLaughlin, B. 1989. Type Epiphenomenalism, Type Dualism, and the Causal Priority of the Physical. *Philosophical Perspectives* 3: 109-35.

Millikan, R. 1989. Biosemantics. *Journal of Philosophy* 86: 281-97.

Papineau, D. 1987. *Reality and Representation*. Oxford: Basil Blackwell.

Putnam, H. 1975. The Meaning of 'Meaning'. *Language, Mind, and Knowledge*, ed. K. Gunderson, 131-93. Minneapolis: University of Minnesota Press.

Sosa, E. 1984. Mind-Body Interaction and Supervenient Causation. *Midwest Studies in Philosophy* 8:271-81.

Van Fraassen, B. 1980. *The Scientific Image*. Oxford: Clarendon Press.

Van Gulick, R. 1989. Metaphysical Arguments for Internalism and Why They Don't Work. *Representation*, ed. S. Silvers, 151-60. Dordrecht: Kluwer Academic Press.

Wilson, R. 1995. *Cartesian Psychology and Physical Minds*. Cambridge: Cambridge University Press.

Yablo, S. 1992. Mental Causation. *The Philosophical Review* 101:245-80.

7

The Causal Powers of Belief:
A Critique of Practical Realism

THEO MEYERING

1   Introduction

Professor Baker's book (Baker, 1995)[1] is admirable, forthright and well-argued. There is much in Practical Realism I wholeheartedly sympathize with. However, there are also some critical nuts to crack. My main contention will be that mental causation requires that belief states are internal states of a subject, being in fact states of a subject's brain. Furthermore, knowledge of brain states is in principle relevant, with corrective potential, *vis-à-vis* propositional attitude explanations of human behavior. As a preamble to the discussion of these propositions I will take issue with Professor Baker's insistence that the notion of cause should be defined by our prevailing explanatory practices rather than by any purportedly *a priori* insights into the metaphysics of causation. Finally, I propose and discuss various arguments in favor of a thesis of *relative* autonomy of the special sciences, while opposing the *radical* autonomy thesis as advocated in Professor Baker's version of Practical Realism.

---

[1] All references to Professor Baker's book *Explaining Attitudes. A Practical Approach to the Mind* (Cambridge: Cambridge University Press, 1995) are abbreviated as EA.

Explaining Beliefs: Lynne Rudder Baker and Her Critics.
Anthonie Meijers (ed.).
Copyright © 2001, CSLI Publications.

Thus, I am afraid the bulk of my paper may be one-sidedly devoted to criticism of Practical Realism rather than to the many points of intellectual agreement. All I can plead in mitigation is that my critique is intended to strengthen Practical Realism rather than undermine it, thus benefiting the many points in Practical Realism worth saving and elaborating.

2 Action-at-a-Distance? Methodological Problems Facing Relational Psychology

Baker takes Fodor to task for inconsistently allowing relational classifications in the *special* sciences while at the same time prohibiting relational taxonomy in *psychology*. In the following I wish to defend Fodor against this charge. My main concern, however, is not with the merits or demerits of Fodor's theory of 'narrow content' as such. Rather what I want to focus on is the urgency and indispensability of the quest for intelligible interlevel relationships between different levels of explanation. Thus I intend to give a rather lengthy reconstruction of Fodor's arguments in order to then use them as a foil for developing more tenable and more sophisticated solutions to the methodological problems he is rightly seriously concerned about.

Fodor [the Fodor before *The Elm and the Expert* (Fodor, 1994)] has vigorously defended 'narrow content' as the only admissible taxonomy for a truly scientific psychology. This theory was more or less forced on him given his general methodological position according to which a causal-nomological model of explanation holds for science *tout court*. Whether it is folk psychology, cognitive science or information semantics, science, according to Fodor, always aims at finding explanations involving genuine, context-free, causal laws. (Fodor, 1991b)

In the course of time Fodor has defended this theory of narrow content with great agility, advancing a variety of arguments in support of it. First, Fodor (Fodor, 1980) propounded a *semantic* argument, invoking the so-called formality condition and an associated 'methodological solipsism'. Later, Fodor (Fodor, 1991a) developed a *modal* argument by insisting that purely conceptual connections (such as the 'wide' connection between our 'water thoughts' and H_2O) are causally inert and thus irrelevant for the purposes of scientific taxonomy. However, Fodor's main argument is a *methodological* one. In brief this argument states that the science of psychology is concerned only with computational processes taking place *within* the skull and supervening on underlying neurophysiology. In those processes distal context can play no causal role. Consequently, it cannot be an admissible factor in the scientific explanation of behavior.

In a discussion with Burge, Fodor (Fodor, 1987) spelled out these claims in terms of a combination of two principles, which are often confounded. One is the principle of what he calls *methodological individualism*, that is, the thesis that scientific taxonomy should be based exclusively on causal powers. The relevant passages constitute an ineluctable challenge for anyone who believes that causation and individuation can go different ways, as Burge (with Professor Baker possibly following in his wake) maintains.

However, it is important to realize that Fodor's principle of methodological individualism, which he himself presents as a 'mandatory methodological principle' (Fodor, 1987, 1991[a]) does not by itself exclude or prohibit relational taxonomies. As Fodor explicitly states,

> ...there is nothing to stop principles of individuation from being simultaneously relational and individualistic. *Individualism does not prohibit the relational individuation of mental states*; it just says that no property of mental states, relational or otherwise, counts taxonomically unless it affects causal powers. (Fodor, 1987, p. 42).

This, I submit, is a muddle only to those who have neglected to appreciate that in order to prohibit relational taxonomy in psychology Fodor needs, *and supplies*, a second principle, viz. his well-known principle of *methodological solipsism*. The latter principle, unlike the former is a metaphysical *option*. It is the principle that causal powers supervene on local microstructure, and in particular, in the psychological case, that the mind's causal powers supervene on local neural structure (Fodor, 1987: p. 44). That is to say, in the mechanisms subserving mental processes the neurons respond to *local* inputs; they are blind to distal facts, and *a fortiori* to semantics. This is not at all an implausible principle - indeed in Fodor's view mind/brain supervenience (or /identity) is our only plausible account of how mental states could have the causal powers that they do have. I take this to be Fodor's main motive and overriding concern: in the final analysis the causal transactions invoked in causal explanations of human behavior presuppose, and perhaps must ultimately be spelled out in terms of, *local* processes operative *here and now*. But as I said, unlike the former principle this at least is a principle that is debatable in principle (and one which Professor Baker may debate in fact).

Fodor's critical position, in its application to psychology, can thus be summarized in the following sequence of theses:

1. The principal aim of science is successful generalization.

2. The success of generalizations depends largely on the extent to which the underlying taxonomy reflects truly existing causal powers ('cuts nature at the joints').
3. Ergo: scientific taxonomy should respect all and only causally relevant factors. Or (*corollary*): good taxonomy does not apply causally inert distinctions, which may hamper successful generalization.
4. Mental causation is mediated through *local* microstructure.
5. Possible relations with distal factors in space and time do not causally affect the *modus operandi* of mental processes: any differences between me and my possible 'twin brother' on 'twin earth' (molecularly identical with me, but with a different history and environment) are *ecological* or *evolutionary*, but not *psychological* in kind.
6. Ergo: for taxonomical purposes of a *scientific* psychology, non-causal relations with distal factors are entirely irrelevant.

Having said all this, the challenging question for those who, like Baker, advocate a wide propositional attitude psychology is this: how is it that beliefs, individuated in terms of broad contents, can be held to be causally explanatory, and causally explanatory in virtue of their contents, without any account of how they relate to relevant local processes filling the bill so to speak of the causal transactions invoked?

3 Mental Causation and Radical Externalism

Needless to say, the problem of mental causation looms large in current debates surrounding cognitive science. It comes mainly in two forms, one presupposing a functionalist account of mental properties, the other presupposing some form of externalism about intentional content. For functionalists the problem is how to account for mental causation if mental properties are functional properties and functional properties 'don't do any real work'. Here a satisfactory answer can be given, I believe, by distinguishing between causal efficacy and causal relevance, and by arguing that content is causally relevant without being causally efficacious (Jackson, 1996; Jackson & Pettit, 1988; Dretske, 1993). On this solution our 'localist' intuition of causation - the view, that is, that causation, if anything, has got to be something here and now - can be maintained, inasmuch as causal relevance *is* a matter of *hic et nunc*: what I am believing now causally explains what I am doing now, assuming that mental nature is in some important sense in common between *Doppelgänger* (Jackson, 1996).

For externalists, however, the problem seems to be much worse. How on earth could content properties which are not intrinsic (syntactical or neurological) properties ever be causally explanatory? As McGinn puts it:

'According to externalism, contentful states are identified by reference to entities that lie outside the subject's body ... [Yet] what happens at the causal nexus is local, proximate and intrinsic: the features of the cause that lead to the effect must be right where the causal interaction takes place.... [T]he causal powers of a state must be intrinsically grounded; they cannot depend essentially upon relations to what lies quite elsewhere.' (McGinn, 1989, p. 133)

How does Professor Baker propose to address this issue? I believe one can distinguish between two distinct though interrelated strands in Baker's argument. One is the general recommendation contained in Practical Realism to treat causation as an *explanatory* notion. The other, related, line of argument is to note the many cases both within science and in common sense explanatory practices where we explain in broad or relational terms using extrinsic classifications, and then to raise, with Professor Baker, the rhetorical question:

Now which should we give up - the proposed standards of [explanatory] adequacy or the examples [of successful nonpsychological causal explanations]? I think there is no contest. (EA 119)

Let me begin with the first suggestion. Treating causation as an explanatory notion, of course, is diametrically opposed to a widely shared view stressing the independence and primacy of our metaphysical insights into causation, which in turn dictate standards of causal-explanatory adequacy. Baker turns the table against this. Instead of attributing primacy to our metaphysical intuitions and the attendant standards of causal-explanatory adequacy, she insists on taking explanatory practices as primary, and adapting our metaphysics to them. There is an appealing argument supporting this claim. For clearly, if causes were to be the kind of things that lie altogether beyond our explanatory ken, they would certainly become irrelevant as guides to our explanatory practices. In that case the pragmatist would surely be right to insist that we had better revise our metaphysical intuitions rather than declaring our successful explanatory practices to be null and void. Thus our epistemic notion of what we can possibly come to know and explain certainly puts constraints on what we can conceive causes to be. But Baker's motive for Practical Realism is much weaker than the case just imagined. Her charge is not - cannot be - that our *a priori* notions of cause and causality have rendered explanation *as such* impossible; but the much weaker charge that these *a priori* notions and the attendant standards of causal-explanatory adequacy rule out a special *class* of explanations, viz. macro-explanations. My objections to her are threefold:

1. I believe she throws in the towel much too early. The skeptical dilemma between cherished metaphysical intuitions and plausible ex-

planatory practices both within and outside of psychology is far from unresolvable.

2. The problem of action-at-a-distance involved in macro-explanations posed especially for radical externalism or relationalism as advocated by Professor Baker cries out for philosophical analysis and resolution.

3. There is a *dialectic* between *a priori* notions of causal-explanatory standards on the one hand and explanatory practices on the other.

Let me begin with the latter point. I believe we cannot just let causes be derivative concepts depending on whatever may be our explanatory practices. In fact standards and practices are mutually corrective forces resulting in an ongoing dynamics of gradually more and more sophisticated practices. Let me give an example. I believe the problem of explanatory asymmetry provides a case in point. Thus to avoid puzzles about barometer readings 'explaining' storms and shadow lengths 'explaining' flagpole heights Wesley Salmon (Salmon, 1984) has proposed that all explanation must be causal. 'Cause' in his view should not be taken as a primitive concept. Instead Salmon has tried to give a noncircular account of the difference between causal processes and what he calls 'pseudo-processes'. The relevant point for our purposes is that Salmon's proposal is one where causal-explanatory standards dictate and constrain our explanatory practices. Inasmuch as science is to uncover real causes, it must discard pseudo-processes as mere shadows of the true explanatory mechanisms to be found elsewhere.

However, the further development of this case is even more to the point. For Sober (Sober, 1985) has convincingly argued against Salmon that some explanatory processes, though based on pseudo-processes, are nevertheless quite legitimate. Thus the quantitative characterization of the concept of heritability is defined with respect to pseudo-processes (viz. in terms of parent phenotypes yielding similar offspring phenotypes), yet heritability has more than just heuristic or predictive utility, it can be genuinely explanatory, according to Sober. If Sober is right, his recommendation would amount to a case that is the converse of Salmon's example cited above, viz. one where explanatory *practices* correct and refine causal-explanatory *standards*. Generally speaking, I think, it is uncalled for, as Baker does, to turn the tables against the metaphysicians and take the opposite extreme of letting practices alone dictate what would be viable notions of cause and of attendant standards of causal-explanatory adequacy. Indeed, the dialectic just described seems to be much more in the spirit of Practical Realism as advocated and aptly described by Professor Baker elsewhere. To be sure, she does insist on taking her philosophical clues from reflection on human practices rather than from some overarching theory claimed to have *a priori* credentials. However, she goes on to qualify her Practical Realism significantly when she states that '[f]rom the more pragmatic perspective, theory and practice must be brought into reflective equilibrium.' (EA p. 20) It is precisely this dialectic, which I would want to endorse. It implies among other things that to consult our current explanatory practices alone would be consulting no more than yesterday's philosophical lessons. In other words, although metaphysics shouldn't be the sole measure of all things, it certainly is an independent, and possibly critical factor operative in shaping tomorrow's resulting practices.[2]

Now one of those metaphysical intuitions is the *hic-et-nunc* character of causal processes. How does Baker's radical relationalism propose to handle this problem? Or would this be a particularly good example of a case where we can simply brush aside our metaphysical intuitions and allow action-at-a-distance obscurantism with no further account of how on earth distal events may be causally related? Or perhaps we should, with Professor Baker, take a more defiant attitude and proclaim in defense that since there are so many macro-explanatory practices *outside of* psychology, we are also entitled to rely on them for the purposes of strictly *intentional* explanations, and either plead non-guilty by association, or plead guilty, but then guilty in company too good to feel overly worried?

4   The Local Character of Causation

There are various strands to the issue of causation being operative *hic-et-nunc* that need to be carefully disentangled. One is the question of *reductionism*, or the replaceability of macro-explanations by explanations that

---

[2] Perhaps Professor Baker might wish to deny that there is any tension between on the one hand her claim that explanatory practice rather than causal-explanatory standards should fix the notion of a cause and on the other Practical Realism's endorsement of reflective equilibrium between the two. Thus she might wish to distinguish between on the one hand standards derived from scientific methodology and on the other standards derived from *a priori* metaphysics, such as Kim's or Davidson's views. However, I am not at all convinced that this is a principled distinction rather than a mere matter of degree. *A priori* metaphysics, though possibly operative at a higher level of conceptual abstraction, is historically speaking no more exempt from the dialectic between standards and practices than are the standards of scientific methodology. Thus it was under the impact of the emergence of modern science that the Aristotelian metaphysics of the four causes gave way to mechanicist metaphysics allowing no mode of causation other than efficient causation. Conversely, action-at-a-distance theories in modern science have always been exposed to critical pressure from the metaphysical intuition that causation is local and contiguous (or, as the case may be, distributed across fields).

only mention locally operative causes and effects. Indeed, Professor Baker seems to be seriously concerned that the ultimate ambition of what she dubs the Standard View[3] is the reduction of psychological to neurological explanations. Thus she contrasts the Standard View with the Practical Realist view by stating that '[a]ccording to Practical Realism, believing that *p* is an *irreducible* fact about a person' (my italics; EA 23). Elsewhere she says:

> If the 'brain explain' thesis is true, then belief explanations are replaceable
> by brain-state explanations of the same phenomena. (EA 138)

However, I believe this is a red herring. Not only because many of those who adopt the Standard View in one way or another profess to be non-reductive materialists and would balk at being ascribed a replaceability thesis of the sort imputed to them by Professor Baker (this inspires for example Van Gulick's critique of Baker's analysis (Van Gulick, 1994)). But also, and more importantly, because whatever reductive tendencies may animate defenders of the Standard View should be conceived of as attempts to understand explanatory relations between different levels *each of which is already taken seriously in itself*, rather than as an unending quest for ever deeper foundations whereby, in Roger Sperry's words, ultimately everything gets explained in terms of virtually nothing.

How then do things stand with the action-at-a-distance problem posed especially urgently for externalism? If the content of belief and desire is broad, involving things in the subject's environment, history or linguistic community, then *Doppelgänger* will no longer be psychologically alike. My behavior will no longer be explicable just in terms of what it is about me ('here') doing my act ('now'), in terms, that is, which I would share with any *Doppelgänger*. I believe this is a problem philosophers cannot afford to neglect. Fodor for one has taken the problem seriously enough to come up with a radical solution. As I have amply detailed, his proposal (Fodor, 1980, 1987, 1991a) was to distinguish a special kind of causal explanatory content ('narrow content'), which is supposed to be causally efficacious and operative here and now. However, the notion of narrow content being a content that is not semantically evaluable is an implausible psychological category. Human action, it seems to me, can only be explained and predicted by beliefs that are taken to be *true* and by desires that yearn to be *satisfied*.

---

[3] According to Professor Baker, what she calls 'the Standard View' holds that 'beliefs are (or are constituted by) brain states [i.e.] that for every belief token, there is a brain-state token that constitutes the belief.' (EA 7)

How then does Professor Baker propose to respond to this problem? As I have indicated, Professor Baker explicitly appeals to the many cases of macro-explanations where we causally explain in relational terms without worrying about implementing mechanisms or about here-and-now intuitions concerning causal efficacy. As she says:

> Part of my strategy is to show that *nonpsychological* causal explanations in general do not require that explanatory properties be physically realized internal states; and, some philosophers to the contrary notwithstanding, there is no compelling reason to require that explanatory properties cited by *psychological* causal explanations be physically realized internal states either. (EA 23-4)

Indeed, examples of macro-explanations adverting to distal states of affairs generally abound in the social sciences. Professor Baker herself gives an extensive example from economics. Even in physics and astronomy examples of macro-explanations are not difficult to come by. Thus, Fodor's own example of a planet being a body with the relational property of being under the influence of a sun provides a case in point. Yet, one must be aware of the limitations of Professor Baker's strategy. To be sure, relational properties often do inform us about causal origins, and thus the information they provide is in this sense undoubtedly highly relevant for explanatory purposes. This is even more pertinent in the case of explaining *behavior*. Knowing the distal objects causally responsible for the information-sensitive states of human subjects is undoubtedly of great *explanatory* importance. At the very least it may tell us which thing's properties it is that are being encoded inside the subject, even if it may not tell us which properties of that thing are being encoded (Jackson, 1996). However, these observations do nothing to solve the problem of here-and-now causal efficacy, as opposed to that of causal relevance in some wide sense. The problem of causal efficacy concerns the question which properties of my internal states here-and-now are causally responsible for making my arm move, or whatever. And an answer to this question must surely advert to local properties of my internal states. In this respect the example of the planet as an example of a relational category generating *bona fide* macro-explanations should offer little solace to radical externalists. As Jackson (Jackson, 1996) reminds us, even though 'planet' may be relationally defined, it is the *local* properties of the gravitational field operative *where* the planet is *at* the time in question that make the planet move in its characteristic fashion around a sun. Thus the appeal to macro-explanations being offered in good conscience elsewhere in science does not lay to rest our worries about how what we believe and desire can have causal efficacy here and now, if content is not a here-and-now property to start with.

A possible way to solve the riddle for externalism is to accept that there is narrow content after all, and that it is, *pace* Fodor, truth conditional content. Lewis (Lewis, 1994) has offered some sobering thoughts to remind us that not all content is wide. He warns us not to jump to the conclusion that just any belief sentence is susceptible to Twin Earth examples. In fact, the scope of these examples is much more limited than is generally assumed. They thus leave plenty of room for content that is independent of what one is acquainted with. In an important sense, therefore, you and the brain in a bottle and Davidson's Swampman and Oscar and Twoscar have a lot of content in common (e.g. that square pegs don't fit round holes; or that the stuff you have heard of under the name 'water' falls from clouds).[4] Also it is important to remind ourselves that intentional states *per se* are not broad

---

[4] One referee for this volume has objected to the idea that narrow content might have truth conditions. Specifically he has raised doubts about whether the Lewis examples are of any help here. There certainly are deep issues here that I am afraid cannot all be adequately addressed within the scope of this paper, let alone of this footnote. Let me try to tackle just one particular point of criticism. One of the Lewis examples as rendered by the referee runs as follows: 'The stuff I have heard of under the name "water" falls from clouds'. My critic then goes on to argue that my twins and I will not be expressing type-identical beliefs by our utterances of this same form of words since the expressed beliefs will differ in their truth-conditions: 'only "I" will figure essentially in the truth-conditions [...] - no possible twin who isn't me will.' The point at issue, I suppose, is the vexed question whether beliefs *de se* can be reduced to beliefs *de dicto*. Assume they cannot (an assumption I share), would this suffice to show that 'egocentric' beliefs, inasmuch as they make essential reference to the *actual* speakers or thinkers of the utterances in question, cannot, so to speak, leave any narrow content to be *shared* by actual thinkers and their Doppelgänger? I am far from convinced that this is the only, or the only plausible, way to resolve the issue. For one thing, there is a natural intuition that Doppelgänger do share the same beliefs (or alternatively: desires) when expressing the same form of words, even though this commonality is reflected only in the self-ascribed properties of egocentric propositional attitudes, not in the conditions under which their respective beliefs are true. And then again, the truth-conditions of egocentric propositional attitudes do not vary, as they do in the typical cases of broad content, as a function of changes in context *outside* the subject, but only as a consequence of the fact that I and my twins are numerically distinct. On this count, then, egocentric beliefs should come out narrow, not broad: their contents are shared between Doppelgänger and their truth-conditions do not depend on their subjects' surroundings.

Secondly, my critic doubts whether narrow contents 'construed as mappings from pairs of contexts and internal representational states to broad contents' are useful explanatory constructs in psychological theory formation. *Au contraire*, I believe they are *indispensable* for it! Narrow content descriptions allow us to explain subjects' interactions with typical causes and effects in actual and possible environments *regardless of whether these environments are actual or not*. I submit such explanations are entirely analogous to explanations in terms of dispositional properties shared by intrinsic duplicates (cf. Braddon-Mitchell & Jackson, 1996).

and that, contrary to widespread opinion, intentionality is not a relation, given the fact that many intentional objects do not even exist. Jackson has expressed an admittedly deflationary view on broad content which I would like to endorse:

> whenever someone is in an intentional state with broad content, what makes it true that they are in such a state is the combination of the narrow intentional state they are in with certain connections between that narrow state and their surroundings, including especially the causal origin of the narrow state. (Jackson, 1996, pp. 402-3)

As Jackson elaborates, this proposal handles the here-and-now problem without excessive repudiation. Whenever for purposes of psychological explanation we impute beliefs and desires to subjects in terms of broad contents, we are in fact doing two things simultaneously: we give information about causal origins or environmental effects *and* we state that, underlying these external facts, there is some local current fact about them which settles what they believe or desire in the narrow sense and which explains their actions. The (broad) beliefs we thus attribute to ourselves and others in explaining our actions have narrow content components which we and our *Doppelgänger* have in common. These explain our actions in terms of some narrow local facts that are either causally efficacious (if identical with some neurological property) or at any rate causally relevant (if not), but at least they will be local. At the same time nothing prevents one from categorizing those narrow states widely, bringing in historical, social and environmental factors that reach well beyond the confines of the head or the body, thus characterizing the state in question as a *broad* intentional state. For example, frogs may be said to detect flies and rattlesnakes mice, given the standard *habitat* their detection systems are attuned to. Furthermore, given attendant desires, they will act predictably. And so do we when thirsty and spotting a glass of beer. Relational, functional, even teleological as these taxonomies may be, they do not change the essentially *local* causal facts. It would be a gloomy day when our classifications were to change the causal facts. But they don't, and the weather is just fine.

5 Baker's Control Test for Explanatory Adequacy

In trying to explicate how beliefs can explain Professor Baker proposes a simple Control Test for determining whether one has a causal explanation. She is aware that the test has limited applicability: it purports to provide only a sufficient condition for a causal explanation; many causal explanations will elude the test. The test is very much in the spirit of Richard Miller's remark that 'all means of control are causes, even if the converse is not true.' (quoted in EA 122) Thus the Control Test proposes the following:

> An occurrence of F in circumstances C causally explains an occurrence of G in C if: (i) If an F had not occurred in C, then a G would not have occurred in C; and (ii) given that an F did occur in C, an occurrence of G was inevitable. (EA 122)

However, I believe there may be several difficulties with this proposal, modest as it may seem to be. Suppose a red-hot piece of coal burns a piece of paper. It is true that if the coal hadn't been red, it wouldn't have burnt the paper. Yet its redness did not cause the burning. Rather, the redness and the burning find their common cause in the hotness of the piece of coal.

Again, we often don't know the true causal mechanisms, yet some rough and ready counterfactuals would come out true. Thus it might be true to say: 'If the crew hadn't eaten the lime, they would have developed scurvy'. And yet we now know it wasn't (exactly) the lime, but the Vitamin-C it happened to contain, that prevented the scurvy. Similarly it might be true to say: 'If Sara hadn't been out in the sun, she wouldn't have developed a suntan', yet it wasn't the sun that caused the tan but rather, and importantly more precisely, the UV-radiation it emitted.

Perhaps my earlier example of heritability as a measure of the correlation between parental and offspring phenotypes provides an even better true-to-life 'meta-test' of how well the Control Test's counterfactuals test for causality. Ever since August Weismann's formulation in 1889 of his principle of the continuity of what he called the 'germ plasm' (which we now call the genome) we know that parental phenotypes do not cause offspring phenotypes; rather, each traces back to a common cause - the parental genotypes. Yet the theory of quantitative inheritance for which Francis Galton laid the foundation provides a successful tool used even now by plant and animal breeders to predict and explain the changes they produce by artificial selection. If ever there was a successful instrument of control, it was this theory. The counterfactuals it yields are all true. And yet we now know perfectly well that parental phenotypes are not *causes*.

Yet, we have to be very careful in drawing the right conclusions from the previous arguments. What they show is that the causal character of macro-explanations is, to say the least, very precarious. The Control Test for causal explanatoriness as proposed by Professor Baker simply falls short of adequately discriminating between genuinely causal processes and mere pseudo-processes. However, what these arguments do not show is that macro-explanations as such should be banned. Or that macro-explanations are second-rate at best, with no more than merely instrumental or provisional value, to be abandoned as soon as knowledge of the true causes comes in. Rather, the truth, I believe, lies somewhere in the middle. On the one hand, contrary to the claims of Practical Realism and in line with the 'brain-explain' thesis of the Standard View, macro-explanations cannot just stand on their own. There is no ground for *radical* autonomy of any of the so-called special sciences. Whenever macro-explanations are being offered, there is always a warranted presumption that in principle a more detailed account can be given of the causal powers of the macro-properties invoked in terms of some relevant implementing mechanisms operative *at the next level down* in some more or less determinate functional hierarchy of sciences and their respective domains. Thus classical genetics may look to cytology for an explanatory extension just as cytology in its turn may do so with respect to molecular genetics (Kitcher, 1984; Gasper, 1992). On the other hand, the justification of causal claims made in macro-explanations does not require the truth of any claims of radical reducibility - as Kitcher (Kitcher, 1984) has argued, explanatory *extension* simply does not entail explanatory *replacement* - nor need we go 'all the way down' to account for the causal relevance of higher order properties: their explanatory legitimacy does not depend on the availability in principle of some ultimate causal theory of fundamental physics, in which causal powers can be accounted for in terms of the intrinsic qualities of quarks or of any other fundamental particles of micro-physics. In the following section I will amplify on the varying metaphysical and methodological status of macro-explanations and on their varying relationship to lower-level explanations in terms of implementing mechanisms.

6 The Varying Functions of Macro-explanations and the *Relative* Autonomy of the Special Sciences

There are, I believe, at least four reasons to retain and to positively value macro-explanations in general.

1. First they are obviously useful in cases where we want to explain and predict, but have no more than a rough indication where to locate the relevant cause and how to specify it. In some such cases our explanations may turn out to be genuinely causal after all, but perhaps only lacking in the fineness of their grain. These are philosophically innocent cases. Thus brewers in the 19th century used yeast without the foggiest notion of enzymes being the true causal mechanisms responsible for fermentation. In other cases, however, our explanation may not be genuinely causal at all but may turn out to be based on a pseudo-process, for example, if we were to explain the current position of the shadow of a car on the shoulder of the road by reference to its earlier position and its velocity. Similarly perhaps - or so it has been argued - mental causation, for all we know, may be noth-

ing but the shadow of physiology (in ignorance we are all captives in Plato's cave, mistakenly taking shadows to be true causal agents).

2.   By contrast, the second reason for upholding macro-explanations has to do with cases where our explanatory preference is driven not so much by ignorance but rather by a well-motivated positive need for *functional abstraction*. In such cases the real causal agent may be a member of a disjunctive class, each of which would have had the same result and all of which share a second-order functional property, which is thus rightly singled out as the causally relevant factor. Thus if you have an headache, you are well advised to take a familiar analgesic rather than to look specifically for acetylsalicylic acid (the stuff contained in aspirin). Our advice would be guided by the insight that any old painkiller would do. The corresponding explanation, say, of the relief of the headache, in terms of the functional property of the pill as being analgesic is what Jackson and Pettit (Jackson & Pettit, 1988; Jackson & Pettit, 1990) call a *program* explanation. By contrast, a *process* explanation of the same phenomenon would cite the actual chemical agent (the acetylsalicylic acid, as the case may be) operative in the given case. Such a process explanation, in spite of appearing to give more detailed information would, on the contrary, rather be less informative than the corresponding program explanation couched in terms of more general functional properties. Process explanations are often lacking in what Wilson (Wilson, 1994) has called 'causal depth'. They are not resilient across slight counterfactual changes as program explanations are. The weakness of process explanations is precisely that they are what Garfinkel (Garfinkel, 1981) in the context of explanations in the social sciences has called *hyperconcrete*. These considerations demonstrate the special explanatory potential of functional explanations and thus their indispensability over and above what process explanations may have to offer. They thus count against what Kim has labeled the problem of explanatory exclusion and thus refute his theory of supervenient causation with the attendant charge of epiphenomenalism in the case of mental causation.

3.   The foregoing considerations were based on the *multiple realizability* of the macro-properties on relevant lower level properties. However, even more powerful arguments in favor of the indispensability of macro-explanations advert to *multiple supervenience* rather than to multiple realizability. An analogy with dispositional explanation may illustrate the point. For dispositions also fail to produce causal effects on their own independently from their categorical base. And yet their explanatory power clearly differs from, or exceeds, that of their bases. This becomes intel-

ligible when we recognize that one and the same categorical base 'realizes' more than one disposition. Even so, only one of those is usually relevant for a given event. Thus Mary's death is related to the electrical conductivity of her aluminum ladder. But the categorical base thereof (the cloud of free electrons permeating the metal) also 'realizes' such diverse dispositions as the thermal conductivity or the opacity of the metal.[5] Clearly, a proffered explanation for the tragic accident that cited only the underlying categorical base would be incomplete, or even misleading, but in any case *objectively* less informative than one that cited no more than the relevant disposition. Moreover, the accident would have occurred even if another categorical base had realized the same disposition of electrical conductivity. Thus, this disposition is apparently relevant and its actual categorical base is causally efficacious. Together this constitutes good reason for calling the disposition in question causally relevant.

This analogy may cast light also on the question why functional explanations cannot be reduced to causal explanations. The reason constitutes the mirror image of the phenomenon of multiple realizability, often cited in such contexts. For the irreducibility of dispositional explanations clearly does not consist in the fact that a given disposition can be realized by otherwise unrelated categorical bases, but precisely in the opposite fact that a given categorical base does not identify which of the dispositions realized is explanatorily relevant in a given case. In other words, it is not multiple realizability but rather *multiple supervenience* of dispositions onto one and the same subvenient categorical base that necessitates citing that disposition, which is responsible for the given effect. Thus the special character of higher levels of organization in nature can be vindicated in principle, and more effectively than by the conventional appeal to multiple realizability. They necessitate the need for macro-explanations with the causal depth and the theoretical appropriateness corresponding to the grain of the explanatory level in question.

4. Finally, once the semi-reality of higher levels of organization is thus recognized, the putative non-supervenient character of typical externalist relational connections becomes equally manageable and intelligible. All that is needed for this is simply to expand the supervenience base [as Peter Menzies (Menzies, 1988) has proposed, drawing on Goldman's theory of actions level-generating other actions]. Context thus becomes part of a 'wide' system with corresponding levels of organization, in which typical

---

[5] The example is due to David Lewis (Menzies, 1988). Also cf. Jackson & Pettit, 1990.

boundary conditions are consistently realized, causing typical special effects that help to maintain the system in question. Taken in this way, context functions no longer as an accidental variable in the environment, *in tandem* with which 'narrow' output functions of a subject or organism, that are already *independently* interpretable, will happen to produce predictable distal effects. On the contrary, context now emerges as part of a coherent integrated system with complex causal interactions constituting the basis for the 'wide' functional agreement or physical and social relatedness of the subject to its environment.

Now, while the four reasons just formulated certainly count against causal and explanatory reductionism, thus supporting a *relative* autonomy for propositional attitude psychology as Baker would certainly want to maintain, nothing has been said so far to prevent one from identifying beliefs with brain states residing within the head and occupying certain causal roles. And nothing prevents a functionalist from insisting (plausibly, to my mind) that such roles be categorized widely. Content would thus be a matter of the wide functional role of a subject's internal brain states. Indeed, we could be Australian type-type identity theorists and say that the environmental relations crucial for content are part of what makes it true that an internal state is the content that it is; and yet the content itself is not a relation to the environment but is precisely that internal state that happens to mediate between perceptual inputs and behavioral outputs in a way characteristic of the content in question. As Jackson (Jackson, 1995, p. 267) says: 'The answer to the familiar puzzle - how can a relation to the environment drive behavior? - is that it cannot. But it can provide explanatory information and play a role in determining that a non-relational state is a certain content.'

Thus my argument, though consistent with a thesis of *relative* autonomy of psychology as a special science, is inconsistent with the *radical* autonomy advocated by Professor Baker. Thus I am not at all persuaded that, as Professor Baker maintains, no discovery about a subject's internal organization could trump intentional explanations of his behavior (EA 142; EA Ch 6). This is a bold claim indeed, conjuring up reminiscences of Cartesians proclaiming that all *cogitations* are necessarily conscious; or reminiscences of Bishop Berkeley proclaiming the principle that no idea itself unperceived can be the cause of perceiving any other idea. After the breakdown of rational and introspective psychology and its replacement towards the end of the 19th century by experimental psychology we have come to rather different conclusions! Quite similarly the currently rapid development of the neurosciences may certainly be expected to yield insights that will correct and constrain theory formation in cognitive science and psychology. It would seem that propositional attitude psychology can hardly be immune from such developments. At any rate such counterexamples as put forward by Block (Block, 1981) and Peacocke (Peacocke, 1983) would certainly seem to cast doubt on Professor Baker's claim. Imagine a system that would look exactly like a human being, but whose movements were in fact produced by a vast, pre-programmed, internal look-up table that matches every possible pattern of sensory input to a given output that is appropriate given that input and the system's past history. Wouldn't we feel inclined to withdraw our earlier intentional explanations for the system's behavior as in fact falsified by the discovery of its actual internal make-up?

However, I have another more general and less artificial consideration to offer to the same effect. We have said that intentional explanations cannot be reduced to, or replaced by, physical explanations. Yet it is one thing to claim this much, and quite another to maintain that there is no possibility in principle of corrective interaction between different levels of explanation altogether, including in particular corrective interaction between neuroscience and intentional psychology. Above I have tried to outline some forceful arguments against causal or explanatory reduction. Even so, causal or explanatory reduction does not exhaust the possible, and possibly fruitful, relations and interactions that may exist between different levels of explanation in the sciences. Thus Kitcher (Kitcher, 1984) has similarly developed strong arguments showing that classical genetics cannot be reduced to molecular genetics. And yet he has held open, and developed, the notion of what he calls *explanatory extension* (or elaboration) of a higher order theory in terms of entities and processes postulated by a relevant lower level theory. And the important point he wished to emphasize in developing this notion is precisely that such explanatory extensions usually have *critical* and *corrective* force *vis à vis* the higher level theory. In this context let me remind you again of Weismann's theory of the continuity of the genome. This theory dramatically corrected, though did not replace, our insight into the nature of the processes determining the heritability of phenotypical traits.

7 Conclusion

Let me wind up my argument with the following comparison. It strikes me that to claim *radical* autonomy for intentional psychology, as Professor Baker seems to argue, or to say that belief explanations cannot in principle be overturned by future neuroscientific insights into the workings of the brain (EA 142; EA ch. 6) comes dangerously close to a theologian's claiming that the stories the Bible tells us can only be evaluated in terms of properly 'biblical evidence' and that theology is in principle immune from critical results derived from extra-theological empirical sources. By contrast, I submit that the only thing that would render theology (or any other science) *radically* autonomous and altogether beyond the reach of any corrective impacts from other empirical sciences is when it declared itself to be pure and unadulterated mythology.

In brief, my critique of Professor Baker's Practical Realism carries good news as well as bad news. On the one hand I do believe, *pace* Professor Baker, that belief explanations, though irreducible, are nevertheless in principle liable to be trumped by future insights into the internal economy of the brain. If this is sad news, so be it. But the good news certainly contained in my paper is this: propositional attitude psychology is no mythology. On the contrary, as may be manifest from these pages, it lies wide open to constructive criticism.

8 References

Baker, L. R. 1995. *Explaining Attitudes. A Practical Approach to the Mind.* Cambridge: Cambridge University Press.

Block, N. 1981. Psychologism and Behaviorism. *Philosophical Review* 90, 5-43.

Braddon-Mitchell, D. & Jackson, F. 1996. *Philosophy of Mind and Cognition.* Oxford: Blackwell.

Dretske, F. 1993. Mental Events as Structuring Causes of Behavior. In A. Mele (Ed.), *Mental Causation.* Oxford: Clarendon Press: 121-36.

Fodor, J. A. 1980. Methodological Solipsism Considered as a Research Strategy in Cognitive Psychology. *Brain and Behavioral Sciences* 3, 63-109.

Fodor, J. A. 1987. *Psychosemantics; The Problem of Meaning in the Philosophy of Mind.* Cambridge, Mass.: The MIT Press.

Fodor, J. A. 1991[a]. A Modal Argument for Narrow Content. *Journal of Philosophy*, 88 (1), 5-26.

Fodor, J. A. 1991[b]. You can Fool Some of the People all of the Time, Everything Else being Equal: Hedged Laws and Psychological Explanations. *Mind* 100, 19-33.

Fodor, J. A. 1994. *The Elm and the Expert. Mentalese and its Semantics.* Cambridge, Mass.: The MIT Press.

Garfinkel, A. 1981. *Forms of Explanation: Rethinking the Questions in Social Theory.* New Haven (CT): Yale University Press.

Gasper, P. 1992. Reduction and Instrumentalism in Genetics. *Philosophy of Science*, 59 (4), 655-670.

Gulick, R. van 1994. Are Beliefs Brain States? And if they are what might that explain?. *Philosophical Studies* 76, 205-215.

Jackson, F. 1995. Essentialism, Mental Properties and Causation. *Proceedings of the Aristotelian Society* XCV, 253-268.

Jackson, F. 1996. Mental Causation. *Mind*, 105 (419), 377-413.

Jackson, F. & Pettit, P. 1988. Functionalism and Broad Content. *Mind* XCVII (387), 381-400.

Jackson, F. & Pettit, P. 1990. Causation in the Philosophy of Mind. *Philosophy and Phenomenological Research L (Supplement)*, 195-214.

Jackson, F., & Pettit, P. 1990. Program Explanation: a General Perspective. *Analysis* 50, 107-117.

Kitcher, P. 1984. 1953 and All That: A Tale of Two Sciences. *Philosophical Review* 93, 335-373.

Lewis, D. 1994. Reduction of Mind. In S. Guttenplan (Ed.), *A Companion to the Philosophy of Mind.* Cambridge: Blackwell.

McGinn, C. 1989. *Mental content.* Oxford: Basil Blackwell.

Menzies, P. 1988. Against Causal Reductionism. *Mind* XCVII, 551-74.

Peacocke, C. 1983. *Sense and Content.* Oxford: Oxford University Press.

Salmon, W. 1984. *Scientific Explanation and the Causal Structure of the World.* Princeton: Princeton University Press.

Sober, E. 1985. A Plea for Pseudo-Processes. *Pacific Philosophical Quarterly*, 66, 303-309.

Wilson, R. A. 1994. Causal Depth, Theoretical Appropriateness, and Individualism in Psychology. *Philosophy of Science*, 61 (1), 55-75.

8

Contextual Realism:
The Context-dependency and the
Relational Character of Beliefs[1]

ALBERT NEWEN

In *Explaining Attitudes* and in the leading article of this volume, Lynne R. Baker criticizes the claim of the so-called Standard View that beliefs are constituted by neural states, i. e. that belief-tokens are constituted by tokens of neural states. My aim is to show that she does not present convincing arguments against the Standard View but only arguments similar to the well-known arguments for the externalism of beliefs. However, since she grants that the Standard View is compatible with externalism there remains no real argument against the Standard View. If one takes the relationality and the context-dependency of beliefs into account then it is still possible to maintain a version of the Standard View. After a detailed criticism of Baker's Practical Realism, I outline a version of the Standard View called 'Contextual Realism' according to which beliefs are understood as being constituted by neural states relative to a given context.

---

[1] I would like to thank Rimas Cuplinskas and Kai Vogeley for many helpful comments.

Explaining Beliefs: Lynne Rudder Baker and Her Critics.
Anthonie Meijers (ed.).

1 Central Claims of Practical Realism

'Practical Realism' is a theory about the metaphysical status of beliefs put forward by Lynne R. Baker in her book *Explaining Attitudes*. To distinguish her view from the so-called Standard View she begins with the following rough explanation:

> According to Practical Realism, (1) concepts of belief and the other attitudes do genuinely apply to human beings, (2) attributions of attitudes are often true without qualification (i. e., not in some second-class sense), (3) attitudes causally explain behavior. However - and this is what distinguishes my position from the Standard View - (4) there is no metaphysical requirement that the attitudes be constituted by particular brain states. (Baker, 1995, 6-7)

To understand just what is the difference between Practical Realism and the Standard View, one must concentrate on the last point which states that there is no metaphysical requirement that the attitudes be constituted by particular neural states. This claim is meant to express the denial of the Standard View, according to which beliefs are identical with, or are constituted by neural states.[2]

To evaluate the claim of Practical Realism, I shall investigate the arguments Baker puts forward against the Standard View in the leading paper of this volume and in her main book. This will allow me to specify her metaphysical claim. Furthermore, I shall evaluate this claim and show that her arguments are not sufficient to deny the Standard View.

2 The Central Claim of the Standard View

The minimal general claim of the Standard View has the following form:

> Beliefs are token-identical with or constituted by *internal* states of a system capable of having beliefs.[3]

Practical Realism denies this; Baker claims that beliefs cannot be identical with or constituted by the *internal* states of a system:

> Against Ryleans, but with the proponents of the Standard View, I hold that belief explanations are causal explanations; against proponents of the Standard View, but with Ryleans, I hold that attitudes are not particular internal states. (Baker, 1995, 28)

---

[2] Baker, 1995, 12.

[3] '(...) each instance of each belief is identical with, or is constituted by, an instance of a particular brain state.' Baker, 1995, 12. This minimal general claim of the Standard View encompasses very different theories, e. g. type-identity theories, token-identity theories, constitution theories, functionalism; Baker, 1995, 7-11.

The main point of Practical Realism is that beliefs cannot be characterized by internal states, because they are essentially relational:

> So Practical Realism should be considered not a form of behaviorism but a form of radical relationism. (Baker, 1995, 155-156)

> This has the consequence that 'physical realization or constitution is simply irrelevant to the justificatory, explanatory, and predicative uses to which we put beliefs.' (Baker, 1995, 148)

To evaluate Baker's main claim about the nature of attitudes I shall concentrate on the explanation of properties.[4] The central question is: What is the relation between the property of having the belief-token that p and the property of having a certain neural-state[5]? A proponent of the Standard View claims that the relation in question is either a *token-identity relation* or *a relation of being constituted by* that holds between having a certain neural state and having a belief-token. Baker accepts that neural states are necessary for human beings to have beliefs, but denies that this allows us to draw any further (non-analytic) implications that characterize the relation between neural states and belief-tokens.

3 Arguments for Radical Relationalism

Before I look at Baker's arguments I would like to point out the role of externalism according to Baker. She concedes that externalism is compatible with the Standard View:

> What makes a particular brain state a belief that p (say, a belief that water is good to drink) may be determined partly by the believer's relations to her environment, as so-called externalists have it... (Baker this volume, 18)

Nevertheless, she claims that her main argument against the Standard View is an argument for the relationalism of beliefs. Being charitable, it follows that she believes that her arguments for relationalism show something essentially more and different from the relationalism that has been argued for by the leading externalists (Putnam 1975, Burge 1979). I purport to show that this is not the case and that she therefore does not present any convincing argument against the Standard View.

---

[4] Beckermann, 1996, 414-417.

[5] In speaking about neural states I leave the question open, whether it would be more appropriate to speak of states or processes. Although I restrict myself to human beliefs, the arguments put forward can be extended to all systems to which we are prepared to ascribe beliefs. The point of this paper is to present an argument that a relation of *being constituted by* holds between belief states and their material basis in a given context.

To defend the claim that beliefs are relational Baker argues as follows:

> Having certain neural states is, presumably, necessary for people to have beliefs; but it does not follow that for a person to have a particular belief, there is a neural state that constitutes that belief. Compare: Horses win races; legs have states. Having certain leg states is, presumably, necessary for horses to win the races; but it does not follow that for a horse to win a particular race, there is a leg state that constitutes the winning of the race. (Baker, 1995, 153, 154)

The example is not very well chosen, because 'win' is a success verb (in Rylean terms) while 'believe' is not. The adequate comparison would be between the property of winning a race and the property of knowing that p, because knowing that p implies that it is a fact that p and winning the race implies that the horse was the first one in a group of horses. Because of these implications, success verbs unambiguously describe relational properties. The property of believing that p should be compared with the property of running and then the argument loses its intuitive appeal:

Compare: Horses are running; legs have states. Having certain leg states is, presumably, necessary for horses to run; but it does not follow that for a horse to run in a particular situation, there are leg states that constitute this running.

If one puts it that way, no strong argument remains. But there is still an argument that supports context-dependency: The property of running is essentially characterized relative to contextual facts. Running is moving on the ground (in contrast to flying as moving in the air or swimming as moving in the water). Furthermore, running is a special way of moving on the ground, since we distinguish walking from running. Running might therefore be characterized as the quickest way a living being can naturally move on the ground. However, snakes never run even when they are moving quickly. This shows that running is furthermore a special way of moving on the ground involving using one's legs and moving them quickly. What counts as legs and moving them quickly is determined relative to the legs of human beings and relative to the way human beings move their legs while doing what we call 'running'. This is not a complete characterization of the property of running, but it shows that this property is essentially context-dependent.

Does the relationality of winning-states or the context-dependency of running-states imply that a winning-state or a running-state of a horse cannot be token-identical with or constituted by its leg state? I will argue that it does not.

The reason Baker seems to have in mind is based on the relational character of winning and the context-dependency of running: One can only win a race relative to a convention of running games which implies that there are several participants and we obviously characterize running states relative to the way human beings move their legs while moving quickly. As we have shown, Baker wants to argue against the Standard View even if it includes the claims of externalism. This means she has to show that there is a relationality that is different from the dependency of beliefs on objects and from the dependency on the linguistic community and their conventions because both kinds of dependency are part of externalism (Putnam 1975, Burge 1979). But there are just those two kinds of dependencies which are characteristic for states of winning and of running. Presupposing externalism the analogous claim of the Standard View is that the winning state of the horse is identical with or constituted by the leg state of the horse given the relation to other horses and our conventions concerning horse races.

Baker seems to have the idea that 'winning' presupposes some social or cultural processes and that these processes are something extraordinary which are different from what was discovered by externalists. This reading is also confirmed by the following remarks:

> Much of our mental life is relational and specific to culture - even though what is culture-specific takes place against a background of broader mental patterns like paranoia, euphoria, etc. I expect neuroscience to illuminate these broader mental patterns (like paranoia and depression); I am less sanguine about neuroscientific illumination of the vast portions of mental life that are specific to culture. (Baker this volume, 31)

If social or cultural processes were shown to be nonreducible to the entities that are accepted by the Standard View including externalism then this would be an argument against the Standard View. But Baker does not present any argument of this kind and there is a strong intuition that the social conventions that are characteristic for 'winning'-states are not essentially different from the conventions of a linguistic community as accounted for by externalists. The 'social' character of the conventions seems to be the same whether linguistic or nonlinguistic conventions of a community are involved. So there remains no argument against the Standard View based on the social character of beliefs but only an argument for standard externalism if we presuppose that social and cultural processes cannot be explained according to individualism. Even this presupposition is still part of an open dispute.

4 Beliefs as Counterfactuals

We often use the notion of belief to attribute a disposition to someone, e. g. when I attribute to a normal adult the belief that $17 + 23 = 40$ in a context in which the person is sleeping or is doing anything other than thinking about mathematics, then I am characterizing his or her disposition to correctly answer the mathematical question 'What is the sum of 17 + 23?'. Beliefs as dispositions can be characterized by counterfactuals. Baker not only claims this, but also that this is the only way to characterize beliefs:

> The claim of Practical Realism is that counterfactuals, and counterfactuals alone, reveal the nature of belief. (Baker, 1995, 167)

The counterfactual analysis given by Baker includes a positive and a negative clause. For example, Smith's belief that it might rain in Seattle can (in standard situations) be roughly characterized by the conjunction of the following counterfactuals:[6]

i.   If Miller had borrowed Smith's only umbrella and Smith believed that she was about to go to Seattle and Smith always wants to keep dry, then Smith would ask Miller to return her umbrella; and

ii. If it is not the case that (Miller had borrowed Smith's only umbrella and Smith believed that she was about to go to Seattle and Smith always wants to keep dry), then it would not be the case that Smith would ask Miller to return her umbrella.

This is obviously only one characteristic combination of a situation and a type of behavior that characterizes the belief that it might rain in Seattle. Ryle called such a belief an example of a multi-track (not a single-track) disposition. The main claim of Baker is that such an analysis is the only analysis that can be given of beliefs, including belief-events as manifestations of belief-dispositions. The reason for this claim is that (i) and (ii) describe some *a priori* connections between attitudes and behavior relative to our language competence and our standard knowledge about folk-psychological rules. Baker seems to presuppose that this *a priori* status of (i) and (ii) is compatible with any a posteriori analysis of beliefs in terms of neural states (together with objects and conventions conceded by externalism) and concludes that an a posteriori analysis, firstly, cannot be a necessary truth and, secondly, is in any case irrelevant for an analysis of beliefs. Let us begin with an argument against Baker's second point, which she illustrates by the following example:

> (G) If a member of the school board believed that the school budget would raise taxes too much, and he wanted to keep his pledge to stop tax increases, then (ceteris paribus) he would vote against the school budget. (Baker 1995, 173-174)

> So, the Practical Realist makes two points: If (G) is implemented by some mechanistic process, the mechanism need not be a neural mechanism; and

---

[6] Baker, 1995, 162.

in any case, the adequacy of (G) does not depend on the discovery of any mechanisms, neural or not. (Baker 1995, 176)

The counterfactual analysis (G) represents an a priori connection between the 'if'-part and the 'then'-part of (G). If all counterfactuals characterizing a belief have this a priori status, the question arises whether or not it is possible to find any psychophysical correlation (a posteriori) that could reveal the nature of a belief. Baker seems to deny this solely on the grounds of the a priori status of folk-psychological counterfactuals. But this conclusion cannot be drawn, because the epistemological category of 'a priori / a posteriori' has to be distinguished from the metaphysical category of 'necessary / contingent'. In principle, a neural characterization of beliefs can be a necessary truth a posteriori. In this case a neural description (including the objects and conventions accepted by externalists) would capture the nature of beliefs at least as well as the folk-psychological characterization. There is no argument which excludes this possibility unless it is shown that the folk-psychological characterization is in principle the only possible characterization of beliefs. The fact that experts are not yet able to present such a neural characterization a posteriori of a belief does not imply that it is in principle impossible to do so. Furthermore, if one concedes externalism - as Baker does - it is plausible to expect some psychophysical correlation relative to special external conditions. I will explain this in more detail in the next paragraph by distinguishing different kinds of external conditions that may constitute a relevant context for psychophysical correlations. But the fact that no argument is presented which shows that there cannot be a neural characterization of a belief that is a necessary truth a posteriori is sufficient to deny at least one of Baker's premises. She claims:

2.221   If T is necessarily true, then it is necessary that human brains are organized the way that T claims.

2.222   It is not necessary that human brains are organized in the way that T claims.

According to Baker 'T' is a sign for any version of the Standard View, T is a 'noneliminative theory according to which particular beliefs are particular brain states' (Baker this volume, 19). Conceding externalism we can add that T is a noneliminative theory according to which particular beliefs are particular brain states relative to special external conditions. T essentially includes a theory T+ involving the claims about correlations between neural states in external conditions and belief states and T includes some theory T* about the individuation of brain states. On the one hand, premise 2.221 is only true if we interpret the phrase 'that human brains are organized the way that T claims' as claiming 'that the psychophysical correlations are organized the way that T+ claims'. The latter can be a necessary truth a posteriori according to the Standard View as I already explained. There is especially no knock-down argument against an identity theory .[7] If we accept such a necessary truth a posteriori, then premise 2.222 is false. On the other hand, premise 2.221 is false, if we interpret the phrase 'that human brains are organized the way that T claims' as claiming 'that human brain states are organized the way that T* claims'; because obviously the brain states of a human being could have been different. This would render 2.222 a true premise in this case. So, there is no reading of the premises according to which both premises are shown to be true. Therefore the argument is insufficient.

In the next paragraph I would like to distinguish different kinds of external conditions that may be relevant when arguing in favor of psychophysical correlation rules. The function of this paragraph is twofold: Firstly, these distinctions allow us to show by comparison that many external conditions are already presupposed by our characterization of *physical* dispositions and, secondly, we can undermine the intuition that mental states are not characterizable by neural states.

To reveal the nature of mental dispositions and events it might be helpful to compare a belief with a disposition of a mechanical object. The example I propose is the disposition of a car to brake well, i. e. to decelerate quickly upon application of the car's brakes without the wheels locking. I shall argue that the case of beliefs is strictly analogous to that of the car's disposition, and that in both cases there is a relation of *being constituted by* that holds between the property of braking well and the property of having a certain brake mechanism or between the property of having a belief that p and the property of having a certain neural mechanism.

5 Relational Properties and Context-Dependency

To characterize different kinds of external conditions relevant for beliefs I introduce a distinction between relationality and context-dependency. Whether a property is relational or not can be distinguished from questions concerning its context-dependency. To have a neutral term for all entities that may have properties, I use the term 'system' (including all kinds of objects).

(rel) The property p expressed with the monadic predicate 'p' is a *relational property* of a system S if and only if the fact that S has p implies that

---

[7]Compare the rejection of the three main arguments against the identity theory (the Zombie Argument, the Knowledge Argument and the Modal Argument) in Perry 2001.

there is an individual object to which S stands in a relation which can be expressed by a (relational) predicate that is part of 'p'.

If in 2001 Peter has the property of being married to Anne then this is a relational property because it implies that Anne exists and that Peter is bound by a relation to Anne which is expressed by the predicate 'being married to'. The intuitive content of this definition is that a property is relational only if it can be adequately characterized as a relation between two (or more) individuals. In the case of beliefs relational properties are involved if we have beliefs *de re* while beliefs *de dicto* are nonrelational. We can also illustrate the non-relationality in the case of physical properties. If a car has the property of braking well then this does not imply that another system exists to which the car stands in a relation expressed by the predicate 'is braking'. One may argue that the car only brakes well relative to the surface on which someone drives it. However, this renders the property context-dependent rather than relational.

(con) The property p expressed with the monadic predicate 'p' is a *context-dependent property* of a system S if changing the context can modify the property expressed, i. e. in the context c1 the property expressed by 'p' is p while in the context c2 the property expressed by 'p' is the property pN.

In addition to being relational, the property expressed by 'being married to Anne' is context-dependent because it is essentially defined by the conventions of a society. For example the property expressed would be a different one if divorce would be impossible or if there were legal consequences other than those one is accustomed to in Western society. The counterfactuals characterizing the situations in which the given property is a relevant factor in Peter's behavior would differ relative to such conventions.

It is important to note that the nonrelational property of braking well is context-dependent as well. This property of a car can be characterized by the following counterfactual: If one would use the brake pedal of the car, then it would decelerate quickly without skidding (i. e. without the wheels locking). The essential behavior of decelerating quickly is dependent on a *physical context*. In this sense we can distinguish natural conditions (the road surface being wet due to rain, or slippery due to snow or ice) or cultural conditions (our way of building streets). The property of decelerating quickly is meant to characterize the behavior of a car on dry streets when someone brakes. Furthermore, this property is dependent on a *social context* (with that I mean the habits of a group of people), e. g. the property of decelerating quickly (as opposed to not quickly enough) is determined relative to common driving practice, such as the average speed and the distance kept between cars. Finally, we can check whether the property is dependent on the *linguistic context*. One relevant aspect of the linguistic context is the (actual) utterance context including our linguistic conventions: The property p is dependent on the (actual) utterance context (and independent from possible worlds) if the property could change relative to a modification of the utterance context but could not change relative to a change of the possible world. Using semantic terminology we can characterize the relevant predicate 'p' as being referentially used if the property expressed is dependent on the utterance context. The property of being a person called 'Aristotle' is obviously dependent on the (relevant) possible world and independent of the utterance context if this is understood as the property of being a person called 'Aristotle' in a possible world, the so-called world of evaluation. In the same way, the property of influencing a car's motion in a way called 'to brake well' (relative to a possible world of evaluation) is dependent on the possible world and independent of the utterance context: If the extension of the word 'to brake' not only included decelerating a car but also stopping and parking it then the property expressed by 'braking well' would be different from the property we express by using this predicate in the (actual) utterance context. But the expression 'to brake well' is not used in that way. It is used referentially. Since the expression is always evaluated relative to the (actual) utterance context including our linguistic conventions, the property of braking well (i. e. the property of decelerating a car in a way called 'to brake well' in the actual context) is not dependent on the possible world but on the utterance context. This dependence is called linguistic context-dependency.

To summarize this paragraph: The property of braking well is dependent on a physical and social context, and on the linguistic context, i. e. on the (actual) utterance context. When we attribute the property of braking well we presuppose some standard physical context (dry streets), a standard social context (common driving practice), and a standard linguistic context (including our way of using the verb 'to brake'). Since it is nonetheless a nonrelational property we have good reason to think that it is constituted by some internal mechanism of the car in the standard contexts. Given the standard physical, social and linguistic context, the brake behavior is constituted by the brake mechanism of the car[8], because the following counterfactual is true: Given the standard physical, social, and linguistic context, if you change the brake mechanism of the car, e.g. by installing a so-called ABS-brake-mechanism, then you will change the way the car decelerates.

Compare the false counterfactual: Given the standard physical, social, and linguistic context, if you change the color of the car/the design of the car/the headlights, you will change the way the car decelerates.

---

[8] To keep things simple, I mention the brake mechanism as the only relevant internal mechanism. There are obviously other important aspects as well, e.g. the car's suspension. I also presuppose (in every case) that the driver brakes in an ideal manner.

6   The Context-Dependency of Beliefs

I wish to demonstrate that beliefs are sometimes relational and always context-dependent in at least one of several ways. A belief is relational if and only if it is a de re belief, i. e. a belief about an individual object o which can be expressed by 'A person A believes *of o* that it is F'. There definitely are beliefs de re but there are also beliefs de dicto. Therefore beliefs are often relational, but not always. De dicto beliefs are nonrelational beliefs. To distinguish several forms of context-dependency, I shall first explain the methodological framework:

Beliefs are expressed by utterances, i. e. by sentences being uttered in a context. To characterize the context-dependency of beliefs, we can characterize the context-dependency of utterances. We can distinguish overt and hidden context-dependency.

A sentence uttered in a context c is *overtly context-dependent* if the sentence(-type) alone (independent of the utterance context) does not completely express the belief that is nonmetaphorically expressed by the sentence in the context c. The belief that is nonmetaphorically expressed by the sentence in the context c can be characterized (for our purposes) by the objective truth-conditions of a sentence expressed in a context. If a sentence contains an indicator (e. g. indexicals, demonstratives), the objective truth-condition is overtly context-dependent, e.g. the sentence 'He is a famous psychologist' uttered by someone while pointing at Freud expresses a belief about Freud and it is true if Freud is a famous psychologist. The sentence 'It is raining' is also overtly context-dependent because uttered in Bonn now, it expresses the belief that it is raining in Bonn now. The sentence 'I already had breakfast' is overtly context-dependent as well, because, uttered in a context in which someone asks me whether I am hungry, I am not expressing the belief that I have had breakfast earlier in my life, but the belief that I already had breakfast this morning.[9]

Overt context-dependency demands the substitution or the addition of words to completely express a belief by a sentence(-type). Beliefs expressed by utterances involving indicators are a special class of relational beliefs. Even if one removes the overt context-dependency by substituting or adding words, hidden context-dependencies remain: The sentence-type (not having any overt context-dependency) would express different beliefs in different contexts. The examples will make clear what I mean. There are several kinds of *hidden context*-dependency analogous to the forms of context-dependency distinguished in a car's property of braking well.

---

[9] Precisely how such cases should be characterized is a question that must be answered by a theory of semantics and pragmatics. Recanati, 1993; Newen, 1996.

Physical context-dependency (the relevance of the physio-chemical structure): A belief that p expressed by a sentence s in the context c is physically context-dependent if it would change together with a modification of the physical context; e.g. a belief about a physical substance. A belief that water is healthy is physically context-dependent because it is a belief about the substance we call 'water' *in our world.* Since water has the chemical structure H_2O in our world, it is a belief about the substance with the chemical structure H_2O. If water had the chemical structure XYZ, then an utterance of the sentence 'Water is healthy' would express a belief about the substance with the chemical structure XYZ.[10]

Social context-dependency (the relevance of social conventions): A belief that p expressed by a sentence s in the context c is socially context-dependent if the belief is dependent on the habits or (nonlinguistic) conventions of a society. If A believes that John is married to Anne, this belief is socially context-dependent, because the concept of being married to someone is dependent on our social conventions. In a society with essentially different marriage conventions, one would be expressing a different belief with the same sentence 'John is married to Anne'.

Linguistic context-dependency (the relevance of linguistic conventions): A belief that p expressed by a sentence s in a context c is linguistically context-dependent if the belief is dependent on the linguistic conventions of a speech community.

This is well illustrated in the examples given by Tyler Burge.[11] If a belief is expressed with the sentence 'Mary has arthritis' then relative to an utterance context in our speech community this sentence expresses the belief that Mary has an inflammation of the joints, because arthritis is defined as an inflammation of the joints. If in an utterance context of another speech community 'arthritis' covered a broader class of inflammations, for example inflammations of the joints or the bones, the sentences would express the belief that Mary has an inflammation of the joints or the bones. This illustrates that beliefs are linguistically context-dependent.

---

[10] Putnam, 1975. Since a substance is not an individual this is not a case of a relational belief. If someone has a belief about an individual piece of a substance then this is a case of a relational belief.

[11] Burge, 1979.

Subjective context-dependency (the relevance of background beliefs): A belief that p expressed by a sentence s in a context c is subjectively context-dependent if the belief is dependent on the subjective background beliefs of an individual.

This can be illustrated by a variant of Burge's example: Suppose Peter belongs to our speech community and expresses his belief by uttering the sentence 'Mary has arthritis in the thigh'. Since arthritis is defined as an inflammation of the joints, it is impossible that Mary has arthritis in the thigh, since there are no joints in the thigh. But Peter has many correct beliefs about arthritis. Therefore Peter understands what 'arthritis' means, but he has only an incomplete understanding. Although Peter has this incomplete understanding, the belief he expresses is a belief about arthritis, since he is a member of our speech community and has a partial understanding of the expression. Because of the division of linguistic labor[12] Peter is still relying on the meaning of 'arthritis' that it has in our speech community. But how should we characterize the content of Peter's utterance?

Contrary to what standard semantics (often) presuppose, there is no *one* way to characterize the belief expressed by Peter's utterance. We must distinguish the *objective content* of his utterance from the *subjective content*.[13] The objective content of an utterance is the objective (or standard) proposition expressed by the utterance; the objective proposition expressed can be characterized by the truth condition of an utterance relative to the standard physical, social and linguistic background independent of any deviate subjective background beliefs. The subjective content of an utterance is the proposition characterized relative to all relevant subjective background beliefs of an individual. In the case of Peter's utterance 'Mary has arthritis in the thigh' the objective proposition expressed can be characterized as the truth-condition that the sentence is true if Mary has an inflammation of the joints in the thigh (an irrational belief). Since Peter has the false belief that arthritis is an inflammation of the joints or the bones, the subjective proposition expressed in this context is that Mary has an inflammation of the joints or the bones in the thigh (a rational belief). According to the Fregean criterion of distinguishing thoughts, one utterance token can express different thoughts.[14] Only the objective content of the utterance is irrational, but not the subjective one.

---

[12] Putnam 1975.

[13] Perry 1993; Haas-Spohn 1995; Newen 1996.

[14] Newen in press.

In summary: Beliefs are sometimes relational and they are always context-dependent at least in one of several ways. If we compare the varieties of context-dependency of a physical property like braking well with the varieties of context-dependency of beliefs we can see that only the subjective context-dependency is something which is not found in the case of physical properties. In comparison, beliefs can be dependent on the subjective background beliefs of an individual. This makes beliefs characterized in this way dependent on other beliefs and therefore introduces a holistic aspect of beliefs. All these relevant beliefs are beliefs of one individual. I will not discuss the question here whether relational beliefs can be completely described in nonrelational terms: If beliefs are nonrelational, then the holism is intra-individual; if beliefs are at least sometimes relational in a non-reducible manner then a physicalism of beliefs has to be a holistic physicalism.

Since Baker grants that the Standard View is compatible with externalism, all the arguments for the relationality and the context-dependency of beliefs are not arguments against the Standard View. The only problematic aspect is the holistic character of beliefs but - as I have noted - a move towards holistic physicalism may resolve this.

7   Undermining the Argument Against Type-Identity Theories

In her argument against type-identity theories, Baker relies on the following premise:

> 2.2321   If T is a type-identity theory, then T will not be confirmed by neuroscience

The argument for this premise runs as follows:

> According to type-identity theories, for every belief-type, there is a type of brain state N such that necessarily, S believes that p if and only if S's brain is in a state of type N. Even relativized to species, type-identity seems way too strong. For type-identity would require that there be a single brain state such that everyone who believes, e. g., that millions died in World War II, be in that state. But that seems wrong. (Baker this volume, 21-22.)

In her reasoning Baker presupposes that a type-identity theory has to be an internal theory. If one grants the an identity theory can be combined with externalism then the identity claim can be a true claim combining a belief description, on the one hand, and a description of a neural state and the relevant context, on the other. If one grants this possibility - and Baker does it by conceding externalism to her critics - then there is no longer any argument against this version of the Standard View.

8 Against Baker's Empirical Conjecture

Baker's argument against the Standard View is essentially based on an empirical conjecture concerning the possibilities of neurobiology. Her intuition is that neuroscientists are able to explain special moods of a human being (e. g. depression, paranoia, euphoria, dejection, confusion) but that they will never be able to explain propositional attitudes (Baker this volume, 30). She concedes that 'a neuroscientist can understand about mood, alertness, and sense of balance by understanding the mechanism inside my head.' (Baker this volume, 31). But she is very skeptical concerning the prospect of neuroscientific analysis of beliefs:

> 2.23222   It is false that: neuroscientists in the long run are able to identify particular neural tokens as tokens of the belief that p (for any belief that p) (*Empirical Conjecture*) (Baker this volume, 22)

One reason to support this claim is according to Baker the fact that there are large individual differences in brain functions. There is e. g. the well-known phenomenon of plasticity in young brains: In young infants who suffer from brain damage we can observe a reorganization of the brain such that healthy areas of the brain assume novel functions. However, this does not imply that there is no correlation between belief states, on the one hand, and brain states, on the other, but rather that the correlation is a complicated one – one which has to account for the history of individual brain development.

I believe that recent development in neuroscience allows one to be more optimistic than Baker is. We are now beginning to discover the neural correlates not only of emotional states but also of specific cognitive states. Although neuroscience is not yet in a position to investigate the neural correlates of specific propositional attitudes, there are e. g. interesting studies which investigate the neural correlates of decision making.[15] Furthermore, neuropsychiatrists are investigating the neural correlates of the capacity to attribute propositional attitudes to other people. Pioneering work has been done by Christopher Frith and his group in London focussing on so-called theory of mind studies, in which the capacity of the attribution of mental states to other persons is studied.[16] Frith and his colleagues have shown that the activation of the medial frontal cortex (especially anterior cingulate cortex) is correlated with the theory of mind-

---

[15] Libet 1985.

[16] Frith 1992 and 1994.

capacity. Recently we investigated in a collaborative study an extended theory of mind paradigm (Vogeley et al. 2001). In this study we investigated the neural correlates of third-person-attribution of propositional attitudes in contrast to first-person-attribution. Firstly, this study confirmed Frith's results with respect to attribution of mental states to other people as reported previously in classical theory of mind studies (e. g. Fletcher et al. 1995). As new result, it was shown that self-attribution of mental states to oneself is associated with additional activation in the right temporoparietal region.[17] There is strong evidence that there is a neural correlate of the capacity to self-ascribe propositional attitudes which is at least partly different from the neural correlate of the capacity to make of third-person-ascriptions. Both capacities are basic constituents of human social interaction. Therefore we have presented two probably specifically human cognitive capacities that can be successfully investigated on the neural level.

The development of neuroscience can be described such that scientists began by discovering the neural correlates of some basic emotional states like depression or primitive cognitive states like visual experience.[18] Recently, neuroscience went on to discover more complex cognitive states (like theory of mind-capacity and the capacity of self-attributing attitudes) and there is no conclusive argument presented so far that it is in principle impossible to continue research in this direction. If neuroscientists begin to investigate individual beliefs in the future, they will however have to develop operational criteria which account for the relationality and the context-dependency of beliefs.

Furthermore, there is a general argument against Baker's empirical conjecture. According to her view, neural states are necessary for having beliefs, because of the neural organization of human beings, but more cannot be said about the relation between neural states and beliefs. This is implausible because not any neural state can implement any belief in a given internal and external context. If we presuppose an internal and an external context (i. e. the history and biography of a specific person, on the one hand, and his or her standard physical, social, and linguistic environment, on the other) then it is plausible that there are only certain types of neural states that can implement a specific belief. To argue for this intuition I rely

---

[17] Vogeley et. al. 2001.

[18] There are many aspects we presently understand concerning visual experience. On the other hand, there are also problems that are not solved, e. g. the phenomenal quality of an experience. However, there is no conclusive reason that this cannot be understood within a physicalist framework. Compare Perry 2001.

on Kim's principle that there cannot be two complete and independent causal explanations of one phenomenon: A folk-psychological explanation of a bodily movement as well as a neural explanation of the same bodily movement are characterized by Baker as complete and independent causal explanations. It follows that she denies Kim's principle. But Kim's principle is based on good reasons. If one accepts that one bodily movement can be explained by two complete and independent causal explanations then one must claim that the folk-psychological cause (a belief and a desire) is independent of the neural cause of the same bodily movement. But then it remains a mystery how a belief (in combination with a desire) can cause a bodily movement. If one accepts the scientific view that bodily movements are only possible if some motoneurons are active then either there is a systematic correlation between the folk-psychological cause and the neural cause or we must endow causal powers to propositional attitudes which are not correlated to neural states. The latter move would imply that it is in principle a mystery as to how beliefs cause behavior. Although we do not yet sufficiently understand how the brain works there is no reason to buy into a position which denies that we could ever discover the neural correlates of beliefs and understand e.g. how they relate to behavior. Against Baker my empirical conjecture is that science will discover neural correlates of beliefs but that these correlations will be described relative to the relevant contexts described above.

9 Outline of an Alternative View

In this final paragraph I would like to outline a version of the Standard View which accounts for the relationality and context-dependency of beliefs. The View is called Contextual Realism. To present this view I characterize the physical property of braking well and compare it with the mental property of having a belief.

To characterize the relation between the car's brake mechanism and the way the car decelerates, we distinguish properties (as dispositions) from their manifestations (as events). We thus get the following table:

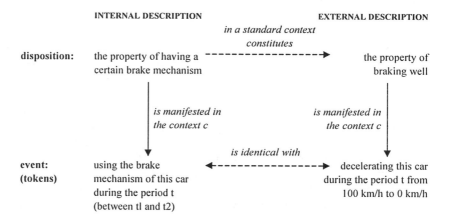

Table 1

On the level of events, it seems plausible that the relation of *being identical with* holds: Given the actual context (someone is driving the car with a speed of 100 km/h on a highway) using the brakes of this car during the period t (between t1 and t2) is identical with decelerating the car during that time-period from 100 km/h to 0 km/h. If we individuate events as spatio-temporal entities then we are describing the same event. The fact that the event is described internally or externally is no reason to make an ontological difference here. We are dealing with two descriptions of one event.

What is the analogous relation at the level of dispositions? The relation can be described as follows: Given a standard physical, social and linguistic context, the property of having a specific brake mechanism is necessary and sufficient for attributing the property of braking well. But if the context changes, the internally described property remains the same while the externally described property may change: If a standard physical context were such that roads are usually extremely slippery, having the said brake mechanism might not be sufficient for braking well. In the same sense, if a standard social context is such that people always drive at a distance of 5 m from the car in front of them regardless of their speed, the common brake mechanism would probably not be sufficient to guarantee braking well, because the car would never decelerate quickly enough to prevent accidents at high speeds. Because of this difference, the internally described property is not identical with the externally described property and the relation between the two properties is also not that of one constituting the other. Nevertheless, if we presuppose a standard context, the relation can be described as one of constitution. The internal property X constitutes the external property Y of a system S in a context c if the following counterfactuals hold:

i.   If the system S would not have the internal property X *in a standard context c*, it would not have the external property Y.
ii. If the system S has the internal property X *in a standard context c*, it has the external property Y.

Having a certain brake mechanism is the internal property of a car that constitutes in a standard context the external property of braking well. In the following I try to make it plausible that the same relation of context-dependent constitution holds between neural states or processes and beliefs. Let me present the analogous picture and then I will explain the details:

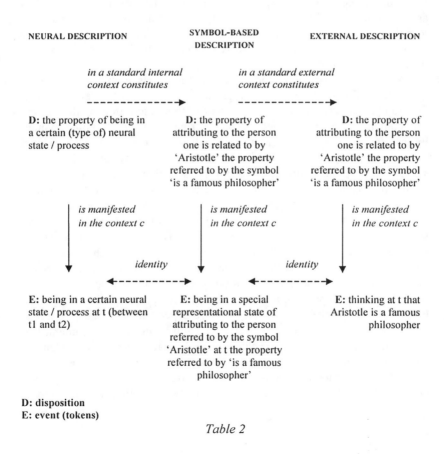

NEURAL DESCRIPTION	SYMBOL-BASED DESCRIPTION	EXTERNAL DESCRIPTION
	in a standard internal context constitutes ------>	*in a standard external context constitutes* ------>
D: the property of being in a certain (type of) neural state / process	**D**: the property of attributing to the person one is related to by 'Aristotle' the property referred to by the symbol 'is a famous philosopher'	**D**: the property of attributing to the person one is related to by 'Aristotle' the property referred to by the symbol 'is a famous philosopher'
↓ *is manifested in the context c*	↓ *is manifested in the context c*	↓ *is manifested in the context c*
identity <------>	*identity* <------>	
E: being in a certain neural state / process at t (between t1 and t2)	**E**: being in a special representational state of attributing to the person referred to by the symbol 'Aristotle' at t the property referred to by 'is a famous philosopher'	**E**: thinking at t that Aristotle is a famous philosopher

D: disposition
E: event (tokens)

Table 2

To explain this view in more detail I will illustrate that we can distinguish three ways of describing beliefs which I call a neural, a symbol-based and an external description of a belief. Let us illustrate this by using the belief *de re* expressed by the utterance 'Aristotle is a famous philosopher'. A belief *de re* is a belief about an object o that is expressed by using a referential singular term r and a predicate F while uttering the sentence 'F(r)'. A referential singular term is either a proper name, a referentially used definite description or an indicator (e. g. demonstratives or pure indexicals). The use of these terms has the consequence that the belief expressed is a belief about the object determined in the actual utterance context. The object remains the same for all possible worlds that are relevant for determining the truth-value of the content of the utterance (so-called circumstances of evaluation).[19] If we describe this belief externally the content of the belief is standardly characterized by the proposition which consists of the object and the externally characterized property: < Aristotle; being a famous philosopher >. This content can also be roughly attributed to a believer by saying 'A believes, with respect to Aristotle, that he is a famous philosopher'.

A second description of the same belief abstracts from the relationally or contextually fixed objects or properties and relies on the relevant symbols to characterize a belief. Therefore I call this description symbol-based. The content of the same belief can be described in a symbol-based manner by making the following attribution: A believes of the person he is related to by using the symbol 'Aristotle' that he has the property referred to by the symbol 'is a famous philosopher'. A third description presupposes a version of the identity theory: The same belief can then be described by a special neural state of a person at a certain time (and in a special context).

The properties of having certain beliefs and of being in certain neural states are related in a way analogous to the way in which the property of braking well and the property of having a certain brake mechanism are related. It was demonstrated that the main difference between these cases is only a difference in the nature of the respective context-dependencies. Beliefs are context-dependent in more ways than the property of braking well. Beliefs and properties like braking well are dependent on a standard external context, i. e. a standard physical, social and linguistic environment. Beliefs, however, have an holistic character and are furthermore dependent on the history of the thinker: A symbol-based description of the belief expressed by the utterance 'Aristotle is a famous philosopher' presupposes that the thinker has learned to use the symbol 'Aristotle'. Which symbols

---

[19] Kaplan, 1977/1989.

we learn and are able to use while thinking is determined by our individual history. We label the relevant biographical aspects as well as the relevant background beliefs of a thinker the *internal* context, in contrast to the *external* context given by the standard physical, social and linguistic environment. These forms of context-dependency do not in any way present us arguments to show that beliefs could not be constituted by neural states. If one accepts that these context-dependencies are relevant then one can still maintain the position of Contextual Realism.[20]

Of course, this is only a very sketchy picture but the framework can be made more explicit. The leading question is whether beliefs are reducible to neural states. A *strong* version of property reduction should explain the fact that the system S has the property p in the following way:[21]

S1   It is implied by general laws of nature that all systems with the microstructure C1, C2, ... Cn, O (C1 ... Cn being parts of the system and O being the organization of the parts) have (the characteristic features of) the property F.

S2   The system S has the microstructure C1, C2, ... Cn, O.

S3   The system S has (the characteristic features of) the property F.

If we accept the arguments which support externalism we have to make changes of the schema of explanation but we do not have to give up the Standard View. We still can defend a *weak* form of reduction which would account for relationality and context-dependency:

W1   It is implied by general laws of nature that all systems which are **in the relevant internal** and **external context k** and have the microstructure (C1, C2, ... Cn, O), C1 ... Cn being parts of the system and O the organization of the parts, have (the characteristic features of) the property F.

W2   The system S has the microstructure (C1, C2, ... Cn, O) and it is **in the relevant internal and external context k.**

W3   The system S has in k (the characteristic features of) the property F.

In the case of beliefs the following explanation can be expected:

---

[20] It is still an open question whether the relationality and context-dependency of beliefs could be accounted for by an internalist theory. But this will not be discussed here. Since Baker concedes externalism I take it for granted in my criticsm.

[21] Beckermann, 1996, 416 (my translation).

B1   It is implied by general laws of nature that all (intentional) systems (with central nervous systems) which are in a standard internal and external context k and are in the neural state (or process) N, believe that p.

B2   The (intentional) system S (with a central nervous system) is in the neural state (or process) N and is in a standard internal and external context k.

B3   The (intentional) system S believes in k that p.

Finally, I would like to illustrate this view with regard to artificial neural networks. If we characterize two neural nets N1 and N2 differing in the number of elements, their connections and respective configuration then, strictly speaking, we are dealing with two different types of neural nets. Although the nets are of different types, they can be trained to accomplish the same task, e.g. to distinguish between squares, triangles and circles on the basis of a visual input. Thus the net states of N1 and N2 that are relevant in realizing the recognition of a given square are different. The neural nets then may have the same cognitive state, i. e. recognizing a square, realized by different neural net states. But it does not follow that the act of recognition is not constituted by the relevant net states. It only follows that a certain net state alone is not a sufficient constitutive basis. The recognition is constituted by a certain net state together with the type of relevant context (the relevant context can be characterized e. g. by the present input, the connectivity, initial configuration and learning history of the net). This short look at neural nets illustrates the argument I have given in the case of human beliefs. Even if one belief is realized by different types of neural states it does not follow that beliefs are not constituted by neural states. A belief state (token) is according to my view constituted by a neural state(token) together with the relevant internal and external context of the believer. This constitution relation can in principle be characterized by general psycho-physical laws of the following form: If a person A is in a neural state of type N and in a context of type C then A has a belief of type B.

In conclusion: Baker does not present arguments that essentially differ from arguments for externalism. Since she accepts that externalism is compatible with the Standard View she does not present any conclusive arguments against the Standard View. Furthermore, if one accepts the arguments for externalism then one can defend Contextual Realism as a version of the Standard View which accounts for the relationality and the context-dependency of beliefs.

References

Baker, L. R. 1981. On Making and Attributing Demonstrative Reference. *Synthese* 49, 245-273.

Baker, L. R. 1987. *Saving Belief.* Princeton, Princeton University Press.

Baker, L. R. 1995. *Explaining Attitudes. A Practical Approach to the Mind.* New York, Cambridge University Press.

Beckermann, A., Flohr, H., Kim, J. (Eds..) 1992. *Emergence or Reduction?.* New York, de Gruyter .

Beckermann, A. 1996. Können mentale Phänomene neurobiologisch erklärt werden? In: Roth, G., Prinz, W. (eds.): *Kopf-Arbeit. Gehirnfunktionen und kognitive Leistungen*, Berlin, 413-425.

Burge, T. 1979. Individualism and the Mental. *Midwest Studies in Philosophy,* 4, 73-121.

Fletcher, P.C., Frith, C. D., Baker, S. C. , Shallice, T., Frackowiak R. S. & Dolan, R. J. 1995. The Mind's Eye – Precuneus Activation in Memory-Related Imagery. *NeuroImage* 2, 195-200.

Fodor, J. 1987. *Psychosemantics. The Problem of Meaning in the Philosophy of Mind.* Cambridge Mass, MIT Press..

Frith, C. D. 1992. *The Cognitive Neuropsychology of Schizophrenia.* Hillsdale.

Frith, C. D. 1994. Theory of Mind in Schizophrenia. In A. S. David, J. C. Cutting (eds.): *The Neuropsychology of Schizophrenia*, Hillsdale, 147-161.

Haas-Spohn, U. 1995. *Versteckte Indexikalität und subjektive Bedeutung.* Berlin, Akademie-Verlag.

Heil, J. 1992. *The Nature of True Minds.* New York, Cambridge University Press.

Kaplan, D. 1989. Demonstratives. An essay on the semantics, logic, metaphysics, and epistemology of demonstratives and other indexicals. In: J. Almog, J. Perry, H. Wettstein (eds.), *Themes from Kaplan*, Oxford, 481-563 (Manuscript 1977).

Libet, B. 1985. Unconscious Cerebral Initiative and the Role of Conscious Will in Voluntary Action. *Behavioral and Brain Sciences*, 8, 529-66.

Newen, A. 1993. How to Fix the Reference of 'that' in Demonstrative Utterances. In: Meggle, G., Wessels, U. (eds.), *Analyomen 1.* Proceedings of the 1st Conference 'Perspectives in Analytical Philosophy', Berlin, de Gruyter, 493-508.

Newen, A. 1996. *Kontext, Referenz und Bedeutung: Eine Bedeutungstheorie singulärer Terme.* Paderborn, Schöningh-Verlag.

Newen, A. 1997. The Logic of Indexical Thoughts and the Metaphysics of the 'Self'. In: Künne, W.; Newen, A.; Anduschus, M. (eds.), *Direct Reference, Indexicality and Propositional Attitudes*, Stanford, CSLI Publications, 105-132.

Newen, A. in press. Fregean Senses and the Semantics of Singular Terms. In: Newen, Nortmann, Stuhlmann-Laeisz (eds.), *Building on Frege. New Essays on Sense, Content, and Concept,* Stanford: CLSI Publications.

Perry, J. 1993. *The Problem of the Essential Indexical and other Essays.* New York, Oxford University Press.

Perry, J. 1997. Reflexivity, Indexicality and Names. In: Künne, Newen, Anduschus, M. (Eds.): *Direct Reference,* Indexicality *and Propositional Attitudes,* Stanford, CSLI.

Perry,J. 2001. *Knowledge, Possibility, and Consciousness.* Cambridge Mass., MIT Press.

Putnam, H. 1975. The Meaning of 'Meaning'. In: Gunderson, K. (ed.): *Minnesota Studies in the Philosophy of Science,* 12, (Language, Mind, and Knowledge), Minneapolis, University of Minneapolis Press.

Recanati, F. 1993. *Direct Reference. From Language to Thought.* Oxford, Blackwell.

Ryle, G. 1949. *The* Concept *of Mind.* London, Hutchinson.

Spohn, W. 1997. Begründungen a priori - oder: ein frischer Blick auf Dispositionsprädikate. In: W. Lenzen (Ed.): *Das weite Spektrum der analytischen Philosophie*, Festschrift für Franz von Kutschera, Berlin, de Gruyter.

Vogeley, K., Bussfeld, P., Newen, A., Hermann, S., Happé, F., Falkai, P., Maier, W., Shah, N.J., Fink, G. R., Zilles, K. 2001. Mind Reading: Neural Mechanisms of Theory of Mind and Self-Perspective. *NeuroImage* 14, 170-181.

9

Collective Beliefs and Practical Realism: Giving Relations their Proper Metaphysical Due

ANTHONIE MEIJERS

Philosophers of mind and action have a sober diet. They often concentrate on rather simple cases, like raising one's arm, or believing that the cat is on the mat, or that grass is green. One of the merits of *Explaining Attitudes* is that it has extended the discussion in the philosophy of mind to non-psychological intentional explanations of economic, legal, political, and social phenomena. I will discuss in this chapter another neglected category of explanations: Psychological intentional explanations of *collective* phenomena in terms of *collective* intentional states. These constitute a very important category in the explanation of behavior in everyday life, in legal contexts, and in the political and social sciences. It is also a category where the limitations of the Standard View, as defined by Baker, become very clear. Let me give a few examples:

(1) The Security Council decided to send UN troops to the Balkans, because it believed that such a move was necessary in order to restore law and order.

(2) After Exxon was held responsible for the Alaska oil disaster, its management reviewed the internal environmental regulations.

(3) The orchestra performed Lully's first opera extraordinarily well, knowing that a CD would be made of it.

Explaining Beliefs: Lynne Rudder Baker and Her Critics.
Anthonie Meijers (ed.).
Copyright © 2001, CSLI Publications.

(4) A coalition of European countries effectively blocked new world-trade regulations, so as to protect their home markets.

(5) We intend to finish our discussions at 12.30, in order to have enough time for lunch.

These are common examples of situations in which collective actions, collective intentions, and collective beliefs are attributed to collective agents. In this chapter, I will deal rather briefly with the various conceptions of these phenomena. Rather than making a detailed analysis, my strategy will be to assume what I believe to be a plausible conception of collective beliefs, and then to evaluate how the Standard View and Practical Realism compare in their ability to take into account these beliefs in the explanation of collective actions.[1]

What is at stake in these discussions is not only the ability to account for a particular class of intentional states. The truly important issue is whether Practical Realism can become a *full-fledged* theory of the attitudes. Decisive in this respect is the ability to account for the notion of a *practice*. As Baker says, 'Practical Realism is a metaphysical view based on practice', and 'the nature of the attitudes is best revealed by their operation in our practices'.[2] However, the notion of a practice has remained rather vague in philosophical discussions from Wittgenstein to Rorty and beyond, and Baker also does not say much about it. Practices consist of, among other things, such social phenomena as rules, joint actions, collective judgments, collective beliefs, and collective commitments. Thus the notion of collective intentionality will play an important role in the analysis of practices. The ability to account adequately for collective intentional phenomena can therefore be seen as a crucial test for Practical Realism. Assuming it succeeds in refuting the Standard View, does it have the potential to develop a full-fledged, positive alternative account based on practices?

In the first section of this chapter, I will discuss the notions of a collective agent and of a collective belief. Next, I will explore the Standard View's ability to account for collective attitudes. The third section is devoted to a possible Practical Realist account. My conclusion will be that Practical Realism is in a much better position to account for collective intentional phenomena than the Standard View. In the fourth section I will discuss the objection that the superiority of Practical Realism only holds if collective agents have beliefs in a literal sense. If not, my arguments can even be used against Practical Realism. I will argue that if we make a more

---

[1] See for some recent developments in the theory of collective intentionality Gilbert, 1998.

[2] *Explaining Attitudes*, 20.

fine-grained distinction between the cognitive attitudes of believing and accepting, collective attitudes *can* be literally attributed to collective agents. The final sections of the chapter focus on relations and relational properties. These notions are of great importance for the Practical Realist. I will conclude that although Practical Realism is in a much better position to account for collective intentional states, it has so far failed to give a positive theory of the relational character of propositional attitudes.

1 Collective Beliefs and Collective Agents

Let me start with the rather uncontroversial statement that collective beliefs are the beliefs of collective agents. The Security Council, the orchestra, or the management of an organization believes that p. I will use as a general expression for collective beliefs the expression '*we* believe that p'. Here, the collective agent is the subject of the belief, as opposed to the individual belief '*I* believe that p', where the subject of the belief is an individual agent. In the belief 'I believe that *we* believe that p', the 'we' is part of the propositional content of the belief, and such a belief would therefore not count as a genuine *collective* belief.

The expression 'we believe that p', however, has different readings. First, there is the rather noncommittal reading, according to which all the individuals concerned have the belief that p, or that it is a widespread belief among them. Here the collective 'we' is regarded as an aggregate, i.e., as the simple summation of the participating individuals. An opinion poll usually reflects the beliefs of an aggregate, but does not reveal the beliefs that are collectively held. The aggregate reading does not pose a new problem for either the Standard View or Practical Realism, since it regards the attribution of a collective belief as an attribution of an individual belief, together with a certain distribution of this belief among the members of the group.

Secondly, there is an extreme reading of 'we believe that p', according to which a collective belief is the belief of a super-agent or a super-mind, i.e., of some collective entity which exist *independently* of individuals. I believe that Ockham's razor will quickly cut out these superfluous entities. We don't need them in order to account for collective intentional states and collective actions. From a political point of view such an extreme reading is dangerous, too, since it suggests that there are intentions and actions in history or in the social world that are independent of the intentions and actions of individuals (like, for example, the Will of the People or the course of events dictated by the Zeitgeist). And, it will be argued, we can't take responsibility for these intentions and actions.

I am sympathetic to Margaret Gilbert's interpretation of Durkheim, from which follows an account of collective agents similar to the one I have developed in my work on communication and collective intentionality.[3] According to Durkheim, in his treatise *The Rules of Sociological Method*, social groups arise from a special *synthesis* of individual agents. As such, they give rise to new ways of thinking, feeling, and acting, i.e., to collective intentional states and practices. Collective beliefs, then, are not a sub-category of individual beliefs, but constitute a category of their own. When Durkheim says that social facts exist outside individual consciousness, his remark should be interpreted in the context of the idea that these facts have social groups as substrata, i.e., individuals in association. They exist outside individual human beings *only* in the sense that they cannot be completely reduced to facts about individuals. They are, however, not independent of the individuals that constitute the social group. I will call this third approach the *relational* reading of 'we believe that p'.

According to the relational view, the collective 'we' in 'we believe that p' consists of individuals standing in certain relations. They come in various types, depending on the kind of individuals that participate and the kind of relations between them. A top-down organized company or an army is different in this respect from a football team, the Security Council, or an ad hoc group of philosophers discussing Baker's theory of the attitudes at a conference. Nevertheless, to repeat my point, it is only individuals standing in certain formal or informal relations who constitute collective agents. The relational position taken here is in between the reductionist aggregate reading and the non-reductionist extreme reading of 'we believe that p'.

The main reason why the aggregate reading of 'we believe that p' does not work, is that a collective belief involves agreements and commitments between the members of the group, in order for the belief to be a collective belief. The simple summation of beliefs among the individual members will not do, since they are not logically sufficient for a group belief. To use one of the earlier examples, if all the members of the Security Council individually believe that sending UN troops would be necessary to restore law and order in the Balkans, this would not count as the belief of the Council. They might not even know of each other's belief in this situation, for example because they never mentioned it. But even if they did know, this would not

[3] Gilbert, 1992, *On Social Facts*, Chapter 5; Meijers, 1994. *Speech Acts, Communication and Collective Intentionality; Beyond Searle' Individualism;* Meijers, 1999a, Believing and Accepting as a Group. See also Tuomela, 1995, *The Importance of Us; A Philosophical Study of Basic Social Notions,* Chapter 9, for a similar approach.

make much difference.[4] Even if an opinion poll reveals that all the members of the Council individually believe that sending UN troops would be necessary, and they all know about the opinion poll, these beliefs still would not count as the belief of the Security Council. In order for it to become the belief of the Council, they have to meet and jointly accept this belief as the belief of the Security Council. Such a collective belief has consequences which individual beliefs do not have. For example, representatives of the Council can act on this belief in international negotiations, the Council itself will decide upon further actions which follow from this belief, members will be committed to sticking to their belief even if they change their mind or simply don't have an opinion on the matter, etc. The aggregate reading cannot account for these phenomena.

Thus, collective beliefs are not the beliefs of individual agents, or of an aggregate of individual agents, but of related subjects. They are always 'collectivity involving', as Margaret Gilbert puts it. To show this, she constructs an ingenious example, which I will present in a slightly modified version. Imagine two committees of the university, say the Food Committee and the Library Committee, which, coincidentally, have the same members. According to Gilbert, it seems quite possible to say without contradiction (a) that most members of the Food Committee believe that budget cuts would be disastrous for the library, and that this is common knowledge in the Food Committee; (b) that the same goes for the members of the Library Committee; (c) that the Library Committee believes that further budget cuts would be disastrous for the library, whereas the Food Committee does not have an opinion on the matter. Gilbert's conclusion, which I support, is that it is not logically sufficient for a group belief 'we believe that p' either that most group members believe that p, or that there be common knowledge within the group that most members believe that p.[5] It requires a collective agent in the sense of the relational reading discussed above.

Both the Security Council example and the committee example reveal a crucial aspect of collective attitudes. They involve commitments among the members of the group, where both the procedure of accepting and the type of commitments that follow from it depend on the structure of the group concerned. As Durkheim said, collective beliefs have 'coercive power' in

---

[4] This also applies to the idea that collective beliefs are individual beliefs plus common knowledge about the beliefs of other participants. 'We believe that p' is then taken as shorthand for the expression 'I believe that p', and 'I believe that everybody else in the group believes that p', and 'I believe that everybody in the group believes that everybody in the group believes that p', etc.

[5] *On Social Facts*, 273.

that individual members are restricted in their subsequent actions because of their collective belief. And others may rightly correct them if they do not live up to this belief. Contrary to individual intentionality, collective intentionality involves a web of normative relations.

2   Collective Beliefs and the Standard View

Given this conception of collective agents and collective beliefs, can the Standard View account for these phenomena? And can it handle such relational notions as agreement, commitment, or joint acceptance? The Standard View is committed to the idea that for every belief there is a brain state that realizes that belief. In Baker's formulation, its minimal commitment is:

(SV)   For all persons S and propositions p, S believes that p only if there is some neural token, n, such that (i) n has the content that p, or means that p, and (ii) S tokens n.[6]

For our discussion here it is useful to distinguish between two versions of the Standard View: The internalist or non-relational version, and the externalist or relational version. The former adheres to the idea that intentional states are constituted solely by the *intrinsic* properties of the brain. The latter version allows for *extrinsic* or relational properties in its account of intentional states.

The internalist adherent to the Standard View has basically two options with regard to collective intentional states. Either he takes collective beliefs to be different from individual beliefs and tries to incorporate them in his ontological framework; or he opts for a reductive strategy, according to which collective beliefs are a special class of individual beliefs. Such a reductive strategy is the aggregate approach mentioned above, or a more sophisticated one that uses, for example, recursive notions like common knowledge or mutual belief to account for the relatedness of agents that hold intentions or beliefs collectively. Since I have already suggested why I believe such a reductive strategy will not work, I will discuss only the first option.

The non-reductive Internalist holds that all intentional states, *including collective intentions and beliefs*, are constituted by the intrinsic properties of the brain. Their ontological descriptions do not involve relations to the natural or social world. The idea is sometimes formulated in terms of the metaphor of a brain in vat: According to the internalist, we can have all the intentionality we have, even if we are radically mistaken about the outside

---

[6] See Chapter 2 of this volume.

world, even if we are a brain in a vat. This constraint immediately brings to the fore why it is impossible for the non-reductive internalist to account for collective intentionality: The internalist is forced to hold two incompatible ideas at the same time. On the one hand, he regards relations to the outside world as non-essential for the individuation of intentional states (illustrated by the brain in a vat), whereas on the other hand, he has to regard relations as essential for collective intentional states if the account given above is correct. As we have seen, the *we* in 'we believe that p' is not an isolated individual or a super-agent, but a network of connected individuals called a collective agent. The individuals involved stand here in certain relations and have commitments and obligations, due to the intentions and beliefs they collectively hold.

If both the reductive and the non-reductive *internalist* version of the Standard View fail to account for collective intentional states, is there an *externalist* way out for the adherent to the Standard View? I will focus here on Fred Dretske's account of the attitudes, since it seems the more promising of the various proposals: It explicitly incorporates external relations in the causal explanation of intentional actions.[7] Dretske reformulates Baker's formulation of the minimal commitment of the Standard View in the following way:

> For every belief that p (for any p), there is some neural state or other in the
> believer (a token of some neural type) that means that p.[8]

His reformulation is intended to make it clear that adherents of the Standard View are committed only to token-token identity and not to the stronger type-type identity. Also missing from Dretske's reformulation is the original reference to persons, since he only talks about beliefs and neural states.

What is crucial in his account of belief is the distinction between a neural state on the one hand and its meaning on the other. Like many philosophers of mind, Dretske is convinced by the arguments of Putnam and Burge which show that meaning is to be construed externally: Meaning does not supervene on the intrinsic properties of the brain, but on the wider social context. What makes a mental state *mental*, i.e., a state having content or meaning, is a network of *external* facts that exist outside a person.[9] It is

---

[7] See his *Explaining Behavior: Reasons in a World of Causes*, Cambridge 1988, especially Chapter 4: 'The Explanatory Role of Belief', and his chapter in this volume.

[8] Dretske in this volume, p 47

[9] Ibid., p 42.

only in virtue of its relations to the outside world that a belief has meaning, and here Dretske and Baker agree.

But when it comes to the explanation of behavior, Dretske rejects a straightforward externalist account. He defends the idea that beliefs are causally efficacious only in so far as they neural states. 'Relational states of S do not have to be brain states *unless* they control (as beliefs are thought to control) bodily movements. Then you need them *inside* with their hands on the steering wheel'.[10] The analogy with a vending machine is illuminating. A coin has meaning not in virtue of its intrinsic properties, but because of our monetary system. When we use a coin in a vending machine, it is in virtue of its intrinsic properties (weight, size, shape) that it does the job it does (deliver drinks or food), and not in virtue of its monetary value. The latter is causally irrelevant, according to Dretske. Note that such an account cannot describe the events happening as the transfer of property rights caused by the paying for a drink. As a matter of fact, it can only describe the events on a physical level.[11]

Dretske's account does not make meaning epiphenomenal. Meaning does figure in the explanation of behavior, but in a very different way. To make this clear, Dretske introduces his well-known distinction between the structuring cause and the triggering cause of behavior. The coin mentioned above starts a sequence of events in the vending machine, which results in its delivering drinks or food. As such, it is a triggering cause. But there is also a structuring cause, for it is only because the vending machine has been designed and built to be sensitive to items like coins that these events happen in the first place. Meaning, according to Dretske, is like a structuring cause. Neural states have acquired the control over bodily movements they have *in virtue of* what these states mean or indicate about their external circumstances.[12]

I don't need to go into further details of Dretske's position in order to answer the question whether an externalist adherent of the Standard View, like Dretske, can take into account *collective* intentional states. And my answer will be negative. The collective belief 'we believe that p' has a collective agent 'we' as its subject. Its content and meaning are specified in the 'that p' clause. This belief has to fulfill the Standard View condition that 'for every belief that p (for any p) there is some neural state or other in the

---

[10] Ibid, 43.

[11] In such an account, Dretske is also not allowed to use such notions as food or drink. They do not belong to the physical vocabulary.

[12] *Explaining Behavior*, 88.

believer (a token of some neural type) that means that p'. Since brains or neural states are not distributed over more than one person, this condition amounts to a commitment to individualism, i.e., to the idea that ultimately all intentionality is the property of individual brains. Collective beliefs have to be reduced, then, to individual beliefs. The aggregate reading of 'we believe that p' shows what such a (problematic) reduction might look like.

Dretske's externalist version of the Standard View allows for semantic externalism, which is concerned with the *content* of a mental state, and not with its *subject*. His account in terms of structuring and triggering causes is meant to provide an explanation of why certain neural structures in individuals are in place. Relations *between* individuals that constitute a collective agent, such as claims and obligations, cannot be taken into account this way. That requires a very different form of relationalism (see below).

3 Collective Beliefs and Practical Realism

Practical Realism is not committed to the idea of beliefs as brain states. It does not specify a priori metaphysical constraints on causes for behavior. Its ontology is much more liberal. In this section I will give a rough sketch of a possible Practical Realist account of collective beliefs, using the theory of beliefs developed in *Explaining Attitudes*.[13]

The point of departure for the Practical Realist account will be our successful explanatory practices, where we attribute collective intentional states to collective agents. The examples given earlier show common situations where we explain the behavior of collective agents in terms of these states. The Security Council decides to send UN troops, because it *believes* that this will restore law and order, etc. These explanations also allow for the prediction and manipulation of behavior, assuming that collective agents act rationally.

The first claim a Practical Realist will make with respect to collective beliefs, is what I will call Baker's ontological claim. A collective belief is a global state of a collective person, and not a state of any proper part of this person. It is definitely not a brain state of one or of all of the participating individuals. Practical Realism is therefore compatible with what I earlier called the relational reading of the belief 'we believe that p', but also with the extreme reading of this belief. In *Explaining Attitudes*, Baker approvingly quotes Dennet saying 'the subject of all the intentional attributions is the whole system (the person, the animal, or even the corporation or na-

---

13 Especially Chapter 6: 'Belief without Reification'. References between brackets in this chapter are to *Explaining Attitudes*.

tion)' (153, note 3). Baker's ontological claim formulated in the case of collective beliefs is stronger than the one in the case of individual beliefs. Not only brain states but also propositional attitudes of individuals are insufficient for collective beliefs, even if these attitudes are understood in a Practical Realist way. Remember the case where all the members of the Security Council have a certain belief, as revealed by an opinion poll, without the Council having the relevant collective belief. Certain brain states or individual beliefs may be a necessary condition for the having of collective beliefs, but they are clearly not a sufficient condition.

The second claim the Practical Realist wants to make with respect to collective beliefs is what I will call Baker's epistemological claim, since it concerns the attribution of beliefs. It is the claim that whether a collective agent has a particular belief is determined by what the agent does, says, and thinks under various circumstances, whereas what the agent would do may be specified intentionally (155). Whether collective agent CA believes that p, depends on there being relevant counterfactuals true of CA. They reveal the nature, or are indicative, of having the collective belief that p, or - put the other way around - the collective belief that p manifests itself in such a way that these counterfactuals are true of CA.

This claim does not imply that a collective agent's believing that p is identical with a *particular* set of counterfactuals being true. Given holism, where beliefs are part of a network of intentional states, the set of relevant counterfactuals is different for different agents having the same belief. This is another way of saying that every belief is always *from a point of view*. Counterfactuals need to be specified from this point of view. It is remarkable that Baker says virtually nothing in *Explaining Behavior* about the indispensability of a first-person point of view for the analysis of intentional states. This is an important issue for Practical Realism, since the specification of the conditions for having a particular belief is agent-specific.

With regard to Baker's epistemological claim, there is an asymmetry between individual and collective beliefs. In the case of the former, the counterfactuals specify the actions, thoughts, and statements of *individual* agents required in order for the attribution of the belief to be true. In case of the latter, the counterfactuals specify what *collective* agents will do, think, or say. But it does not follow from this latter specification what the relevant actions, thoughts, and statements of the participating individuals will be. These, however, jointly make up the collective ones and are decisive for the true attribution of a belief to a collective agent. There is underdetermination here with respect to the relevant individual actions. For example, if the Security Council decides to send UN troops to the Balkans, the required actions of the individual member states are not yet determined: Italy, or Holland, or any other country willing to participate, may send troops. Since a given collective action may be realized by a great many individual actions, the counterfactuals do not, and cannot, specify the actions of the individuals involved, in order for the belief attribution to be true. Only at the global level of the collective agent are these actions, thoughts, and statements specified by the counterfactuals.

Collective beliefs also pass Baker's Control Test for causal explanation (122), though a single collective belief will only occasionally explain behavior. Beliefs are part of a web of intentional states (beliefs, intentions, and desires). It is this intentional web that explains why an agent did what she did in a particular situation. Baker's test for the causal explanation of collective action can be formulated as follows. Using my earlier example of the Security Council, the test would be: The Security Council's belief that restoring law and order is necessary *causally explains* the decision to send troops in a particular circumstance C if (i) if the belief had not occurred, troops would not have been sent in C, and (ii) given that the belief occurred in C, the decision was inevitable. There are definitely circumstances where both (i) and (ii) are true, and where collective beliefs will pass Baker's control test and thus will causally explain the collective actions of the Security Council.

My sketch of what a Practical Realist account of collective beliefs could be already shows, in my view, that Practical Realism is superior to the Standard View in its ability to account for collective intentional phenomena. It is not forced to adopt an individualistic ontology or a reductionist strategy. It can also easily incorporate our everyday explanatory practices with regard to collective intentional behavior, while passing Baker's test for causal explanation.

4   An Objection and Reply

The conclusion so far may be questioned in two ways. It may be argued that (i) collective agents are not agents in a literal sense and (ii) that even if they were, they are not able to have beliefs in the same sense that individuals have. As a result, the argument in favor of Practical Realism turns out to be an argument against it, since it allows for the attribution of beliefs that are clearly counterintuitive from the opponent's point of view.[14]

The first part of the objection has already been addressed above. Collective agents are agents in a literal sense if understood in a proper way. In section 1 I argued for a relational reading of 'we believe that p', a position in between a reductionist approach (collective agents are aggregates of in-

---

[14] The objection was made by an anonymous referee.

dividuals) and a collectivist approach (collective agents are superagents). In the analysis of collective action a pluralist approach is clearly necessary. Though there are cases where an aggregate reading of 'we believe that p' is appropriate (the opinion poll case), not all cases are like that. The Security Council is a clear case where such a reduction is not possible. It is composed of individual member states acting *together,* where these members are bound in their actions by *relations* (agreements, commitments, claims). This makes it impossible to understand their collective actions in terms of the reductive, summation view. At the same time the Security Council, as a collective agent, can *literally* be said to decide on a future action, to send troops to the Balkans, to be responsible for the outcome of such action, to have reasons for its actions, etc. These decisions, actions, responsibilities and reasons cannot be attributed to the individual nations making up the Council. This is shown by the fact that individual states may have voted against these actions, or may have no opinion about them, whereas they are responsible for these actions *qua* members of the Security Council.

The second part of the objection questions whether beliefs can be literally attributed to collective agents. To understand why the opponent both has a point and has not, it is necessary to make a more fine-grained distinction between the various attitudes involved. The notion of belief used so far is a general cognitive notion that contains, among other things, the propositional attitudes of believing (in a narrow sense), accepting and holding true. The relevant distinction for the issue at stake here is between belief and acceptance. In this chapter I will not give an in depth analysis of these attitudes, but only sketch an account that addresses the opponent's concerns.[15]

There are obvious asymmetries between individual beliefs and collective beliefs of the relational, *non*-aggregate type. Groups do not have minds or consciousnesses. If accessibility to consciousness is a requirement to have genuine beliefs (which is, for example, Searle's position), then groups evidently do not have beliefs in a literal sense.

Following Bratman and Engel, we may list a number of properties that distinguishes the propositional attitude of believing a proposition from the attitude of accepting a view. Firstly, beliefs are normally not subject to direct control, they are involuntary, whereas acceptances are voluntary. To accept a view means to use a certain proposition as a valid premise in one's practical deliberations. Acceptance is a pragmatic notion. It is not only in-

---

[15] I discuss the relation between believing, accepting, and holding true in the case of collective agents extensively in Meijers (1999a) and Meijers (2001). For a general analysis in the individual case see Bratman (1993), Engel (1998) and Engel (2000).

formed by epistemic considerations, but by prudential ones as well. We may accept a view that we believe is likely to be false, for example if we act on a worst-case scenario.

If we apply the voluntary - involuntary distinction to collective beliefs, it turns out that they are more like acceptances than beliefs proper. The main reason is that collective beliefs require some sort of assent by the members of the group for the belief to be a collective belief. As we have seen in the case of the Security Council, for a belief to be the belief of the Council, the members have to meet and jointly accept this belief as the belief of the group. Otherwise it will be just the belief of the members taken individually (analogous to the opinion poll case).

Secondly, beliefs aim at truth, whereas acceptances aim at utility or pragmatic success. Beliefs represent the world as it is, not the world as we would like it to be. Acceptances, on the other hand, take into account action-oriented considerations, in addition to epistemic ones. This property points again in the direction of the collective acceptance of a view. This is shown, among other things, by the fact that collective beliefs are context bound in a much stronger sense than individual beliefs. What a group is willing to believe depends on the situation it is in. Genuine beliefs are not like that. We believe that Lynne Baker is professor of philosophy at Amherst, regardless of the context we are in. It is also shown by the fact that a group may believe a proposition that none of its members believes individually, for example in the case of a compromise. A selection committee may accept the view (as opposed to believes) that person P is the best candidate for the job, though no member believes this individually.

A third property that distinguishes beliefs from acceptances is that beliefs are shaped by evidence and are subject to an ideal of integration, whereas acceptances need not be based on evidence en require only coherent policies. This property also suggests that collective beliefs are more like the acceptance of a view than belief proper. A collective belief is part of a coherent policy of a group, and not so much part of an integrated true view of the world.

A final distinguishing property is that beliefs come in degrees, whereas acceptances are qualitative. Beliefs have subjective probabilities, acceptances are a matter of all or nothing. Since collectively believing that p requires an act of agreement among the members of the group, where agreeing is qualitative, we have again evidence in favor of the acceptance view of collective beliefs.

I conclude from this discussion that collective beliefs should be understood on the model of the acceptance of a view, rather than of belief proper. In this respect my opponent has a point. If we unpack the global cognitive notion of belief, it turns out that a collective belief is in fact the collective acceptance of a view. Our analysis has to be refined in this respect.

On the other hand, this result in no way undermines the arguments given above for the superiority of Practical Realism. Though collective agents do not collectively believe that p in a literal sense, they *collectively* accept a view in a literal sense. This collective attitude cannot be reduced to individual attitudes, for it involves relations (commitments, claims and obligations) among the individuals making up the collective agent. As we have seen in Section 2, the Standard View has serious problems accounting for these relational aspects of collective attitudes, even in its externalist version. The arguments given in favor of Baker's Practical Realism therefore equally apply to collective beliefs conceived as the collective acceptance of a view. My opponent's objection thus fails to undermine the arguments in favor of Practical Realism.

However, if Practical Realism is to become a genuine alternative to the Standard View, it needs to be based an account of one of its main ontological categories: Relations and relational properties. That will be the topic of the next section.

5   Relations Given Their Proper Metaphysical Due?

Many philosophers nowadays accept the critique of an internalist conception of mind and meaning formulated by Burge and Putnam, among others. From their arguments it follows that content and meaning cannot be solely 'in the head'. This is, however, to a large extent a negative thesis: It tells us what mental states are *not*. When it comes to the positive thesis, however, many externalist accounts have little to offer with respect to the external, relational character of the mind. Though Practical Realism constitutes an alternative that is much more promising than many of its competitors, it also lacks an elaboration of what Lynne Baker calls its 'radical relationalism' (156). Refuting a non-relational account of the attitudes is clearly not enough here.

If we try to characterize Baker's idea of radical relationalism, we may come up with the following theses:

a. propositional attitudes supervene globally; i.e., to have a propositional attitude, a person needs to stand in a certain relation to her environment (11).

b. consciously entertaining propositional attitudes supervenes globally; i.e., to entertain a propositional attitude, a person needs to stand in a certain relation to her environment (189).

c. *all* mental phenomena, including first-person episodes, supervene globally; i.e., to have a mental phenomenon, a person needs to stand in a certain relation to her environment (this would, for example, also apply to the experience of pain).

I am not sure whether Baker would subscribe to the third thesis; she does, however, explicitly subscribe to the first two theses.

One of the aims of *Explaining Attitudes* is 'to give relations their proper metaphysical due' in the analysis of intentional phenomena (63). From what I have said so far, it will be evident that such an approach is indeed necessary, and that the analysis of collective actions and collective attitudes only adds weight to this observation. Baker, however, devotes only a few passages to relations. She finds it difficult to express relational properties in two-place predicates (63), and she gives a short definition of relational properties without further analysis:

R is a relational property if and only if: x's having R entails that there is some y distinct from x (63).

Such a definition is, in an important sense, incomplete in that it does not specify what y has to do with x, if anything. The point of a relational property is that it *relates* x and y. Baker also mentions that a Leibnizian view of relations is seriously incomplete. Such a view holds that a relational property can be explicated in terms of the intrinsic properties of its bearer, together with intrinsic properties of other things in the world (116).

If relations are to play such a central role in the account of intentional phenomena, we may rightly ask for a more elaborate account. What are relations and relational properties from an ontological point of view? Is the concept of a relation primitive? What is the difference between, for example, causal relations, intentional relations, and normative relations? What do we mean exactly when we say that beliefs are relational states of persons? Is the notion of a person relational, too? Or, to put these questions more generally: How do relations fit into the overall ontological framework of Practical Realism? Here I believe a lot of work needs to be done in order to develop a full and credible alternative account. This would make a fascinating research program. Assuming that relations are not reducible to intrinsic properties,[16] I will explore in the remainder of this section the relata to which the mental state of believing relates. The negative thesis that beliefs do not supervene on intrinsic properties is much easier to establish than its

---

[16] See the appendix to this chapter.

positive counterpart, where it needs to be specified what exactly is related by the relational state of a belief.

6 Beliefs and Their Relata

According to Baker, beliefs are global states of persons and the nature of belief is best revealed by its operation in practice (20). Whether or not a person believes that p, depends on what this person would do, think, or say in various circumstances. The state of believing that p thus is to be specified counterfactually (22). Baker's claim here is not that facts about beliefs are nothing over and above facts about counterfactuals, but rather that the nature of a belief is revealed by counterfactuals about the believer (21). Two obvious candidates for the relata of beliefs emerge from her account: Persons and practices. This is not to say that belief states are necessarily to be expressed in terms of two-place predicates, as Baker rightly observes, but that persons and practices will be among the relata of the relational state of believing.

Externalists such as Baker defend the idea that beliefs are relative to social and linguistic practices. But what does it exactly mean to say that a belief state is relative to, and thus related to, a practice? Are these practices simply a condition for having particular beliefs, among other conditions? That seems to be too modest a claim. Externalism originated in the problem of the *ontology* of intentional states, where the externalist argued that meaning and content cannot be 'in the head'. For a large class of mental states, social and linguistic practices determine the content of these states. Social practices, however, constitute such an imprecise category that they can hardly be used to individuate beliefs: How, on this basis, can one distinguish between, for example, the belief that tenure is important for academic life, and the belief that tenure is *usually* important for academic life?

Another approach would be to regard beliefs as states that relate believers to counterfactual situations. Whether or not a person believes that p, depends on what this person would do, think, or say in various circumstances. Baker herself, however, emphasizes that though counterfactuals reveal the nature of beliefs, they are not *identical* to the relational state of believing. Furthermore, it would raise a number of questions with regard to the ontological status of counterfactual situations and the type of relation that a believer has to these situations. This illustrates again, in my view, that Practical Realism needs to have an elaborate account of relations before it can be a genuine alternative to the Standard View.

Baker also defends the idea of beliefs as relational states of *persons*. The notion of a person is therefore important for the Practical Realist and requires a more detailed analysis.[17] If we want to know what persons need to be like in order to have intentional states, it is obvious that they need to be more than simple bodies. Persons can figure in counterfactuals, i.e., they are able to think, act, and speak, whereas bodies only move, or utter sounds. The concept of a person therefore needs to be much more substantial. A person is at the very least a possible subject of a belief, able to act in counterfactual situations.

Counterfactuals specify what kind of action A person P *would* do in situation S, given the belief that p. The relation between S and A, however, is underdetermined, as we have seen above. Baker indirectly refers to this underdetermination when she mentions the Gore / Quale case: From a given belief, one cannot derive a *particular* set of counterfactuals (156). A background of other beliefs, intentions, desires, etc, needs to be added in order to narrow the gap between S and A. But even adding such a background does not solve underdetermination completely, because not every belief, desire, or intention needs to be taken into account in a situation S. From A's point of view, only certain beliefs may matter, and the ones that matter may have different weights. These observations suggest that the concept of a person includes the concept of a *point of view*. Counterfactuals specify what persons would do, say, or think given their belief that p and their particular point of view. Since a point of view itself consists of beliefs, among other things, this implies that beliefs do not come in isolation. In order to be able to believe that p, one has to already have a number of other beliefs, which is a familiar point in philosophy.

If my analysis here is right, persons and beliefs are intertwined and the concept of a person is a relational one. To be a person means to have certain belief states, and the idea of a person as nothing more than a *possible* subject of beliefs is an illusion. More analysis is obviously needed here, but my discussion shows again that if beliefs are conceived as relational states, the terms of these states cannot be taken for granted.

7   Conclusion

In this chapter, I have argued that Practical Realism is superior to the Standard View in its ability to account for collective intentionality. Practical Realism is not forced to adopt a reductive or individualistic strategy, while

---

[17] Baker has recently given an elaborate account of persons in her book *Persons and Bodies; A Constitution View.*

it can incorporate causal explanations of actions that refer to collective beliefs, desires, and intentions.

The ability to account for collective intentional states is also crucial for Practical Realism. In Baker's theory of the attitudes, the notion of *practice* is a core concept. This notion entails the notion of collective intentionality, since practices consist of collective actions, intentions, beliefs, and desires, among other things.

The objection that collective agents do not literally have collective intentional states was rendered harmless by introducing a more fine-grained distinction between the cognitive attitudes of believing and accepting.

I also argued that if Practical Realism is to become a full-blown alternative to the Standard View, it has to be based on a systematic account of relations. Such an account needs to include an analysis of the *relata* of mental phenomena, a topic largely ignored by externalists. Although it claims to be a form of 'radical relationalism', Practical Realism is still 'radically' incomplete in this respect.[18]

References

Baker, L.R. 1987. *Saving Belief; A Critique of Physicalism.* Princeton: Princeton University Press.

Baker, L.R. 1995. *Explaining Attitudes; A Practical Approach to the Mind.* Cambridge: Cambridge University Press.

Baker, L.R. 2000. *Persons and Bodies; A Constitution View.* Cambridge: Cambridge University Press.

Bratman, M. 1993. Practical Reasoning and Accepting in a Context. *Mind* 102, 1-15.

Dretske, F. 1988. *Explaining Behavior: Reasons in a World of Causes.* Cambridge (Mass.): MIT Press.

Engel, P. 1998. Believing, Holding True, and Accepting. *Philosophical Explorations* 1, 140-151.

Engel, P., ed. 2000. *Believing and Accepting.* Dordrecht: Kluwer.

Gilbert, M. 1992. *On Social Facts.* Princeton: Princeton University Press.

Gilbert, M. 1998. In Search of Sociality. *Philosophical Explorations* 3, special issue on social atomism and holism,

Griffin, N. and A.C. Lewis, eds., 1990. *The Collected Papers of Bertrand Russell, Volume II: 1896-1899.* London.

Meijers, A.W.M. 1994. *Speech Acts, Communication and Collective Intentionality; Beyond Searle's Individualism.* Leiden.

---

[18] I am grateful to anonymous referees for their comments on an earlier version of my paper.

Meijers, A.W.M. 1999a. Believing and Accepting as a Group. In Meijers (1999b).

Meijers, A.W.M., ed., 1999b. *Belief, Cognition and the Will.* Studies in General Philosophy of Science 6, Tilburg: Tilburg University Press, 59-71.

Meijers, A.W.M. 2001. Collective Agents and Cognitive Attitudes. *ProtoSociology,* forthcoming.

Russell, B., 1903/1937[2]. *The Principles of Mathematics.* London, 534 pp.

Tuomela, R. 1995. *The* Importance *of Us; A Philosophical Study of Basic Social Notions.* Stanford: Stanford University Press.

Weinberg J.R. 1965. The Concept of Relation: Some Observations on its History. In *Abstraction, Relation and Induction.* Madison, 61-119.

Appendix: The Irreducibility of Relations

With hindsight we may say that the ontology of substance and (nonrelational) attribute has been a real hindrance in the history of philosophy for developing an adequate understanding of the concept of a relation.[19] This ontology forces one to adopt a reductive strategy of relations, since all properties, including relational ones, have to fit the framework. Russell, among others, has effectively refuted reductive strategies. In this Appendix I will recall some of his arguments to this effect.[20] Russell distinguished between two types of reductive theories: The monadistic and the monistic theory. He describes them as follows: '[g]iven, say, the proposition *aRb,* where R is some relation, the monadistic will analyze this into two propositions, which we may call ar_1 and br_2 , which give to a and b respectively adjectives supposed to be together equivalent to R. The monistic view, on the contrary, regards the relation as a property of the whole composed of a and b, is thus equivalent to a proposition which we may denote by *(ab)r.*'[21]

The monadistic theory has difficulties accounting for asymmetrical relations such as *greater than.* According to this theory, there must be *intrinsic* properties that explain why the relation is asymmetrical. Take, for example, two lines L and M which are identical in every respect, except that L

---

[19] J.R. Weinberg, The Concept of Relation: Some Observations on its History.

[20] The principal texts for Russell's views on the irreducibility of relations are: The Classification of Relations (1899), in *The Collected Papers of Bertrand Russell, Volume II: 1896-1899,* eds. N. Griffin and A.C. Lewis, London 1990, 138-146; and *The Principles of Mathematics,* especially the Chapters 'Relations' (95-100), 'Whole and Part' (137-142), 'Asymmetrical Relations' (218-226), and 'Logical Arguments against Points' (445-455). For an account of the development of Russell's views on relations, see Nicolas Griffin, *Russell's Idealist Apprenticeship,* Chapter 8: 'Relation. The End of Russell's Apprenticeship', 314-369.

[21] 'Asymmetrical Relations', 221·

is greater than *M*. This will be analyzed as *L is (greater than M)*. The adjective is complex, consisting of several parts. The part *greater than* by itself does not discriminate between the terms, since *M* will also have this property in some respect. The asymmetry must come therefore from the inclusion of *M* in the predicate *greater than M*. But on analysis this turns out to be a relation in a disguised form, since *greater than M* is an extrinsic predicate instead of an intrinsic one. The original relation is transformed in a relation between extrinsic predicates. The monadistic theory therefore fails.

The monistic theory is equally flawed. It holds that every relational proposition *aRb* is to be resolved into a proposition concerning the whole which *a* and *b* compose. The proposition *a is greater than b* is analyzed, say, as the proposition *(ab) contains diversity of magnitude*. Asymmetrical relations are a source of trouble here again. *(ab)* is symmetrical with regard to *a* and *b*, and thus the property will be exactly the same in the case where *a* is greater than *b* as in the case where *b* is greater than *a*. 'In order to distinguish a whole *(ab)* from a whole *(ba)*, as we must do if we are to explain asymmetry, we shall be forced back from the whole to the parts and their relation.'[22] The monistic theory is thus unable to explain the *sense* of a relation. These and other arguments show that relations cannot be reduced to intrinsic properties. They belong to a separate ontological category.

---

[22] Ibid., 225.

10

Practical Realism Defended: Replies to Critics

Lynne Rudder Baker

I wish to begin by thanking the contributors to this volume, who have put so much energy into reading my work, criticizing it and making helpful suggestions. Instead of engaging in tedious point-by-point combat, I shall organize my replies around a number of topics that, I trust, will be of interest to the general philosophical community. In this way, I hope not only to answer criticisms and to clear up misinterpretations, but also to further philosophical discussion about the attitudes. One dominant theme, shared by a number of my critics, is this: Belief-explanations, and macro-explanations generally, 'cannot just stand on their own,' as Meyering (p. 131) put it. I shall discuss variations on this theme under several of the topics.

The topics that I shall consider are these: (1) Causal Explanatoriness of the Attitudes (Dretske, Elugardo); (2) The 'Brain-Explain' Thesis and Metaphysical Constraints on Explanation (Antony, Elugardo); (3) Causal Powers of Beliefs (Meyering); (4) Microreduction (Beckermann); (5) Non-Emergent, Non-Reductive Materialism (Antony); (6) The Master Argument Against the Standard View (Dretske, Antony, Elugardo); (7) Relational Properties and Context-Dependency (Newen); and (8) Practical Realism Extended (Meijers).

Before turning to these topics, however, let me clear up a point on which Dretske misinterprets Practical Realism and its difference from the

Explaining Beliefs: Lynne Rudder Baker and Her Critics.
Anthonie Meijers (ed.).
Copyright © 2001, CSLI Publications.

Standard View. According to Practical Realism, believing that p is in the first instance a complex property of a person; what makes it the case that a person believes that p is determined entirely by what that person would do, say or think in various circumstances. The term 'belief' is a nominalization of 'believes that.' Beliefs are not entities that are located at one place 'inside' or 'outside' a person. So it is misleading to say, as Dretske does, that according to Practical Realism, beliefs are 'outside where the observable facts are that are used to tell what people believe and desire.' (Dretske, p. 39) The question of *where* a belief is arises only if one (mis)takes beliefs to be entities, as Standard Viewers do. Although Dretske's 'observable facts' are partly constitutive of S's believing that p, conditions inside S's skin may also be partly constitutive of her having that property. A person's property of believing that p is a relational property 'located' where the person is - just as the relational property of promising to do A is 'located' where the promiser is. In neither case - the case of believing that p or of promising to do A - does it follow that one's internal states are irrelevant to one's having the property in question.

The main difference between Practical Realism and the Standard View is that, according to the Standard View, each belief has a specific location in the brain. That is, on the Standard View, for each instance of a belief, there is a particular neural configuration or token (perhaps 'distributed') that is identical to, or constitutes, that belief. Roughly, the externalist Standard Viewer takes a neural token to be a belief that p partly in virtue of its relations to features of the environment; whereas the internalist Standard Viewer takes a neural token to be a belief that p solely in virtue of the intrinsic properties of the believer. Although the Practical Realist agrees with the externalist Standard Viewer in 'locat(ing) the facts that make mental states mental in [a] network of external facts,' the Practical Realist disagrees with both the externalist and the internalist Standard Viewer in supposing that each belief has a location in the brain. According to any version of the Standard View, beliefs have tokens that are spatiotemporal entities. According to Practical Realism, there are no such *things* as beliefs; rather, believing that p is a relational property of persons.

Of course, the mere fact that believing that p is a relational property does not by itself prevent beliefs from having specific locations in brains. As Dretske points out, what makes the paper in my pocket money are its relational properties; but it is located in my pocket nonetheless. He asks: Why 'cannot we locate the mind in the body (just as we keep our money in our pocket), but locate the facts that make mental states mental...in that network of external - including historical - facts that exist (partially, at least) outside a person (at the time he has the belief)?' (Dretske, p. 42) I do not lack an answer. My answer is that, we can say that our minds are in our bodies (in some metaphorical sense of 'in'); but our mental states do not have specific locations in our bodies - in our brains or kidneys, say. Although minds are like money in that they are what they are in virtue of their relational properties, minds are unlike money in another respect: whereas we can identify a particular piece of metal as a coin of a particular value, we have no way to identify a particular internal-physical-state token as a particular belief token. One's mind (or brain) is not like one's pocket, full of discrete items that can be identified in terms of relational properties like being a U.S. quarter. Now on to the actual arguments.

1   The Causal Explanatoriness of the Attitudes (Dretske, Elugardo)

Dretske takes me to task for my attempts to deal with how attitudes causally explain behavior. He argues that 'beliefs must be brain states in order to explain behavior. He says that beliefs are states that explain the behavior of the person they are states of, and there is no way they can do this unless they exist in (or are states of) the motor control centers - the brain.' (Dretske, p. 42) For reasons that I give in Part II of *Explaining Attitudes*, I think that Dretske's point rests on an erroneous conception of causal explanation. There are no metaphysical constraints on causes. Causes are what successful causal explanations cite. Although I have no analysis of 'causal explanation,' I do provide a bare sufficient condition for an occurrence of one property to explain the occurrence of another property. (*Explaining Attitudes*, p. 122). In general, 'x's having F causally explains y's having G (in the circumstances)' does not entail that the instantiation of F be locatable in some particular place inside x. In particular, 'S's believing that p causally explains S's doing A (in the circumstances)' does not entail that there be anything locatable inside S that *is* a belief that p. To say otherwise, I think, is covertly to place a gratuitous metaphysical constraint on what can be a cause.

Dretske continues: If beliefs are to 'control' bodily movements, then 'you need them *inside* with their hand on the steering wheel.' (Dretske, p. 43) But everything here depends on what is meant by 'control.' I take control to be subordinate to causal explanation. So, if beliefs causally explain (certain) bodily movements, then ipso facto beliefs control those movements. And S's belief causally explains a bodily motion if the following is the case: If S had not had the belief, then S's body would not have moved as it did; and given that S had the belief, then it was assured in the circumstances that S's body moved as it did.

To say that a belief explains Clyde's going to the refrigerator is not to say that there is a particular entity in Clyde's brain, called a 'belief,' that reaches out into the body, so to speak, to pick up and set down legs in the direction of the refrigerator. Rather, a belief that there's beer in the refrigerator explains Clyde's behavior when the behavior is a manifestation of a disposition (e.g., If x wanted a beer, then, other things being equal, x would go to the refrigerator) such that (a) it is one of a set of dispositions that constitute Clyde's believing that there is beer in the refrigerator, and (b) Clyde would not have gone to the refrigerator (other things being equal) if he had not had a set of dispositions that constitute his believing that there is beer in the refrigerator. A necessary condition for Clyde to go to the refrigerator is that his body moves in a certain way, and a necessary condition for Clyde's body to move in the relevant ways is that there be certain neural processes that produce the relevant motions. But these necessary conditions would not have obtained if Clyde had not believed that there was beer in the refrigerator.[1]

Dretske thinks that the account that I give of how attitudes explain behavior at the end of 'Are Beliefs Brain States?' is circular. (Dretske, p. 48-49) So, let me try again. According to the Standard View, if a desire to improve one's social status causally explains one's writing of a check, then one was in a brain state at the time of the writing of the check that just *was* the desire to improve one's social status. I can (and do!) deny this conditional; but I need not (and do not) deny that brains produce bodily motions. If a neural process causes a bodily motion that constitutes, say, a writing of a check, there need be no distinct element in that neural process that is identifiable as a desire to improve one's social status. Yet, on my view, the causal explanation of one's writing of the check may well be that one wanted to improve one's social status.

Let me explain. If one had not wanted to improve one's social status, one's brain would not have moved one's hand in that way at that time. Now the huge unsolved problem is how a person's intentional dispositions (e.g., to improve one's social status) are coordinated with a person's brain's dispositions to go into certain sequences of states (e.g., states that move the hand). Somehow, by mechanisms that I do not think are at all understood, there is coordination of dispositions of the person and dispositions of the brain. A person's disposition to write checks in certain circumstances in order to improve social status is tied to a disposition of the person's brain to move the hand in certain ways in certain circumstances. Even though we have no account of the connection between these disparate dispositions, we do know two things: (a) we know that such coordination exists since part of

---

[1] I spell this out in much greater detail in 'What We Do: A Nonreductive Approach to Human Action' in *Human Action, Deliberation and Causation*, Jan Bransen and Stefaan Cuypers, eds. (Dordrecht Holland: Kluwer Academic Publishers, 1998).

the criterion for wanting to improve one's social status is that one be disposed to do what one thinks will improve one's social status in various circumstances, and one cannot be disposed to do what one thinks will improve one's social status in various circumstances unless one's body moves appropriately in certain circumstances; and (b) however the coordination is effected, it does not require that there be any particular brain state that can be identified with a desire to improve one's social status.

Now let met turn more specifically to the charge of circularity. First, since I am not trying to give 'a reason to introduce attitudes,' there is just no space for circularity. Attitudes, in my opinion, are not 'introduced,' as, say, electrons are. Attitudes are part and parcel of the entire commonsense framework by means of which one makes it through the day. Second, I want to respond to the charge that 'the pattern we need the attitudes to explain is only a pattern that is created by the attitude explanation.' (Dretske, p. 46) To see that this is not a consequence of my view, consider our attribution of character traits. Suppose that inspection of Frank's verbal behavior reveals a pattern of telling the truth, even when it would be to Frank's advantage to lie. We may explain this pattern by saying any of the following: Frank has a policy of not saying what he believes to be false, or Frank is just trying to win our confidence so that he can defraud us later, or Frank does not realize when it is to his advantage to lie. But the behavioral pattern of telling the truth is not 'created by the attitude explanation.' The behavioral pattern is there independently of any explanation. Indeed, there is room for rational disagreement about the explanation of Frank's truthtelling. So, it is incorrect to charge that 'the pattern we need the attitudes to explain is only a pattern that is created by the attitude explanation.' (Dretske, p. 46)

I take it to be obvious that what one believes affects what one does. As I have argued in several places, I do not think that proponents of the Standard View have a satisfactory account of this fact. The only proponent of the Standard View who tells a remotely plausible story about the causal relevance of beliefs is Dretske himself.[2] But even Dretske admits that his view 'does not make what is believed and what is desired (i.e., content) relevant to what we do....' (Dretske, p. 45) So, I do not think that the Standard View has a thing over Practical Realism in terms of showing how what one believes affects what one does.

---

[2] See, Fred Dretske, *Explaining Behavior: Reasons in a World of Causes* (Cambridge MA: MIT/Bradford Books, 1988). I criticized his account in 'Dretske on the Explanatory Role of Belief,' *Philosophical Studies* 63 (1991): 99-112, to which Dretske replied in 'How Beliefs Explain: Reply to Baker,' *Philosophical Studies* 63 (1991): 113-117. See also my response to Dretske's reply in *Explaining Attitudes*, pp. 57-62.

Let me conclude this section by responding to two of Elugardo's points (Elugardo, p. 111) about my view of the causal explanatoriness of belief. In *Explaining Attitudes*, I gave three conditions for an explanation (pre-theoretically) to be a causal explanation. Elugardo offers a counterexample. He says that the following satisfies the three conditions, but is not a causal explanation:

> The Elugardo Thanksgiving feast was held at [Ray Elugardo's] house in 1996 because it was [his] turn to host it.' I'll bite the bullet: This is a causal explanation - albeit not a very informative one. The reason that Elugardo thinks that this is not a causal explanation is that the 'fact that it was [his] turn to host it does not causally trace the fact that the dinner was held at [his] house on Thanksgiving Day, 1996. (Elugardo, p. 113)

I have two comments: (a) The purported explanation does cite an event that is in the causal history of the dinner: its being Elugardo's turn to host the dinner led to Elugardo's belief that it was his turn to host the dinner; since Elugardo is a dutiful family member, his belief that it was his turn to host the dinner led to the dinner's being at his house. So, in fact, we can trace a causal path from its being Elugardo's turn to host the dinner to the dinner's being at his house. (b) Whether or not a causal explanation allows us to trace a casual path through space and time from *explanans* to *explanandum* is irrelevant anyway. Think of social, political and economic explanations; we can know *that* one thing makes a difference to another without any idea about *how* it makes a difference. For example, you can know that the gnomic sayings of Allen Greenspan, Chairman of the Federal Reserve, make a difference to your prospects for a job in business without being able to trace a causal path from Greenspan's mouth to the person who hires you.

Elugardo has another counterexample - this one directed toward the Control Thesis. Here is the Control Thesis:

> An occurrence of F in context C causally explains an occurrence of G if: (i) if an F had not occurred in C, then a G would not have occurred in C; and (ii) given that F did occur in C, an occurrence of G was inevitable. (EA, 122)

Here is the counterexample in full:

> Imagine that my brother and I live in the same apartment. He is blind but can hear; I am deaf but I am sighted. To help us know when someone is at the door, the apartment is electrically wired in such a way that our door-bell will ring when and only when the light bulb in our doorway, which is always on, glows dim and bright in an alternating pattern. Because of the internal circuitry, the correlation between the doorbell ring and the light bulb glowing holds as a matter of law. Consequently, you cannot cause the light bulb to alternate between dim light and bright light by pressing the doorbell without also bringing about a situation in which my brother's

eardrums vibrate (when he is home, within earshot, etc.). For, as a matter of law, doing the first is nominally correlated in this context with causing the doorbell to ring, which in turn normally causes my brother's eardrums to vibrate. We may suppose that the doorbell ringing is the only cause of the vibrations in this context. Therefore, given the facts of the case, if the light bulb had not dimmed and then glowed brightly, my brother's eardrums would not have vibrated. And, given that the light bulb did glow in this pattern, the vibration of my brother's eardrums was inevitable. (Elugardo, p. 114)

According to the Control Thesis, then, the light's dimming and brightening causally explains the vibrations in the ear of the blind person who can hear. But, Elugardo says, 'causing the light to alternate between dimness and brightness does not causally explain why my brother's eardrums vibrate in that context.' (Elugardo, p. 115)

Given the context-dependence of causal explanation and the peculiarities of the context with the odd wiring, it is not at all obvious that we should disallow the lights alternating between dimness and brightness in a causal explanation of the vibrating in the brother's ears. The only reason that Elugardo offers for denying that the alternating dimness and brightness causally explains the brother's eardrums' is that 'there is no causal path that traces the second kind of event [eardrum's vibrating] back to the first [alternating dimness and brightness] without bypassing the causal connection between the sound of the doorbell ringing and my brother's eardrums vibrating.' But, is this so? The eardrums' vibrating is caused by the doorbell's ringing, which is caused by (nominally connected to) the alternating dimming and brightening of the light, which is caused by the pressing of the doorbell.

Since we are taking the peculiarities of the wiring to be part of the context (and thus fixed), any event along this path is a causal explanation of the eardrums' vibrating in this context. We have here a predictive / explanatory pattern (i.e., a counterfactual-supporting pattern). As Dennett has said, when one finds a certain kind of predictive pattern, 'one has ipso facto discovered a causal power - a difference in the world that makes a subsequent difference testable by standard empirical methods of variable manipulation.'[3] Instead of showing that there is something wrong with the Control Thesis, Elugardo furnished an unusual case of causal explanation.[4]

---

[3] Daniel Dennett, 'Real Patterns,' *Brainchildren: Essays on Designing Minds* (Cambridge MA: MIT/Bradford, 1998): 112.

[4] For more on causal explanation, see Chs. 4 and 5 of EA, and my 'Metaphysics and Mental Causation' in *Mental Causation*, John Heil and Alfred Mele, eds. (Oxford: Clarendon Press, 1993): 75-95.

2   The 'Brain-Explain' Thesis and Metaphysical Constraints on Explanation (Antony, Elugardo)

Perhaps the most persuasive argument for the Standard View is the argument from causal explanation, which I argued is unsound. Its first premise is the 'brain-explain' thesis:

> IIIa.   Unless beliefs were brain states they could not causally explain behavior.

I attack IIIa in part by means of a thought experiment: If it had turned out that our world was an Aristotelian world, then beliefs would not be brain states. Yet we would have the same causal explanations; beliefs would causally explain behavior in exactly the same way that they do in our world. So, the causal explanatoriness of beliefs does not depend upon their being brain states. Both Antony and Elugardo take issue with my argument. Consider Antony first.

Antony distinguishes between a strong and a weak reading of IIIa, and says that the thought experiment does not refute IIIa on the weak reading.. The weak reading is this:

> IIIa-weak: In any possible world in which beliefs are explanatory, beliefs are physically realized internal states, and in this world those states are brain states. (Antony, p. 76)

It is true that I did not distinguish strong and weak versions of IIIa, but the thought experiment also works to refute IIIa-weak. Suppose that the world had turned out to be an Aristotelian world. (If, as I argued earlier, the Standard View is not necessarily true, then there are no grounds for disallowing that an Aristotelian view is merely possible.) In an Aristotelian world, there is no more reason to think that each instance of each belief is realized by a particular token of a physical internal state than there is to think that each instance of each belief is realized by a particular token of a brain state. It is not as though, had Aristotle been correct, each instance of each belief would be realized, not by a brain state token, but by a token of some other physical-internal state. Aristotle's view is not one that matches up particular instances of mental states with particular tokens of internal physical states, whether the internal physical states are brain states or something else. So, construing 'physical realization' in a way that distinguishes Antony's view from mine, she is just mistaken when she says that the thought experiment about the Aristotelian world 'does not show that beliefs could be explanatory even if they failed to be physically realized *at all*.' (Antony, p. 77)

Antony reformulates the argument that has IIIa as a premise and replaces IIIa with:

1 Unless beliefs were *realized by some kind of physical states*, they could not causally explain behavior. (Antony, p. 77)

With respect to this reformulated argument she has, 'It is clear that the conceivability of an Aristotelian world has no bearing whatsoever on premise (1), which replaces Baker's (IIIa).' (Antony, p. 78) But I was not just proposing that an Aristotelian world is conceivable. Assuming that an Aristotelian world is conceivable, my claim was that had an Aristotelian world been actual, beliefs would still be explanatory without being brain states. From an Aristotelian point of view, beliefs are no more physically realized internal states that are not brain states than they are brain states. So, Antony's reformulated argument is as unsound as the original. For the Aristotelian thought experiment applies to the first premise of her reformulated argument - just as it does to IIIa.

Referring to the argument against IIIa, Antony says that 'the argument does not show that brain states do not *constitute* or *realize* beliefs in the actual world.' Of course, it does not. But the argument against IIIa was not supposed to show that brain states do not constitute or realize beliefs in the actual world. IIIa is a premise in an argument for the Standard View, the argument from causal explanation. My rebuttal of IIIa shows that that particularly tenacious argument for the Standard View is unsound. Nothing more was intended.

Let me elaborate by looking at Antony's example of the explanation of the water's boiling in terms of sufficient heat. (Antony, p. 79-80) She agrees that in an Aristotelian world, an explanation of the boiling of (the stuff that is phenomenologically just like) water in terms of sufficient heat would still be justified. And it 'is up to further investigation to determine what precisely are the mechanisms, if any, that sustain the regularity.' But, she continues, 'none of this has any bearing on the claim that in *this* world, water is H_2O.' Right. But, again, that's not the point. The immediate point is, as Antony has just conceded, that the explanation of the boiling in terms of the heat does not require that (the stuff phenomenologically just like) water be H_2O. I am here trying to reveal as unsound the argument for the Standard View that has as a premise the claim that in order to be explanatory, beliefs must be brain states. Refutation of the Argument from Causal Explanation does not show that beliefs are not brain states; it only shows that one central and tenacious argument for the view that beliefs are brain states is unsound.

Now turn to Elugardo's criticisms of IIIa. - the 'brain-explain' thesis. From now on, I shall use Elugardo's label, '(BET)', for IIIa. So,

(BET) [=IIIa.]   ...[U]nless beliefs were (either identical to or constituted by) brain states, they could not causally explain behavior.

Elugardo objects to the thought experiment about the Aristotelian world. He says that, proponents of the Standard View understand causal explanations in the sense of Aristotle's efficient causation; but if our world had turned out to be Aristotelian, then our belief-explanations would not be causal in the Aristotelian world in the sense of efficient causation. To this, I reply: I was not speaking of Aristotle's view on causation, but ours (whatever that is). If we do not accept Aristotle's four causes, we need not settle on which of the four causes belief explanations invoke. My point was that if we lived in an Aristotelian world in which beliefs are not brain states, then our belief explanations would be causally explanatory to the same degree and in whatever sense that they are now. My argument about the sense in which they are causally explanatory - namely, that they reliably satisfy our explanatory and predictive interests by supporting relevant counterfactuals - is not Aristotelian.

In addition to my argument based on the thought experiment about the Aristotelian world, I argued against (BET) by showing that the general conception of causal explanation that underwrites it is untenable. On Elugardo's recounting, I argued against (BET) on the grounds that it entails a false thesis, (RT):

(RT)   All belief explanations are replaceable by brain-state explanations of the same phenomena.

The claim that (BET) entails (RT) can be restated as what Elugardo calls 'Baker's Premise:' 'If beliefs could not causally explain behavior unless they were either identical with or constituted by brain states, then belief explanations are replaceable by brain-state explanations of the same phenomena.' (Elugardo, p. 105)

Elugardo has an argument against Baker's Premise. He offers a counterexample that just assumes a view that I argued at length was false - namely, the view that an explanation of the destruction of a store by the fact that the building had been set on fire 'metaphysically depends for its causal explanatory power on a deeper explanation that appeals to molecular facts about fires and buildings, soluble goods, etc., and their causal relations.' Since in *Explaining Attitudes*, Chs. 4 and 5, I argued against this approach to causal explanatoriness, I would reject Elugardo's argument here as question-begging. Nevertheless, Elugardo and others (e.g., Antony) have raised enough doubts about 'Baker's Premise' that if I were writing this section today, I would avoid the premise and stick to the argument based on the thought experiment about an Aristotelian world and the argument from the general character of causal explanation.

One reason that defenders of the Standard View are so ardent about the 'brain-explain' thesis is that, either implicitly or explicitly, they impose metaphysical constraints on causal explanations. (cf. Beckermann, Meyering) My rejection of such metaphysical constraints in favor of a more pragmatic approach marks a deep methodological divide between Standard Viewers of any stripe and me. For example, consider Antony's relatively weak version of the Standard View.

Antony and I agree that we do not need to know anything about underlying mechanisms in order to have causal explanations. For example, the highway patrol officer asks you why you were speeding, and you give the true answer that you are late for a meeting. At this point, Antony and I part ways. For Antony takes it to be a metaphysical requirement that 'in order to be a genuine cause of behavior a belief must be (either identical to or realized in) a brain state.' (Antony, p. 79) No doubt there are many underlying mechanisms at work in your brain, but there is no reason to suppose that any particular state of any underlying neural mechanism can be identified with this instance of a belief that you are late for a meeting. The apparent need to impose metaphysical preconditions on belief-explanations stems from acceptance of a comprehensive metaphysical picture - a picture that, in my opinion, is unwarranted. In contrast to those who accept that metaphysical picture, I see no reason to posit metaphysical preconditions that - if the Empirical Conjecture is correct - are undetectable. (And in making that point I am not misinterpreting Antony's Non-Emergent Non-Reductive Materialism.)

So, I am in full agreement with Antony's insistence that ' *(k)nowledge of* the metaphysical preconditions for constituting a cause is never a prerequisite for finding acceptable a proffered causal explanation.' (Antony, p. 78) I also concur that the epistemology of explanation, on which we agree, 'is perfectly consistent with the metaphysical thesis that in order to be a genuine cause of behavior a belief must be (either identical to or realized in) a brain state.' (Antony, p. 79) But consistency is not the issue in the debate over the Standard View. The issue is whether or not we are justified in endorsing some version of 'beliefs as brain states' as a particular metaphysical precondition on belief-explanations. Since all versions of 'beliefs are brain states' are subject to empirical (dis)confirmation - and if the Empirical Conjecture is correct, they will be disconfirmed - it seems risky to me (but not to Antony) to push any version of this doctrine as a metaphysical constraint on belief-explanations.

3 The Causal Powers of Beliefs (Meyering)

Much, if not most, of the disagreement between Meyering and me stems from our different conceptions of causation and causal explanation. There are two main areas of disagreement: (A) On my view, explanatory properties do not need to be locally supervenient on the microproperties of their bearers; i.e., relational properties can be causally explanatory. (B) On my view, a macro-explanation does not need to be buttressed by a micro-explanation to be successful.

A. Professor Meyering provides a forceful argument that causal explanations invoke causal powers that supervene on local microstructure. He quotes McGinn as saying: '[T]he causal powers of a state must be intrinsically grounded; they cannot depend essentially upon relations to what lies quite elsewhere.' Then, Meyering asks pointedly, 'How does Baker propose to address this issue?' (Meyering, p. 123)

Like this: It is just false that causal explanations must invoke causal powers that supervene on local microstructure. If it were true, then much of what we care to explain would fall outside the purview of causal explanation altogether. The kinds of causal explanations of behavior that we actually have typically do not invoke properties that are intrinsically grounded, or that supervene on local microstructure. This is obvious when we look at the *explananda* of interest. The behavior that we want to explain is almost always individuated relationally: Why did the judge dismiss Paula Jones's lawsuit against President Clinton? Why did Professor X vote to hire a person of marginal competence? - Why did John buy a ticket to Rio? No intrinsic properties of the judge or of Professor X or of John could possibly bring about the dismissal of a lawsuit, the vote to hire somebody, or the buying of a ticket to Rio. So, we know in advance that either (a) the properties invoked by causal explanations of ordinary behavior will not supervene on local microstructure, or (b) there are no causal explanations of ordinary behavior.

It is clear that Professor Meyering and I have different basic conceptions of causal explanation and causation. Although he quotes with approval my view that 'theory and practice must be brought into reflective equilibrium,' he seems to think that there is a tension between that view and my rejection of the proposed a priori metaphysical standards of explanatory adequacy. I see no tension here. Taking local supervenience as a constraint on causal explanations would simply rule out the possibility of there being causal explanations of ordinary behavior at all. This is so, once again, because ordinary behavior is itself individuated relationally. So, there is no prospect of reflective equilibrium between taking local supervenience as a metaphysical constraint on causal explanations and any practices of causally explaining ordinary behavior. Therefore, rejection of the local-supervenience constraint is not rejection of reflective equilibrium between theory and practice. Rather, acceptance of the local-supervenience constraint is rejection of causal explanations of behavior in the terms that interest us.

Notice that my line of argument depends on how *explananda* are individuated: Ordinary behavior, for which we want causal explanations, is not individuated in terms of intrinsic properties of the agent. It is not surprising that properties that explain ordinary behavior are not individuated narrowly when what they explain is not individuated narrowly. This line of argument is somewhat different from the familiar arguments about Twin Earth cases. So, I am not relying on the assumption that 'just any belief sentence is susceptible to Twin Earth examples.' (Meyering, p. 127)

Meyering distinguishes between 'the problem of here-and-now causal efficacy, as opposed to that of causal relevance in some wide sense.' What he calls 'the problem of causal efficacy' concerns 'the question which properties of my internal states here-and-now are causally responsible for making my arm move, or whatever. And an answer to this question must surely advert to local properties of my internal states.' (Meyering, p. 127) If the question were, which properties here-and-now bring it about that your arm moves, then I would agree with Meyering that we advert to local properties of my internal states. But that question has almost nothing to do with our concerns to explain behavior. We rarely want to know why your arm moved; we want to know why you voted a certain way - no matter how the vote was taken, whether by raising your hand, or writing on a ballot, or something else. Focusing on the local properties of the internal states that are causally responsible for making your arm move will never yield a causal explanation of your vote. If your vote has any causal explanation, it is not in terms of properties that supervene on your local microstructure. So, to insist on the local-supervenience constraint for causal explanation is to give up on causal explanation of ordinary behavior altogether.

To call rejection of a local-supervenience constraint 'action-at-a-distance obscurantism' (Meyering, p. 125) is simply to use loaded language. And this loaded language is unjustified in light of the fact that the local-supervenience constraint on causal explanation itself has the consequence that ordinary behavior would have no causal explanation at all. Moreover, we all accept explanations that Meyering would describe as 'action at a distance.' For example, why did not B, who was the most qualified applicant, get the job? The explanation is that A started rumors about B, and the potential employer, who believed the rumors, decided not to hire B. Whether or not this is a good causal explanation has nothing to do with whether or not there is a sequence of events beginning with events in A's body and ending with some event in B's body. A can injure B without ever having any physical connection with B.

We no more need narrow psychological explanations (explanations on the basis of intrinsic properties of the individuals whose behavior is to be explained) than we need narrow economic explanations. No one demands narrow economic causation: we can explain why Jones's money went to the ABC pension fund by citing the facts that Jones is a state employee and that payments to the ABC pension fund are automatically taken out of state employees' paychecks. Although the property of being a state employee - which causally explains the diversion of Jones's money to the ABC pension fund - is not an intrinsic property of anybody, no one is tempted to think of economic explanations as tainted. Relational psychological properties are no more suspect than are relational economic properties.

B. Meyering, like many other Standard Viewers, believes that macroexplanations 'cannot just stand on their own.' (Meyering, p. 130) Although Meyering does not reject the explanatory legitimacy of macro-explanations, he says: 'Whenever macro-explanations are being offered, there is always a warranted presumption that in principle a more detailed account can be given of the causal powers of the macroproperties invoked in terms of some relevant implementing mechanisms operative at the next level down in some more or less determinate functional hierarchy of sciences and their respective domains.' (Meyering, p. 130) What Meyering describes here is a very substantial metaphysical view that I do not share. My view is this: Domains of different sciences may or may not be nested in the way that Meyering's view requires. Reduction is where you find it. You have to look and see. There are no guarantees in advance about the unity of science. I do have a further conjecture: If the sciences do turn out to be unified in the way that Meyering suggests, then many things for which we want causal explanations will not be explainable by any of the sciences.

Since Meyering says that I endorse a thesis of 'radical autonomy for intentional psychology,' let me say again what my view is. I do not hold that any old type of intentional explanation is impervious to the findings of neuroscience. However, I do believe that no future discovery of neuroscience could force us to abandon our global intentional explanatory frameworks. The basis for my belief is not the theological caricature that Meyering proposes at the end of his paper, but is the fact that we - scientists and nonscientists alike - are enmeshed in a comprehensive commonsensical framework, without which science itself would be impossible. Since I give arguments for my outlook both in *Saving Belief* and in *Explaining Attitudes*, I will not rehearse them here.

4 Microreduction (Beckermann)

Beckermann appeals to considerations of the generality of microphysics in defense of the Standard View, as he construes it. He construes the Standard View as the following thesis: Mental properties are either identical with or reducible to physical properties. This characterization of the Standard View is much stronger than mine. Many philosophers who are proponents of the Standard View in my sense - e.g., functionalists, philosophers in Jerry Fodor's camp - would deny that mental properties are either identical with or reducible to physical properties. For example, Jerry Fodor gives a spirited argument against reductionism in 'Special Sciences.'[5] Fodor holds that every instance of a mental property is an instance of some physical property or other; but he denies that for every mental property M, there is a physical property P such that every instance of M is an instance of P. That is, Fodor denies that mental properties are either identical with or reducible to (in a familiar and intuitive sense) physical properties. And of the Standard-View contributors to this volume, Antony, Dretske and Elugardo would reject both identity and reduction of mental properties to physical properties.

So, my construal of the Standard View is more encompassing than is Beckermann's. But what is important are the positions in question, not which ones that we assign a certain label like 'Standard View.' Since Beckermann argues for a reductionist view, he would reject the nonreductive view that belief-tokens are merely constituted by neural tokens, no matter what the view is called. Since I oppose both nonreductive and reductive versions of 'beliefs are brain states,' I continue to prefer my broader characterization of the Standard View. Nevertheless, Beckermann's construal of the Standard View is at least part of what I consider the Standard View. So, I want to discuss Beckermann's thesis that I shall call '(BC),' short for 'Beckermann's Construal of the Standard View:'

(BC)   Mental properties are either identical with or reducible to physical properties.

Beckermann gives a careful account of (BC), by defining 'identity' and 'reducibility.' He begins with C.D. Broad's distinction between mechani-

---

[5] Jerry Fodor, 'Special Sciences' in *Representations* (Cambridge MA: MIT/Bradford, 1981): 127-145.

cally explainable properties and emergent properties, which he summarizes in two definitions, (ME) and (E)). This 'distinction between mechanically explainable and emergent properties,' says Beckermann, 'far better captures the intuitive difference between reducible properties and properties that cannot be reduced to more fundamental properties much better than all other accounts have been able to....' (Beckermann, p. 59)

I do not think that Broad's distinction between mechanically explainable and emergent properties does capture the intuitive difference between reducible and irreducible properties. For one thing, the reducible/irreducible distinction is exhaustive (every property is one or the other); but the mechanically-explainable/emergent distinction is not exhaustive. To see this, note that (ME) and (E) have the same first clause, (a): 'The statement 'For all x: if x has the microstructure $[C_1, ...,C_n; R]$, then x has the macroproperty F' is a true law of nature,' where x has the microstructural property $[C_1, ...,C_n; R]$ if and only if x consists of the parts $C_1, ...,C_n$ which stand in the (spatial) relation R to each other. (Beckermann, footnote 6) So, if there is a system that has macroproperty F, and that consists of the parts $C_1, ...,C_n$ standing in the (spatial) relation R to each other, and if there is no law of nature of the relevant form, then the property F is neither mechanically explainable nor emergent.

Now consider the property of being married. There is no true law of nature that says: 'For all x: if x has the microstructural property $[C_1, ...,C_n, R]$, then x has the macroproperty of being married.' Therefore, the property of being married is neither mechanically explainable nor emergent, according the definitions (ME) and (E). But the property of being married, like every other property, is either reducible or irreducible. So, the intuitive difference between reducible and irreducible properties is not adequately reflected in the distinction between mechanically explainable and emergent properties.

On Beckermann's account of reducibility, (R), a condition for macroproperty F of a system S at t to be reducible to a microstructural property $[C_1, ...,C_n, R]$ is this: 'it follows from the general laws of nature applying to the components $C_1, ...,C_n$, that S at t possesses all features which are characteristic of property F.' (Beckermann, p. 59) Since it does not follow from the laws of nature that anyone with components $C_1,...C_n$ in a certain spatial arrangement is married, the property of being married is not reducible to microstructural properties.

Now consider the mental property of believing that some people are married. According to (BC), the mental property of believing that some people are married is identical with or reducible to a physical property, in Beckermann's sense of reducibility, (R). On (R), if S's believing that some people are married is reducible, then 'it follows from the general laws of nature applying to the components $C_1,...C_n$ that S at t possesses all features which are characteristic of the property' of believing that some people are married.

It seems implausible to suppose that S's having the property of believing that some people are married follows from general laws of nature applying to S's microstructure. For a necessary condition for S to have the property of believing that some people are married is that S have the concept of *being married*. But S can have the concept of being married only in certain social environments, where there are conventions and civil laws. (It's not on account of the fundamental properties of the particles that make up a dog's brain, say, that a dog lacks the property of believing that some people are married.)

So, I do not think that S's believing that some people are married follows from general laws of nature applying to S's components. If that is right, then the property of believing that some people are married is a mental property that is not reducible (in Beckermann's sense) to physical properties. And if it is not so reducible, it is not identical to physical properties either. And if there is a mental property that is neither identical with nor reducible to physical properties, then (BC) is false.

In sum, Beckermann construes the Standard View to be the thesis (BC): all mental properties are identical with or reducible to physical properties, where he understands 'physical properties' nonrelationally. The property of believing that some people are married is a mental property that is neither identical with nor reducible to physical properties in the sense of Beckermann's (R). So, here is a counterexample that falsifies the Standard View as Beckermann construes it. Now let us turn to Beckermann's general metaphysical argument in support of the Standard View as he construes it.

Beckermann calls his general metaphysical argument for (his version of) the Standard View the 'argument from the implausibility of downward causation.' Here is a reconstruction of the argument:

> If (BC) were false, then 'mental properties would at least be emergent, i.e., properties that, even in principle could not be deduced from the parts of the organisms that are their bearers.' (Beckermann, p. 62)
> If any properties are emergent, then there is a gap in nuclear physics: 'atoms are sometimes moved by forces the existence of which cannot be derived from the general laws of nuclear physics.' (Beckermann, p. 63)

Such a gap is implausible. Therefore,

> We have good reason to think that] (BC) is true.

This argument raises very large metaphysical issues that I cannot fully address here. So, I shall focus rather narrowly on this argument (1) - (4). First, I shall comment on the use of the term 'emergent.' The term 'emergent' was defined by (E). (E) has two clauses. A property's being such that 'even in principle [it] could not be deduced from the parts of the organism[] that [is] its bearer' is only a necessary, not a sufficient condition for the property's being emergent according to (E). If we interpret 'emergent' in (1) as it was defined by (E), then (1) is false. For if there is a mental property that is neither identical with nor reducible to physical properties, then (BC) is false. And the antecedent of (1) is true. But it does not follow that mental properties are emergent in the sense of (E). For the definitions of emergence and reduction - (E) and (R) - that Beckermann gives are not exhaustive: a property may fail to be *both* emergent and reducible. And the property of believing that some people are married is such a property. Earlier, I argued that the property of believing that some people are married is not reducible in the sense of (R); and it is not emergent in the sense of (E) for the same reason: There is no true law of the form: 'For all x: if x has the microstructure $[C_1,...,C_n; R]$, then x has the macroproperty of believing that some people are married.' So, on the definition of 'emergence' that Beckermann gives, it is incorrect to suppose that denial of (BC) commits one to the existence of emergent properties in the sense of (E). So, given (E), premise (1) is false.

However, in his general metaphysical argument, Beckermann regards emergent properties as 'properties that, even in principle, could not be deduced from the properties of the parts of the organisms that are their bearers.' And I do hold that mental properties are not deducible from the (nonrelational) properties of the parts of the organisms that have the mental properties. Now according to (2), this view would have the consequence that there would be a gap in nuclear physics. The putative gap is that 'atoms are sometimes moved by forces the existence of which cannot be derived from the general laws of nuclear physics.' I want to show that my view, according to which mental properties are not deducible from the (nonrelational) properties of the parts of the organisms that have the mental properties, does not entail that there is an implausible gap in nuclear physics.

Beckermann is correct to say that I claim that many properties are such that even in principle they could not be deduced from the microstructural properties of the parts of their bearers. But it does not follow from this that such properties could not be deduced from *any* microstructural properties. For example, it is consistent with my view that both (i) the property of believing that some people are married is not deducible from properties of the believer's microstructure, and (ii) the property of believing that some people are married is deducible from the properties of the believer's microstructure together with other microphysical properties borne by other things in the believer's social environment. In short, my view is compatible with what is called 'global supervenience.'

Global supervenience is, roughly, the view that for any two possible worlds that are exactly alike in microphysical laws and in distribution of microphysical particles are exactly alike in every respect. Since my view is compatible with global supervenience, it does not entail that there is an implausible gap in nuclear physics. For if the thesis of global supervenience is true, then there are no changes in macrophysical properties without changes in microphysical properties.

Indeed, my view of mental properties is even compatible with Jaegwon Kim's thesis of strong supervenience, as long as the base properties need not be intrinsic properties of the bearer of the supervening property.[6] If - as is logically possible - my view were combined with a relational form of strong supervenience, then 'downward causation' could be avoided altogether. Putative macrocausation would be merely apparent. All genuinely causally efficacious properties would be properties of fundamental particles.[7] I am not proposing that this is the case; I am only pointing out that my view of the attitudes does not entail 'downward causation.'

In sum: I am not committing myself to any supervenience thesis; indeed, I do not think that we are in any epistemic position to affirm or deny any universal supervenience thesis. My point here is only that I have contravened neither the thesis of global supervenience nor the thesis of a relational form of strong supervenience. If Beckermann understands 'general laws of nuclear physics' in such a way that there still follows from my view a gap in the general laws of nuclear physics, I would not see such a 'gap' as implausible at all.

5 Non-Emergent Non-Reductive Materialism (Antony)

Antony helpfully provides a finer-grained taxonomy of views on the attitudes than I was using. However, I believe that my arguments work as well on the finer-grained taxonomy as they do on the taxonomy that I was using. Although I agree that Antony's taxonomy is more interesting than mine, the differences between our taxonomies are irrelevant to my arguments against the various versions of the Standard View, as I shall try to show. Antony identifies her view as Non-Emergent Non-Reductive Materialism and mine as Emergent Non-Reductive Materialism. (Frankly, at this point, I do not know in exactly what sense, if any, I would answer to the name 'emergen-

---

[6] See Jaegwon Kim, 'Concepts of Supervenience' in *Supervenience and Mind: Selected Philosophical Essays* (Cambridge: Cambridge University Press, 1993): 53-78.

[7] See Jaegwon Kim, 'Epiphenomenal and Supervenient Causation' in *Supervenience and Mind: Selected Philosophical Essays* (Cambridge: Cambridge University Press, 1993): 92-108.

tist.') Taxonomies aside, the main difference between Antony's and my positions is this: Whereas Antony thinks that for each instance of each belief there is a token of a physical internal state that is identical to (or constitutes or realizes) that belief, I do not.

In this section, I just want to point out that Antony's Non-Emergent Non-Reductive Materialism does not escape the net of my arguments against the Standard View. According to any version of the Standard View, particular instances of beliefs should be construed to be particular neural tokens. Antony states her position as follows: 'Representationalists like me believe that the best account of how beliefs cause actions is one that posits mental representations: neural assemblages that are type-identified by their structural (or syntactic) properties, and which properties in turn mirror their semantic properties.' (Antony, p. 84) If there are such 'neural assemblages that are type-identified by their structural (or syntactic) properties, and which properties in turn mirror their semantic properties,' these neural assemblages should be discoverable by neuroscientists. (It seems to me idle to postulate neural states undetectable by neuroscientists.) My Empirical Conjecture is that neuroscientists will not discover neural assemblages with the requisite properties to be construed as instances of particular beliefs. Nothing known about the brain (by me, anyway) offers any hope that the brain is organized in such a way that for each instance of each belief there is a token brain state. If the Empirical Conjecture is correct, then no version of the Standard View, including Non-Emergent Non-Reductive Materialism, is warranted.[8]

Antony criticizes a dilemma that I posed for the Standard View. If any version of the Standard View is correct, then either beliefs supervene on brain states or beliefs are (merely) constituted by brain states.[9] I argue that beliefs do not supervene on brain states. And I argue that if beliefs are merely constituted by brain states, then the Standard-View thesis is explanatorily uninteresting: 'Even when there is an undisputed relation of constitution between an intentionally identified object and material ele-

---

[8] Or, as I put it in ABBS, if the Empirical Conjecture is correct, then no version of the Standard View is true. Elugardo, Antony and others have taken me to task for confusing being unwarranted with being untrue. I can agree with the extreme realist that it is logically possible for a theory to be (forever) unwarranted but true. But granting such logical possibility does not prevent one from plausibly concluding that if a theory is (forever) unwarranted, it is untrue. Certainly, if a theory is (forever) unwarranted, then no one is justified in regarding it as true.

[9] Antony's term of choice is 'are realized by.' Although she uses the term unequivocally, it is often used equivocally in the literature to refer both to supervenience and constitution. So, I avoid the term 'realization.'

ments that constitute it, the constituting elements shed no explanatory light on the constituted object as intentionally identified.' (EA, 183) So, the first horn is false (as Antony agrees without giving me credit for my argument), and the second horn renders the Standard View explanatorily uninteresting.

Antony (rightly) opts for the second horn and objects that 'the thesis that beliefs are constituted by brain states has a great deal of explanatory import-it explains how beliefs can be causes.' (Antony, p. 86) I have two comments: (i) Much of the recent literature on mental causation argues, successfully in my opinion, that even if beliefs are brain states that cause behavior, the fact that a certain behavior-causing brain state is a belief is explanatorily irrelevant.[10] That is, the fact (if it is a fact) that a certain brain state is or constitutes a certain belief is irrelevant to what that brain state causes. It is not in virtue of being or constituting a belief that a brain state causes what it does. So, the Standard View, even if correct, would not show how beliefs qua beliefs can be causes. (ii) In any case, if brain states answering to a Standard-Viewer's description cannot be found, then the 'explanation' of how beliefs can be causes is a mythical one. Appeal to Shoemaker's distinction between core realizations and total realization is to no avail here. If the Empirical Conjecture is correct, then Shoemaker's distinction between core realizations and total realization breaks down: the core realizations would be merely speculative items, like the ether (before Michelson-Morley). And, also like the ether, core realizations are dispensable. What would be relevant for understanding mental causation would be total realizations - which may include the entire brain, and from which it may not be possible to 'factor out' core realizations.

6 The Master Argument Against the Standard View (Dretske, Antony, Elugardo)

Dretske charges me with two mistakes in what he derisively calls 'the "proof"' - the Master Argument against the Standard View: (a) a mistake of supposing that 'a belief that p is always realized in (a token of) the same type of brain state,' (Dretske, p. 48) and (b) a mistake of 'thinking that according to standard theory, mental states are the proper study of *brain* science - i.e., neurophysiology.' (Dretske, p. 47) Neither charge hits home.

---

[10] The issue was raised in 'Mind Matters', by Ernest LePore and Barry Loewer, *Journal of Philosophy* 84 (1987): 630-642. In 'Metaphysics and Mental Causation,' (in *Mental Causation*, John Heil and Alfred Mele, eds. (Oxford: Clarendon Press, 1993: 75-96), I tried to show that, given a certain metaphysical picture, the problem is intractable. As I've mentioned, Dretske is the only Standard-View philosopher I know who has really wrestled with this problem.

A. As to the first alleged mistake, I simply deny that I supposed that 'a belief that p is always realized in (a token of) the same type of brain state.'[11] Rather I suppose this: If 'beliefs are brain states' is an empirical thesis, then the neural tokens that are tokens of a single belief (at least in an individual) must have some neurophysiological features in common. There are both metaphysical and epistemological considerations that support this claim.

Dretske's vending-machine analogy suggests a metaphysical reason for my claim. A slug has the same causal role in the vending machine as a legitimate coin, and it has the same effect as a legitimate coin: both slug and coin bring forth candy bars. If the machine 'keys' only, say, shape and thickness of legitimate coins, then, in order to play the same causal role as the coin, the slug must have the same shape and thickness as a coin. But the slug may be very different from the coin in other physical respects (e.g., it may be made of a different material, have a different color, etc.). Hence, the slug need not be of the same physical type from the coin. Nevertheless, the slug must share with the coin the physical properties that enable it to play the same causal role in the vending machine as the coin. Similarly for token brain states that are (according to the Standard View) token beliefs. Two neural tokens of different physical types may be the same beliefs only they have some physical properties in common. It is in virtue of those physical properties that the two neural tokens have the same causal role.[12]

Let me make this point from a different angle. suppose that beliefs are brain states, as the Standard View claims, but that type-identity is false. My claim is that there still must be salient neurophysiological features in common with O belief tokens (at least within a single individual). Dretske asks rhetorically: 'If O detectors need not have anything in common (besides occurring, or having the function of occurring, in the presence of Os), why must O beliefs have some salient *neurophysiological* feature in common?' (Dretske, p. 49) Here is a straightforward answer:

If particular O detector had nothing in common with other O detectors (besides occurring, or having the function of occurring in the presence of Os), then, in order to be an O detector, it must have detected Os in the

[11] In my characterization of the Standard View, (SV), by saying '(ii) S tokens n,' I meant that the token n occurs in S's brain. After some labor, Dretske ends up interpreting (SV) in the intended way. I take my target to be exactly what Dretske insists it must be.

[12] I take this to be a consequence of functionalism. It is highly unlikely that two neural tokens of different types that a functionalist identifies with a single belief have exactly the same causal role since their causal roles will be affected by the subject's other attitudes. This holism raises a difficulty for individuation of causal roles, and hence a difficulty for construing beliefs in terms of causal roles. But that's another problem, not the one at issue here.

past.[13] Otherwise, it would not have the function of detecting Os. (This is roughly Dretske's view.[14]) If the analogy holds, then if an O belief token (=a neural token) had nothing in common with other O belief tokens (=neural tokens), then, in order to be an O belief, it must have detected Os in the past. But this is impossible: for a belief/neural token occurs only once; so *it* could not have detected Os in the past. Therefore, in order for a neural token to be an O belief token, it must have something in common with other neural tokens that detected Os in the past. And what the current neural token has in common with other neural tokens that detected Os in the past must be a neurophysiological feature. Otherwise, the fact that past neural tokens detected Os would have no bearing on whether or not the current neural token is an O belief or has the function of detecting Os. So, if the analogy between o detectors and O beliefs holds, then a neural token that is an O belief must have some salient neurophysiological feature in common with past tokens that detected Os.

Note that the claim that neural tokens of the same belief type have some neurophysiological feature in common does not entail type-identity of beliefs and brain states. For even if tokens of *different* neurophysiological types were O beliefs, there would have to be many tokens of *each* of the types that could be O beliefs. To be an O belief, or an O detector, or to have the function of occurring in the presence of Os, a neural token can not be a 'one-shot' token that has no salient neurophysiological properties in common with other neural tokens that have detected Os in the past.

So, my claim that on the Standard View, there must be neurophysiological similarities among neural tokens that are tokens of a single belief is not a covert appeal to type-identity. For we have good metaphysical reason to hold that even if type-identity is false, instances of a particular type of belief cannot be neural tokens unless those neural tokens share salient neurophysiological features. And we have good epistemological reason as well. So, turn now to an epistemological consideration.

The claim that belief tokens are neural tokens is supposed to be an empirical claim. There is no reason to accept any empirical claim in the absence of confirmation. The way to confirm the hypothesis that a particular neural token n is a token of an O belief, say, would be to compare the neural token n to other neural tokens that are candidates for being tokens of an O belief. If the neural tokens that are candidates for being tokens of an O belief had no neurophysiological feature in common, there would be no

---

[13] This is true only for natural, not artifactual, O detectors.

[14] See Fred Dretske, *Explaining Behavior: Reasons in a World of Causes* (Cambridge MA: MIT/Bradford, 1988).

way to carry out the comparison: there would be no way to distinguish between a correct identification and an incorrect identification of a particular neural token with an instance of an O belief.[15] A theory that postulates identification of tokens without any way to ascertain whether a given proposed identification is correct is not conformable or disconformable. Hence, if neural tokens that are tokens of the same belief had nothing neurophysiologically in common, then the view that neural tokens are belief tokens would not be an empirical theory.

In sum, my point is different from the mistaken point (a) that Dretske attributes to me. For my point does not presuppose that the Standard View is committed to type-identity of beliefs and brain states. Rather, my point is that in order for a neural token to be a candidate to be a belief that p, it must have some salient neurophysiological features in common with other neural tokens that are candidates (at least in a single brain) to be a belief that p.

B. The second 'mistake' that Dretske charges me with is to think that, according to standard theory, mental states are the proper study of *brain* science - i.e., neurophysiology. 'Why think neuroscience is the relevant science to identify beliefs?' he asks. (Dretske, p. 48) Dretske thinks that the only reason that one would look to neuroscience is that one is covertly assuming type-identity. I have just shown that I do not covertly assume type-identity. There are other reasons for my claim that neuroscience is the relevant science for confirming any version of the Standard View.

The obvious reason is that the Standard View *is* the view that beliefs, if there are any, are brain states; and neuroscience is the science that studies brain states. Unless there are many neural tokens that can be identified as instances of various beliefs, there is no confirmation of the Standard View. And the only science in a position to identify and classify neural tokens is neuroscience.

This conclusion is reinforced when we consider the alternatives to neuroscience that Dretske suggests. Dretske asks: 'Why should not evolutionary biology or the learning history of the organism be the relevant source to consult in determining whether any particular state of the creature is a belief that p?' (Dretske, p. 48) This rhetorical question invites us to ignore the problem that I am pointing to. For he is assuming that we already have picked out a particular state (token) of a type whose evolutionary or learn-

---

[15] This point also speaks to Elugardo's analogy of the Gothic statue. In the case of Gothic statues, we can identify pieces of marble as candidates to be Gothic statues and then investigate whether each is a Gothic statue. But in the case of neural tokens with no neurophysiological similarity, there is no way to distinguish those neural tokens that are even candidates to be instances of a belief that p.

ing history can be checked. But in order to determine whether a particular state (token) of a creature is a belief that p, there must be some way to pick out the state (token) - other than as an instance of the belief that p. In order to see whether or not a particular state (token) is of a type that has a particular evolutionary or learning history, we must be able to pick out the particular state (token) in question. So, the picking out of a particular state (token) of a creature in order to determine whether it is a belief that p is logically and temporally prior to determining whether that particular state is a token of a type that has a certain evolutionary or learning history. For this reason, neither evolutionary biology nor the learning history of the organism is of help in picking out the particular state (token) in question. So, we are back to neuroscience as the science equipped to pick out current token states that are plausible candidates to be instances of belief.

I have no doubt that there is an evolutionary-biological story about how brains enable us to have beliefs. But that does not address the problem I am raising. What I'm calling the Standard View concerns identification of particular neural tokens as instances of various beliefs. This requires that relevant current tokens be picked out in order to determine (perhaps by consulting the evolutionary history of tokens of that neural type) that they are instances of the belief that p. From the point of view of the Standard View, appeal to evolutionary biology or learning history might supplement neuroscience; but neither could replace it without abandoning the Standard View.

Both Dretske and (implicitly) Antony complain about premise 2.221 of the Master Argument in 'Are Beliefs Brain States?' Premise 2.221 concerns noneliminative theories according to which particular beliefs are particular brain states. According to 2.221, 'If T is necessarily true, then the correct account of belief is either a form of species chauvinism or uses the term 'belief' equivocally' - where T be any noneliminative theory according to which particular beliefs are particular brain states. The reasoning supporting 2.221 is that if T is necessarily true, then T reveals the nature of belief; and if T gives the nature of belief, then there is no belief that fails to be a brain state - in which case nothing that fails to have a brain (a computer or a god) could possibly have a belief. Both Dretske and Antony construe the Standard View more broadly than 2.221 allows. Antony in effect says that we should we take the relevant necessary truth to be not, that beliefs are brain states, but, more comprehensively, that beliefs are realized by some kind of physical states.[16]

---

[16] Antony is here attacking my argument from causal explanation in *Explaining Attitudes* (Antony, p. 80.). I am discussing this point in the context of 2.221 on the basis of a referee's criticism that 2.221 is false.

I take the criticism to amount to this: If T is reformulated as T' - a theory about physically-realized states, rather than about brain states - then 2.221 is false: A theory about physically-realized states may be necessarily true without being a form of species chauvinism and without using any terms equivocally. So, let us reformulate the argument for 2.22, letting T' be any noneliminative theory according to which particular beliefs are particular physically-realized states:

2.221*   If T' is necessarily true, then it is metaphysically impossible that Cartesian dualism be true.
2.222*   It is not metaphysically impossible possible that Cartesian dualism be true.
∴ 2.22   T' is not necessarily true.

Premise 2.221* is, I think, uncontroversial. If a theory is metaphysically impossible, then there is no possible world in which it is true; if a theory is necessarily true, then it is true in every possible world. If T' is necessarily true, then it is metaphysically impossible that there be any particular belief that fails to be a particular physically-realized state; if it is metaphysically impossible that there be any particular belief that fails to be a particular physically-realized state, then Cartesian dualism - according to which there are beliefs that are states of an immaterial soul and hence not physically-realized - is metaphysically impossible. So, 2.221* is true.

The controversial premise in the reformulated argument is 2.222*. I have no direct argument for the metaphysical possibility of Cartesian dualism, but I do have an indirect consideration. Along with many Standard Viewers, I have a strong intuition that Cartesian dualism is metaphysically possible (though not that it is true). Perhaps some Standard Viewers think that that intuition is wrong - that Cartesian dualism is not even metaphysically possible. How do we adjudicate?

The only argument that I can think of that would support the metaphysical impossibility of Cartesian dualism is a Kripke-style argument that shows what would lead people to endorse the intuition of the metaphysical possibility of Cartesian dualism and yet be wrong. On a Kripke-style argument,[17] we confuse the metaphysical intuition about the possibility of Cartesian dualism with a similar, but distinct, epistemic intuition. The epistemic intuition is that we could be in an epistemic situation indiscernible from the one that we actually are in, but one in which Cartesian dualism is metaphysically impossible. It is the epistemic intuition, not the metaphysical intuition - the argument would go - that is correct. On

---

[17] I am not attributing any such argument to Kripke himself.

this approach, those who endorse the metaphysical possibility of Cartesian dualism are confusing that metaphysical intuition with the related epistemic intuition. This approach depends on reconstruing the (false) metaphysical intuition about what is metaphysically possible as a (true) epistemic intuition about what is compatible with the evidence that we have.

But this argument against the intuition that Cartesian dualism is metaphysically possible would be a misapplication of a Kripke-style argument.[18] In a Kripke-style argument, what motivates reconstrual of the intuition about metaphysical possibility is the fact that we have *independent reason* to think that the original intuition about metaphysical possibility is false. *Given* that the original intuition about metaphysical possibility is false, we cast about to find why the original intuition seemed to compelling. In Kripke-style argument, what we find is that there is an epistemic intuition (i) that is true and (ii) that we confuse with the original metaphysical intuition. Once we see this, we replace the original metaphysical intuition with the correct epistemic intuition. But the original intuition about the metaphysical possibility of Cartesian dualism not like this at all. We have no independent reason to suppose that the original intuition about the metaphysical possibility of Cartesian dualism is false in the first place.

To see the disanalogy between an intuition that a Kripke-style argument does discredit and an intuition - such as the intuition that Cartesian dualism is metaphysically possible - that a Kripke-style argument does not discredit, consider the (incorrect) metaphysical intuition that heat is not necessarily molecular motion. Given Kripke's essentialism, the discovery that heat is molecular motion disconfirms the original intuition that heat is not necessarily molecular motion. It is that disconfirmation that motivates the reconstrual of the metaphysical intuition as an epistemic intuition. In the case of the Standard View, there has been no parallel *discovery* that beliefs are brain states (or more generally, are physically-realized states). And as I have argued throughout, I take it to be an empirical conjecture that there will be no such discovery. Thus, there is no justification for discarding the original metaphysical intuition that Cartesian dualism is metaphysically possible. The only reason to suppose that Cartesian dualism is metaphysically impossible is a prior commitment to the necessity of the Standard View. In the current context, such a commitment would be obviously question-begging.

Since the only argument that I can think of against the metaphysical possibility of Cartesian dualism is flawed (and since almost all philosophers

---

[18] For a discussion of a different (mis)application of a Kripke-style argument, see my 'Why Constitution is Not Identity' (*Journal of Philosophy* 94 (1997): 599-621, especially 615-619.

since the seventeenth century have believed in the metaphysical possibility of Cartesian dualism), I think that it is reasonable to suppose that the intuition of the metaphysical possibility of Cartesian dualism is correct. But if Cartesian dualism is even metaphysically possible, then it is metaphysically possible that there be a particular belief that fails to have a particular physical realization. In that case, 2.222' is true, and the argument for 2.22 is sound.

Elugardo has several epistemological objections to the Master Argument. I shall respond to two of them. First, Elugardo points out there is confirmation of the view that genes are constituted by stretches of DNA even though there is 'no neurochemical property that they all must have in common in virtue of which they are a particular type of gene.' (Elugardo, p. 98) True enough, but there are complications in the belief case that have no parallel in the DNA case. I doubt that even *within* a given individual S, there is a single type of neurophysiological property that is instantiated on every occasion on which S does something explainable by S's belief that p. To cite an example from 'Are Beliefs Brain States?': Suppose that Jones wants to improve his social status, and believes that the best way to improve his social status is to become well-known in the community. He acts on this belief in various ways: he makes large contributions to charities, becomes active in community organizations, and so on. But (in line with my Empirical Conjecture) I doubt that there is some particular neurophysiological property that is instantiated on each occasion of his acting on the belief that the best way to improve his social status is to become well-known in the community.

Second, Elugardo objects to my use of the term 'confirmation' in premise 2.231 ('If T is contingently true, then T will be confirmed by neuroscience.') I meant to use 'confirmation' univocally, in the sense that Elugardo calls 'experimental confirmation:' ' [T]o confirm T is to have positive instances of its generalization[s].' (Elugardo, p. 100) I agree with Elugardo that it is possible that there be a theory that is true, empirical and yet, in fact, never experimentally confirmed. But, barring a Cataclysmic Event, I think that in the case of T, it is unreasonable to suppose that there will be such a theory that is true, empirical and yet, in fact, never experimentally confirmed. Absence of confirmation in the long run would be strong evidence that there is no true T.

7 Relational Properties and Context-Dependency (Newen)

Professor Newen shares with me important philosophical views. For example, we both emphasize ways in which beliefs are context-dependent. Despite these similarities, however, Professor Newen proposes an alternative to Practical Realism that he calls 'Contextual Realism'. Although he criticizes those versions of the Standard View that disregard the role of context in identifying the content of beliefs, he also argues that an adequate accommodation of the role of contexts (or contextual aspects) in describing the content of beliefs does not imply the denial of the main claim of the Standard view, that human beliefs are constituted by neural states.

First - and perhaps this is a minor point - Newen criticizes my analogy between beliefs/brain states and horserace-winning/leg states. Newen points out that 'win' is a success verb and 'believe' is not. Fair enough, but then in Newen's own example of braking well, 'braking well' is a success verb too. Let me also register a related dissent about the first table in Newen's paper. In the first table, Newen says that the (token) event of using the brake mechanism of the car during the period t is identical with the (token) event of decelerating the car during the period t. I would individuate events more finely, as Jaegwon Kim does, so that use of the brake mechanism would be a different event from deceleration of the car. Intuitively, one would think that use of the brake mechanism (as opposed to being struck by lightning) cause the deceleration of the car.

It is difficult to see to what extent Newen and I disagree because of two important terminological differences. We use the term 'relational properties' and the term 'token' in significantly different ways. Newen defines relational properties by '(rel)', and says: 'The property p expressed with the monadic predicate 'p' is a *relational property* of a system S if and only if the fact that S has p implies that there is an individual object to which S stands in a relation which can be expressed by a (relational) predicate that is part of "p"'. He then defines 'context-dependent properties' by '(con)' as follows: 'The property p expressed with the monadic predicate "p" is a *context - dependent property* of a system S if changing the context can modify the property expressed, i.e., in the context c1 the property expressed by "p" is p while in the context c2 the property expressed by "p" is the property pN.'

As I use the term 'relational properties', the properties that Newen calls 'context - dependent' as well as the properties that he calls 'relational' are relational properties (in my sense). In *Explaining Attitudes* (p. 63), I define 'relational properties' like this: 'R is a relational property if and only if: x's having R entails that there is some y distinct from x.'[19] So, any property whose exemplification depends on a physical, social or linguistic context

---

[19] Also see my discussion of relational properties in my response to Meijers in the following section.

(context-dependent, in Newen's sense) is, in my sense, a relational property. A property P is nonrelational if it supervenes on local microstructure in this sense: Necessarily, if x has P and y lacks P, then there is a microphysical difference between x and y. Any property (like having tenure, or believing that water is wet) that fails to supervene on local microstructure is relational in my sense. So when I say that beliefs are relational, I am saying something broader than what Newen takes me to be saying. If beliefs are context-dependent in Newen's sense, then they are relational in my sense.

A second terminological issue regards the type-token distinction. Proponents of the Standard View presuppose that a belief could only be either a type of neural state or a particular neural token (with or without taking into account the relevant context). When speaking from my own point of view, I do not refer to token beliefs at all. In fact I think that the type-token distinction as it is applied to beliefs in the literature is misguided in that it almost forces us to construe instances of beliefs as entities.

Perhaps I was not sufficiently clear, but one of the things that Newen says about Practical Realism I do not hold. Newen says: 'The main point of Practical Realism is that beliefs cannot be characterized by internal states, because they are essentially relational.' (p. 140) Although it is my view that beliefs are not internal states; and it is my view that beliefs are essentially relational, I do not hold that the reason that beliefs are not internal states is that they are essentially relational. It is possible (although I think it false) that beliefs could be both relational and internal states. (That is what so-called 'externalists' typically hold.) According to externalists, a belief is a brain state in an organism that has a certain relation to a certain environment. Believing that p, then, would be a relational property of a particular brain state. I do not connect being relational with not being an internal state in the way suggested by Newen's paper.

Newen thinks that my view collapses into a familiar thesis of externalism. There's no collapse. I characterize my view as a kind of externalism-minus-the-Standard View. I support my thesis that the Standard View is false by various considerations: (1) by giving many examples of cases where it is implausible to suppose that for each belief, there is an identifiable brain-state that is identical (or constitutes) that belief; (2) by claiming that it is empirically unlikely that a particular brain state could be found for *each* of a person's beliefs; (3) by arguing in detail against one motivation for the Standard View - namely, that the Standard View is needed to undergird mentalistic causal explanation. These are the kinds of considerations that I give as reasons to reject the Standard View.

Newen apparently does not think that these kinds of considerations undermine the Standard View. (Indeed, he doesn't seem to recognize that I have offered these considerations against the Standard View.) Newen says

(p. 143), 'If social and cultural processes were shown to be nonreducible to the entities that are accepted by the Standard View including externalism then this would be an argument against the Standard View. But Baker does not present any argument of this kind....' Of course I don't. No such argument is needed.

Newen goes on to imply that, if my points are to count against the Standard View, I must 'presuppose that social and cultural processes cannot be explained according to individualism.' Of course, no such presupposition is needed or made. The considerations of the sort given above, (1) - (3), are appropriate for rejecting the Standard View without rejecting externalism. The considerations that I offered are clearly relevant to the question of the truth of the Standard View, and they are the ones about which I welcome criticism.

Newen's view is that an instance of a belief is a particular neural state together with a context. He thinks that the natural basis of a belief state (token) is neither a token of a special type of neural state alone nor a particular neural token alone but rather a complex token consisting of a neural state together with the context of the believer. The context of the believer is what Newen calls the internal and external context of a person, i.e., the individual learning history and the standard physical, social and linguistic environment of a person.

Now Newen uses the term 'token' in an unusual way. A token (in the familiar sense) is a particular, something that occurs at a certain time in a certain place. (I eschew the term 'token' for beliefs, because I think that beliefs - unlike, say, baseballs - do not have precise locations.) But as Newen uses the term 'token,' a belief token does not seem to have a precise location either. Since the token is said to *consist*, in part, of the individual learning history, it does not occur at a single time or during a specifiable interval, but is temporally extended indefinitely into the past. (Who's to say exactly when a person's learning history (as opposed to a computer's) began? Since the token is said to consist partly in the individual's social and linguistic environment, it does not occur a single place, but is spatially extended indefinitely away from the believer. Except for the use of the word 'token,' I agree that these factors - neural state, learning history, social and linguistic environment - are relevant to what beliefs a person has. But if I am right, there will not be specifiably different neural states for different beliefs.

Newen illustrates his view with regard to neural nets. 'The neural nets...may have the same cognitive state, i.e., recognizing a square, realized by neural states....The recognition is constituted by a certain net state together with the type of relevant context (the relevant context can be characterized by the connectivity, initial configuration and learning history of the net).' He continues: 'Even if one belief is realized by different types of neural states it does not follow that beliefs are not constituted by neural states.' (Newen, p. 160) Now I fully agree. My argument in ABBS is that it is unlikely that the requisite neural states to identify as beliefs will be found, and that if no neural states that are plausibly candidates to be beliefs are found, then the Standard View should be abandoned. But I am willing to wait and see.

8 Practical Realism Extended (Meijers)

Professor Meijers focuses on an important but neglected class of attitudes: collective beliefs. Consider, for example, 'The Security Council decided to send UN troops to Albania because it believed that it was necessary to re-store law and order.' Meijers convincingly shows that a collective belief, such as that of the Security Council, cannot be understood either as an ag-gregate of individual members' beliefs or as attitudes of some kind of 'su-per-agent' that is independent of individuals. Meijers has done a real service by drawing attention to such beliefs, which, I confess, I had never thought about at all.

Meijers has two aims: First, to compare the Standard View and Practi-cal Realism with respect to how well each can handle collective beliefs; and, second, to use collective beliefs to illustrate how Practical Realism needs to be developed. He shows, on the one hand, that no version of the Standard View can accommodate collective beliefs, and, on the other hand, that Practical Realism can be applied to collective beliefs. But the applica-tion of Practical Realism to collective beliefs reveals a gap in the develop-ment of Practical Realism: What, exactly, *are* relational properties?

Before turning to Meijers' major criticism-that I have not provided an adequate account of relational properties-I want to do two things: (1) Re-spond to a criticism; (2) Shed light on a point on which I think I was un-clear in *Explaining Attitudes*.

1. In applying Practical Realism to collective beliefs, Meijers says something with which I disagree. On my view, if S believes that p, then there are relevant true counterfactuals about what S would say, do or think in various circumstances. Meijers says rightly: 'Given holism, where beliefs are part of a network of intentional states, the set of relevant counterfactuals is different for different agents have the same belief.'[20] But then he goes on to say - and this is where I disagree - 'This is another way of saying that

---

[20] This quotation and the others in this section are from p. 172.

every belief is always from a point of view.' I think that the matter of there being different sets of relevant counterfactuals for different agents having the same belief is not the same as the issue of point of view. Meijers objects that I say 'virtually nothing in *Explaining Behavior* about the indispensability of a first-person point of view for the analysis of intentional states.' And he thinks that for Practical Realism, this is 'an important issue since the specification of the conditions for having a particular belief is agent specific.'

By way of reply, I want to say two things. First, I do not think that the fact that the conditions for having a particular belief are agent specific implies anything about 'the indispensability of a first-person point of view for the analysis of intentional states.' Agent specificity could be couched in wholly third-person terms: If S were in circumstances C, then S would do A. But, second, in fact, I do think that the idea of a first-person point of view is indispensable for understanding what a person is. Although, as Meijers notes, I did not discuss a first-person point of view in *Explaining Attitudes*, I am emphasizing the idea of a first-person perspective in subsequent writings.[21]

2. Meijers notes that I claim that whether an agent 'has a particular belief is determined by what the agent does, says and thinks under various circumstances, where what the agent would do may be specified intentionally.' He calls this my 'epistemological claim, since it is a claim about the attribution of beliefs.' Now I agree that such dispositions to say, think or act in certain ways are indicative of the global state of belief, but I think that such dispositions are more than indicative. On my view, such dispositions are metaphysically connected to belief. If one failed to have any dispositions to say, think or act in relevant ways, then one does not have the belief in question. Indeed, relevant dispositions are both necessary and sufficient (in a noncausal sense) for having a belief that p. Nevertheless, the fact that one is disposed to say or think certain things or to act in certain ways is not the same fact as the fact that one has a belief that p. There are other cases in which we say that A is necessary and sufficient (in a noncausal sense) for B; yet A's obtaining is not the same fact as B's obtaining. For example, the jury's voting 'guilty' is necessary and sufficient (in a noncausal sense) for

---

[21] See 'The First-Person Perspective: A Test for Naturalism' *American Philosophical Quarterly* 35 (1998): 327-348. An earlier version of this paper appeared in German in the proceedings of a 1997 conference at Humboldt University in Berlin on Naturalism. 'Die Perspektive der Ersten Person: ein Test für den Naturalismus,' *Naturalismus. Philosophische Beiträge*, Geert Keil/Herbert Schnädelbach (Hg.), Frankfurt-am-Main (Suhrkamp Verlag). Finally, the idea of a first-person perspective is prominent in my account of persons in my book *Persons and Bodies; A Constitution View.*

the conviction of a defendant who pleads 'not guilty,' but the fact that the defendant is convicted is not the same fact as the fact that the jury votes 'guilty.' For one thing, the fact that the defendant is convicted is a fact about a particular person; and the fact that the jury voted 'guilty' is a fact about a group of people.

So, yes, my claim that whether an agent has a particular belief is determined by what the agent does, says and thinks under various circumstances is epistemological, but not *merely* epistemological. Although I admit that I could have been clearer on this point, I think that metaphysical and epistemological matters are connected in certain ways. It is not that I confuse metaphysics and epistemology; it is rather that I think that metaphysics cannot be done in a vacuum.

Now let me turn to Meijers' main criticism: that I do not provide an adequate account of relational properties.[22] I confess that I do not. Indeed, I am not confident that anyone will come up with an adequate comprehensive account of relational properties. We tend to think of relational properties as expressible by two-place predicates like 'is taller than,' 'is the mother of,' and so on. But this tendency obscures a whole class of important properties that are relational in the sense that they could not be had by a being alone in the universe, but are not expressible by two-place predicates. The reason that they are not expressible by two-place predicates is that we have no idea how to specify exactly what relations must obtain for these relational properties to be instantiated.

Social and intentional properties are among such relational properties that are not expressible by two-place predicates. For example, the property of having tenure is perhaps a relation between a person and an institution. But can we say in nonintentional or physicalistic terms what an institution is, or what properties an institution must have for it to confer tenure? Or consider the property of being a registered voter. In order for someone to be a registered voter, there must be numerous complicated political and social conventions; but there is no way to specify what relations a person must have what nonintentionally-described entity in order for the person to be a registered voter. Yet: we know that Smith has tenure, or that Jones is a registered voter, even though we have no idea of what relation Smith has to what, or what relation that Jones has to what, that makes it the case that Smith has tenure or that Jones is a registered voter. I am not sanguine that there is a single account of relations that can cover even these two cases,

---

[22] On p. 176, Meijers suggests that I may hold that one can experience pain only if one stands in a certain relation to her environment. I would not go that far.

which are similar in that both involve intentional relations to institutions. I am even less sanguine that there will be a single account of relations that can cover all the kinds of relations that Meijers mentions: causal relations, intentional relations, normative relations.

I was hoping to start on the project of 'giving relations their proper metaphysical due' by showing at least three kinds of things: (a) that many properties, beyond those expressible by two-place predicates, are relational in the sense that they could not be exemplified in a world in which only one individual existed; (b) that intentional states like belief depend on all kinds of relations, not specifiable in advance; and (c) that a Leibnizian account that reduces relational properties to intrinsic properties of relata is unsatisfactory. A full account of relations was beyond the scope of my inquiry in *Explaining Attitudes*. However, investigation of relations per se seems to me an important research program, and I would be happy if *Explaining Attitudes* stimulated such research.

Bibliography of Lynne Rudder Baker

Books

Saving Belief: A Critique of Physicalism. Princeton, Princeton University Press, 1987.
Explaining Attitudes: A Practical Approach to the Mind, Cambridge: Cambridge University Press, 1995.
Persons and Bodies: A Constitution View. Cambridge, Cambridge University Press, 2000.

Articles in Journals

The Ontological Status of Persons. *Philosophy and Phenomenological Research*, forthcoming.
Material Persons and the Doctrine of Resurrection. *Faith and Philosophy*, forthcoming, 2001.
Philosophy *in Mediis Rebus*. *Metaphilosophy*, forthcoming 2001.
Reply to Jackson, II. *Philosophical Explorations* 3, 2000: 196-8.
What Am I? *Philosophy and Phenomenological Research* 59, 1999: 151-159.
What is This Thing Called 'Commonsense Psychology'? *Philosophical Explorations* 2, 1999: 3-19.
The First-Person Perspective: A Test for Naturalism. *American Philosophical Quarterly* 35, 1998: 327-348.
Why Constitution is Not Identity. *Journal of Philosophy*, vol. 94, no.12, December 1997: 599-621.

Explaining Beliefs: Lynne Rudder Baker and Her Critics.
Anthonie Meijers (ed.).
Copyright © 2001, CSLI Publications.

Science and the Attitudes: A Reply to Sanford. *Behavior and Philosophy* 24, 1996: 187-189.

Need a Christian Be a Mind-Body Dualist? *Faith and Philosophy* 12, 1995: 489-504.

Content Meets Consciousness. *Philosophical Topics* 22, 1994: 1-22.

Attitudes as Nonentities. *Philosophical Studies* 76, 1994: 175-203. [Reprinted in *The Philosopher's Annual*, Vol. 17, Patrick Grim et al, eds., Atascadero CA: Ridgeview Publishing Co., 1996: 33-62.]

Reply to van Gulick. *Philosophical Studies* 76, 1994: 217-221.

Eliminativism and an Argument from Science. *Mind and Language*, 8, 1993: 180-188.

Dretske on the Explanatory Role of Belief. *Philosophical Studies*, 63, 1991: 99-111.

Seeming To See Red. *Philosophical Studies*, 58, 1990: 121-128.

Reply to Johnson. *Behavior and Philosophy*, 18, 1990: 67-68.

Instrumental Intentionality. *Philosophy of Science*, 56, 1989: 303-316.

Recent Work in the Philosophy of Mind. *Philosophical Books XXX*, 1989: 1-10.

Truth in Context. *Philosophical Psychology* II, 1989: 85-94.

Content by Courtesy. *The Journal of Philosophy*, 84, 1987: 197-213.

A Farewell to Functionalism. *Philosophical Studies*, 48, 1985: 1-13.

Was Leibniz Entitled to Possible Worlds? *Canadian Journal of Philosophy*, 15, 1985: 57-74.

On the Very Idea of a Form of Life. *Inquiry*, 27, 1984: 277-289.

De Re Belief in Action. *The Philosophical Review*, 91, 1982: 363-387.

Underprivileged Access. *Nous*, 16, 1982: 227-241.

On Making and Attributing Demonstrative Reference. *Synthese*, 49, 1981: 245-273.

Why Computers Can't Act. *American Philosophical Quarterly*, 18, 1981: 157-163.

First Person Aspects of Agency. *SISTM Quarterly* 2 (Renamed *Journal of Cognitive Science*), 1979: 10-16.

Indexical Reference and *De Re* Belief. (Jan David Wald, co-author) *Philosophical Studies*, 36, 1979: 317-327.

On the Mind-Dependence of Temporal Becoming. *Philosophy and Phenomenological Research*, 39, 1979: 341-357.

Temporal Becoming: The Argument From Physics. *Philosophical Forum*, 6, 1974-75: 218-236.

Chapters in Books

Materialism With a Human Face. In *Body, Soul and Survival*, Kevin Corcoran, ed., Ithaca NY: Cornell University Press, 2001: 159-180.

What Am I? In *Philosophy of Mind* (Vol. 9 of the *Proceedings of the 20th World Congress of Philosophy*), Bernard Elevitch, ed., Bowling Green: Philosophy Documentation Center, 2000: 185-194.

Die Perspektive der Ersten Person: ein Test fuer den Naturalismus. *Naturalismus. Philosophische Beitraege.* Geert Keil/Herbert Schnaedelbach, eds., Frankfurt-am-Main: Suhrkamp Verlag, 2000: 250-72.

Unity Without Identity: A New Look at Material Constitution. *New Directions in Philosophy.* Midwest Studies in Philosophy 23, Peter A. French and Howard K. Wettstein, eds., Malden, MA: Blackwell Publishers, Inc., 1999: 144-165.

Folk Psychology. *MIT Encyclopedia of Cognitive Science.* Rob Wilson and Frank Keil, eds., Cambridge MA: MIT Press, 1999: 319-20.

What We Do: A Nonreductive Approach to Human Action. *Human Action. Deliberation and Causation* (Philosophical Studies Series 77), Jan Bransen and Stefaan Cuypers, eds., Dordrecht, Holland: Kluwer Academic Publishers, 1998: 249-69.

Persons in Metaphysical Perspective. *The Philosophy of Roderick M. Chisholm* (The Library of Living Philosophers). Lewis E. Hahn, ed., LaSalle, Ill: Open Court Publishing Co., 1997: 433-453.

Functionalism. *Cambridge Dictionary of Philosophy.* Robert Audi, ed., New York: Cambridge University Press, 1995.

Propositional Attitudes. *A Companion to the Philosophy of Mind.* Samuel Guttenplan. ed., Oxford: Basil Blackwell, 1994: 488-493

Instrumental Intentionality. In *Mental Representations: A Reader.* Stephen P. Stich and Ted Warfield eds., Oxford: Basil Blackwell, 1994: 332-344. Reprinted from *Philosophy of Science,* 56, 1989.

Content and Context. *Philosophical Perspectives 8: Logic and Language.* James E. Tomberlin, ed., Altacasdero CA: Ridgeview Publishing Co., 1994: 17-32.

Metaphysics and Mental Causation. in *Mental Causation.* John Heil and Albert Mele, eds., Oxford: Clarendon Press, 1993: 75-95.

What Beliefs Are Not. in *Naturalism: A Critical Appraisal.* Stephen Wagner and Richard Warner, eds. Notre Dame IN: University of Notre Dame Press, 1993.

Has Content Been Naturalized? *Meaning in Mind: Fodor and his Critics.* Barry Loewer and Georges Rey, eds., Oxford: Basil Blackwell, 1991: 17-32.

On a Causal Theory of Content. *Philosophical Perspectives 3: Philosophy of Mind and Action Theory.* 1989 James E. Tomberlin, ed., Altascadero, CA: Ridgeview Publishing Co. 1989: 166-186.

A Farewell to Functionalism. In *Re-Representations: Readings in the Philosophy of Mental Representation.* Stuart Silvers, ed., Kluwer Academic Publishers, 1988. Reprinted from *Philosophical Studies,* 48, 1985.

Cognitive Suicide. *Contents of Thought* (Proceedings of the 1985 Oberlin Colloquium), Robert H.Grimm and Daniel D. Merrill, eds., Tucson: University of Arizona Press, 1988: 1-18; Reply to Charles Chastain, 26-30.

Just What Do We Have in Mind? *Studies in the Philosophy of Mind (Midwest Studies in Philosophy, Vol. X),* Peter A. French, Theodore E. Uehling, Jr., Howard K. Wettstein, eds., Minneapolis: University of Minnesota Press, 1986: 25-48.

Reviews

Review of *The Body in Mind* by Mark Rowlands. In *Mind* 109, 2000: 434-7.

Review of *Having Thought: Essays in the Metaphysics of Mind.* By John Haugeland, in *Philosophy of Science* 66, 1999: 494-5.

Review of *The Nature of True Minds.* By John Heil, in *Philosophy and Phenomenological Research* 55, 1995: 475-78

Review of *Consciousness Explained.* By Daniel C. Dennett, in *The Review of Metaphysics*, 1992: 398-399.

Review of *A Neurocomputational Perspective: The Nature of Mind and the Structure of Science* by Paul M. Churchland. In *The Philosophical Review* 101, 1992: 906-908.

Review of *Judgement and Justification* by William G. Lycan. In *The Philosophical Review* 100, 1991: 481-484.

Review of *Understanding Wittgenstein: Studies of Philosophical Investigations.* By J.M.F. Hunter, in *Canadian Philosophical Reviews* VI, 1986: 69-71.

Review of *Thought and Object: Essays on Intentionality.* Andrew Woodfield, ed. in *Philosophy and Phenomenological Research.* 1984: 137-142.

Review of *Consciousness and the Brain: A Scientific and Philosophical Inquiry.* Gordon G. Globus et al, eds. (Michael Woodruff, co-author), in *Neuropsychologia* 16, 1978: 131-133.

Review of *The Emergent Self.* By William Hasker, forthcoming in *Philosophy and Phenomenological Research.*

Publications for General Audiences

God and Science in the Public Schools. *Journal for Philosophic Exchange* 30, 2000: 53-69..

Should the Humanities Be Saved? *UMass Magazine*, Winter 1999.

Electronic Publications

Comment on Intelligence Without Representations. By Hubert L. Dreyfus, sponsored by the Department of Philosophy and the Cognitive Science Initiative at the University of Houston,
http://www.hfac.uh.edu/cogsci/index.html

Book Symposium on *Persons and Bodies: A Constitution View.* Précis and Replies to Brian Garrett, Harold Noonan, Eric Olson, *A Field Guide to the Philosophy of Mind* (2001) (supported by the University of Rome III, Marco Nani, ed).
http://www.uniroma3.it/kant/field/bakersymp.htm

Name Index